BEYOND
BIRDS
&
BEES

Praise for *B*

"With ca ... es new life into our national no ... cues from other countries' sen ... ly towards a saner and healthier future."

—Michael Kimmel, bestselling author of *Manhood in America and Guyland*

"Filled with sweet, poignant, and laugh-out-loud stories, *Beyond Birds and Bees* is a most accessible and most informative book that will help parents and caring adults become more adept at talking to young people about healthy sexuality. Bonnie J. Rough offers practical advice, gentle encouragement, and is vulnerable enough to let us learn from her own failures and successes. If you're looking for a book that provides a heartfelt and common sense approach to raising sexually healthy children, you've found it!"

—Al Vernacchio, MSEd, author of *For Goodness Sex: Changing the Way We Talk to Teens About Sexuality, Values, and Health*

"Bonnie J. Rough has written a brilliant book about sex, gender, justice, and joy, and it's one that manages to be simultaneously sobering and buoyant. Her main ingredients for raising healthy kids—wonder, humor, and trust—constitute a kind of inspirational worldview, applicable to all aspects of parenting certainly, but even beyond that, to life itself. I'm so glad I read it."

—Catherine Newman, author of *Catastrophic Happiness* and *Waiting for Birdy*

"With humor, humility, and gentleness, Bonnie J. Rough takes us on her journey of discovery and leaves us somewhere surprising and wonderful. Along the way, her practical tips add up to a transformative rethinking of what it means to teach our children about sex. This is a book that can help everybody: parents who know what they're doing, parents who worry they don't have a clue, and the rest of us, too, who never got the loving, tender teaching we deserved."

—Lisa Wade, bestselling author of *American Hookup: The New Culture of Sex on Campus*

"What a gift! Bonnie J. Rough offers a much-needed breath of fresh air in her wonderful new approach to discussing sex, love, and equality with our kids. Her smart, vigorously well-researched, and funny book is a great guide for families to read and discuss as their kids grow up."

—Caroline Grant, Co-director, Sustainable Arts Foundation

"Finally: a parenting book that abandons preachiness for a joyful and thoughtful inquiry into how we might guide our kids, and grow with them, as they become healthy, happy young adults. Bonnie J. Rough's experience in the Netherlands and her wide-ranging research offer an inspiring and practical alternative to help children (and their parents) become more comfortable in their own skins."

—Sonya Huber, author of *Pain Woman Takes Your Keys*

"*Beyond Birds and Bees* is a must-read for every parent. With humor and grace, Bonnie J. Rough invites readers to learn alongside her as she embarks on a journey to understand how we can create truly gender equal societies and raise happy and healthy children who celebrate their own bodies. I wish I'd read this book when my daughters were little, but I'm grateful for it now, because it is never too late to talk openly with our kids about sex, sexuality and our bodies. This book is validating, eye-opening and truly life-changing."

—Kate Hopper, author of *Use Your Words: A Writing Guide for Mothers* and *Ready for Air: A Journey Through Premature Motherhood*

"The conversation Rough starts about sexuality and gender equality in *Beyond Birds & Bees* is one we all need to be having—with our partners, our kids, our kids' teachers, our legislators—well: everybody. Read it. Start talking."

—Jill Christman, author of *Darkroom: A Family Exposure* and *Borrowed Babies: Apprenticing for Motherhood*

BEYOND BIRDS & BEES

Bringing Home a New Message to Our Kids About Sex, Love, and Equality

BONNIE J. ROUGH

SEAL PRESS

Seal Press
Hachette Book Group
1290 Avenue of the Americas, New York, NY 10104
SealPress.com
@SealPress

Printed in the United States of America

First Edition: August 2018

Published by Seal Press, an imprint of Perseus Books, LLC, a subsidiary of Hachette Book Group, Inc. The Seal Press name and logo is a trademark of the Hachette Book Group.

The publisher is not responsible for websites (or their content) that are not owned by the publisher.

Library of Congress Cataloging-in-Publication Data has been applied for.

ISBNs: 978-1-58005-739-4 (paperback), 978-1-58005-740-0 (ebook)

LSC-C

10 9 8 7 6 5 4 3 2 1

To my children

Let us fully realize that sex education is more than a collection of biological facts; it is a preparation for fine living....Boys and girls, and young men and young women, who have grown up with adequate knowledge of sex and its various implications are able to discuss it with self-assurance and sobriety and the saving grace of common sense. And through the extension of this same common sense they may achieve for themselves, for their children and for their fellow-men the good life for all.

—Belle S. Mooney, MD
How Shall I Tell My Child?
1944

Contents

Introduction xiii

PART ONE
HATCH

1 **Dreaming** 3

2 **Dropping the Fig Leaf** 19

3 **Finding Words** 39

4 **Innocence** 51

5 **Privileging Pleasure** 69

6 **The Doctor Is In** 85

PART TWO
FLY

7 **What (In)Equality Is Made Of** 107

8 **Consent** 135

9 **No Cooties Allowed** 143

10 **Spring Fever** 165

11 **The Joy of Sex Ed** 183

12 **Safe Haven** 209

   Conclusion: Bringing It Home 229

Acknowledgments 249
Notes 253
Index 283

Introduction

I was never likely to write a book about sex. I grew up Catholic in a middle-class American suburb where I babysat often, wrote long frilly nature poems, and always waited thirty minutes after eating before jumping into the pool. Despite commendable efforts by my parents and teachers, I was expecting a punctuation mark for my first period, and I thought my breast buds were tumors. By the time I rolled a condom onto a banana in my high school health class, I knew I wouldn't be repeating the exercise anytime soon. My parents had told me they waited until marriage to have sex, and judging by the slinky cat costume in my mom's pajama drawer, their love life hadn't suffered. My inexperience didn't stop me from having boyfriends in high school, but my one earnest attempt at fellatio sent my beau into convulsions of laughter rather than throes of ecstasy. (I'd been thinking *corn on the cob*, not *popsicle*.) Certainly nobody on the yearbook committee nominated me Dr. Ruth's protégé. Maybe more like her cat sitter. And that made me perfectly happy. But as I got older, my naïveté kept me from questioning the lopsided culture I cheerfully called my own.

I met my future husband in college, where it never crossed my mind to enroll in a women's studies class or to join in Take Back the Night marches. It failed to strike me as odd that he got to know my anatomy better than I did. As we signed our marriage license, I took his surname without a second thought. I rather liked that Dan took care of lawn mowing, gutter cleaning, and snow shoveling. I figured he was happy I oversaw flower gardens and everything kitchen-related. (We took turns brushing the cat.) Eventually we had a baby, and that's when the inequity of traditional gender roles began to sink in for me. You might think years of street harassment and condescension at work would have clued me in, but for a long time those dynamics hid in plain sight, too normal to notice. Yet how come, in a modern marriage of equals, Dan and I never discussed how having kids would affect my career—or how my default child care role as a mother meant becoming a father would *not* affect his? Now and then I vaguely wondered what my daughter, by virtue of being born female, was in for. Four years later, our second daughter was born. And some time after that, it finally occurred to me to look up the answer to a pesky little question: What *is* the difference between a vulva and a vagina?

All I can say is that gender equality wasn't something I'd spent much time thinking about, and the birds and the bees just weren't my focus. As a youngster I had gotten by, and as a parent, I figured those details would somehow sort themselves out for my kids—perhaps with a nice pamphlet on a day when I planned to be out of town. I never set out to be a champion of the facts of life.

So what sparked my curiosity? How did I become passionate about exploring attitudes toward sexuality and especially the way we teach our kids about this still largely taboo subject?

Looking back now, I can see that the journey began with my first pregnancy. I felt deep in my body that I knew how to carry, give birth to, and nurture a child, and I was surprised how many controlling (and conflicting) messages came my way about how to behave and look while pregnant, how to give birth in the best possible way, and how to be a good parent. Once my daughter was born, trying to be a perfect mother—even by standards I hand-picked myself—made me stressed and miserable. The other parents I knew in our Minneapolis neighborhood—especially the mothers—seemed just as frustrated and overwhelmed. Our babies were fine (if maybe a tad demanding), but we, their caretakers, were barely hanging on.

When Caroline was almost two, Dan's airline job relocated to the Netherlands, and we moved to the heart of Amsterdam—a city world famous for its openness and tolerance. It was uncanny, but almost as soon as we arrived there, something felt better. As a parent, I felt expected to be human, not superhuman. As a woman, I no longer felt examined and judged—and therefore I soon became newly comfortable in my own skin. I marveled—and sometimes puzzled—at the openness and pragmatism with which Dutch families raised their kids. At first I couldn't put my finger on why things felt so different. But as I eventually learned, this was simply how it felt to live in one of the world's most gender-equal societies.

Shortly after we moved back to the United States, this time to our hometown of Seattle, Caroline's little sister, Libby, was born. No longer angsty about how to take good care of babies, Dan and I now found ourselves worrying about how to raise two happy, healthy daughters as we perceived American gender norms with fresh eyes: pink and blue toy and clothing aisles, early and even earlier sexualization (baby bikinis? "chick magnet" onesies?), and a ubiquitous, withering male gaze. It had always been there—that constant sense of being watched and appraised that every American girl finds a way of living with—but after we'd spent a year and a half without it, the gaze and its wounding power were much more obvious now.

More than anything, I wanted my daughters to grow up without shame. I wanted them to be at home in their bodies and to always speak their needs, desires, and ambitions (except at bedtime, when I just wanted them to go to sleep). I wanted them to always love and be loved in healthy, secure relationships. It turned out that my friends raising sons had analogous concerns as they, too, tried to teach their children to honorably navigate a culture that objectifies bodies, normalizes rape, and rewards a cramped idea of masculinity.

It took time to figure out my next move, but eventually I understood that I needed to relearn how to think about sexuality. I needed to dramatically change my approach when it came to bodies, relationships, and love—urgently, while my children were still young. And once I became aware that raising happy, healthy children would mean acknowledging sex in a whole new way—and might mean dealing in unfamiliar ways with my own uncertainties about intimacy and pleasure—it only took a few conversations with friends to confirm that I wasn't alone in asking questions at the edge of my comfort zone and hoping to find fresh, modern, and realistic answers. Clearly, it was time to bring the birds and the bees into the twenty-first century.

But how?

I had lived in the Netherlands long enough to notice *what* my Dutch friends and their children experienced: super-low teen pregnancy, sexually transmitted infection (STI), and abortion rates; more positive, consensual sexual encounters; better parent-teen relationships; and far more respect and cooperation among genders. But now I wanted to grasp *how* they accomplished all that.

So I decided to take a closer look at what actually goes into raising children to be familiar, comfortable, reverent, and responsible with their bodies—children whose sexual lives are acknowledged, accepted, safe, and not so warped by shame. What had the Dutch been teaching that I was on the verge of leaving out? How, as a parent, could I balance my children's need for health and safety with their right to freedom and pleasure?

To find out, I embarked on a journey of observation, research, and reporting—all the while trying new things in my own household. I soon learned that Dutch parents ask the very same questions we do when it comes to kids and sex: *Must I talk about it? When? How? What should they know?* But they come up with markedly different answers: a range of actions and behaviors, often deceptively small, with the power to shape a more just and free society. I discovered how, from babyhood on, Dutch kids are taught by their parents about healthy sexuality as naturally as they're reminded to eat fresh veggies and look both ways. In Dutch schools, I saw how world-class sexuality education begins with lessons for four-year-olds on body parts, knowing how you feel about being touched (on the arm!), and how to form sound relationships. I discovered the completely unexpected ways in which Dutch adults deal with preschoolers' normal tendencies to put their hands in their pants and "play doctor" with friends. When I joined Dutch parents gathered in a bookshop to hear experts on dealing with puberty, I expected sex-talk sample scripts. To my surprise, the subject was how to keep parent-child relationships close and lines of communication open. Why? Because body changes and sexuality had always been out in the open, of course.

In these pages I write a good amount about what I have learned from watching and listening to Dutch experts, educators, and families.

But this is not a book about them. It's a book about us: Americans who sense that something's amiss in our culture's approach to sexuality—and who suspect that more openness might be part of the solution. This book is written not by an expat waving from afar but by an American parent right here at home who had her own reasons to go looking for solutions to suit the society she knows best. In fact, when my research led me beyond Dutch borders and back to different parts of the United States, I found that plenty of American parents are already doing things the "Dutch" way—but they often keep quiet about going against the norm, which can leave them feeling more alone than they really are.

Allow me to say here that as much as I love giant cheese wheels and bounteous vowels and consummate practicality, I don't mean to argue that Holland is perfect. For one thing, it's a great place for tourists to get run over by bikes. Beyond that, though, and more to the point, plenty of Dutch men and women are capable of being sexist, and they often adhere to old-fashioned gender roles. Despite the fact that schools in the Netherlands are required by law to teach about sexual health, including knowing boundaries and respecting diversity, some still don't. The Netherlands may have been the world's first nation to legalize same-sex marriage, and the city of Amsterdam may be a top LGBTQ+-friendly place to live *and* have 180 nationalities, half of whom identify as ethnic minorities, residing more or less peacefully in one place, but like Americans, the Dutch still do—and will probably always—deal with instances of discrimination. Even though the Netherlands perches in fine company at the tippy-top of world racial- and gender-equality charts, my Dutch friends would be the first to say that they've still got a long way to go toward full fairness. Dutch people are allergic to pompousness, so if they weren't embarrassed to hear they're leading the world in effective sexuality education and egalitarianism, they'd probably be surprised—or skeptical. Still, to me as an outsider, many tantalizing lessons of the Dutch approach stand out. I don't want to cherry-pick, so in this book I explore social context wherever I can. But it's my hope that also, sometimes, just knowing there *is* another way can offer a meaningful beginning.

Some readers may want to know why this book on teaching about sexuality focuses so much on the messages we send to children before they reach puberty. The answer is simple: even for caregivers and educators intent on raising well-rounded, capable children, sexuality is never more neglected than during the crucial foundational years. A child's early stages of development are the best and easiest times to set a healthy, happy course—with no unlearning required later on. My friend Deb, an early childhood educator and the mother of a high school boy, put it this way: "You can't learn self-esteem when you're fifteen. It's really hard to unlearn shame, even if somebody comes along and tells you that you're entitled to your sexuality."

In the end, I came away from my research with an up-to-date, wholly new, and utterly surprising sex education. Certainly fine sexual health, safety, and self-esteem emerge from good sex ed offered early, but so too do respectful relationships, broader opportunities, and gender equality itself. As I searched for a new philosophy, what really caught my interest was the unexpected, the counterintuitive: advice that seemed to fly in the face of conventional wisdom and yet seemed *better* at the same time. In the end, the exciting part of this journey for me hasn't so much been amassing handy data about different types of birth control and which comes first, wet dreams or whiskers, although I did learn plenty of things like that. What excited and scared me most—and still thrills me every day—is the challenge of *wanting something different* for my kids. Not only protection from unintended pregnancy and STIs, not only safety from sexual assault, but also total body autonomy, freedom from shame, an unquestioned right to pleasure, and relationships full of love and respect and intimacy and comfort and delight. In other words, I wanted to learn to accept and stop fearing my children's sexuality—starting when they were still little. I wanted to see if I could learn to welcome that side of life with them. At least, I *wanted* to want those things. This is the book in which I try, and these are the lessons I learned in my better-late-than-never sex education: not the fourth-grade film strip, not the high school boyfriends, and not even the intimacy of coupledom and giving birth, but the new notions that I scrambled to gain when my kids needed a message that seemed to be missing.

Often when I tell someone I'm writing about how Americans teach about sexuality, they'll snort and say, "I think you mean *don't* teach." And they do have a point. Although there have always been exceptions, we all know that a single, awkward birds-and-bees talk with a tongue-tied grown-up is practically an American rite of passage. But that is the past, and this book is about the future. It came about not because I'm a condom-flinging sexpert or an Alfred Kinsey acolyte or even much more adventurous in bed than a beached jellyfish. I wrote it because life handed me a revelation so big, so surprising, and so darn *useful* that I don't dare keep it to myself. I hope this book can revolutionize—or at least advance—the ways we think, act, talk, and teach about sexuality in America. Because to my great surprise, that's what we're really talking about when we peek in the stroller—or drop off at college—and name those simplest of wishes for the future: health, happiness, security, equality, and love.

PART ONE

HATCH

1

Dreaming

One cold Minneapolis morning when my daughter Caroline was not quite two, I stepped out of the shower to find her sitting on the bath mat. She'd toddled across the hall in striped footie pajamas from her little bed. Her short brown hair stood up at the back, tangled from a busy night's sleep.

"Hi," I said.

But she wasn't looking for small talk. With great seriousness, she pointed up at my crotch.

"Daddy," she said.

It took me a moment to realize she was drawing a similarity between my (rather free-range) pubic area and a nice hairy man we knew—my husband and her father, Dan, whose bright laugh and helpful soul and wiry black sprinklings always livened up our home. I seized the moment to explain about the body part she had just noticed—what it's called, what it's for. I made sure to relate it to her in a way she could understand; then I asked if she wanted to know more.

Just kidding! Nothing of the sort even remotely occurred to me. I only kept smiling and shaking my head in wonder at this funny little squirt of a kid as I toweled off and got on with my day. *This parenthood thing—what a trip.*

Funny, though, that moment in the bathroom stuck with me. It seemed both momentous—the very first time my child expressed curiosity about a reproductive body part—and totally unexpected: What was this tiny tot doing expressing curiosity about a reproductive body part? Later that day, I laughingly described the anecdote over the phone to my sister, a fifth-grade teacher, who laughed along with me. She also gently hinted that I couldn't go on just smiling and shaking my head forever. At some point, I would need to turn those moments into conversations.

But as with everything else when it came to raising my first child, I figured I would eventually learn on the fly how to talk about *those* things—about bodies, about reproduction and sexuality, about self-esteem, relationships, and love. As for body parts, Caroline had several down already—nose, knee, belly button—but we were still dealing with some confusion about neck versus throat, and ankle just made *no* sense: leg or foot, fine, but ankle, sorry, no, absolutely nothing there. When it came to naming genitals, "bottom" would surely suffice for now. I just had to trust that Dan and I would figure out the rest in time. Given all of the other things we heard young toddlers needed to learn and do—puzzles! playdates! Mozart! baby class! skipping nap! feeding the ducks! jumping off steps! fighting bedtime!—we already had enough to keep up with. A few anatomical terms could certainly wait. Anyway, I had always heard that when it came to explaining things like where babies come from, parents could just wait until kids asked. And naming my *mons pubis* after a friendly fellow wasn't exactly asking. Or was it?

I hardly had time to worry about it. Like all of the loving parents we knew in our family-filled neighborhood by Lake Harriet (and well beyond), Dan and I were busy figuring out how to raise our child to be safe, smart, happy, healthy, confident, and loved. We wanted her—particularly as a girl—to have a fair shake in life and to know that every child deserves the same good opportunities. But how to get there?

Dan and I had both inherited from our parents a deep belief in children's capacity for independence. Over time we gained confidence that when lovingly given good knowledge, even tiny ones can make good choices. This was a good start. But unfortunately, like any parents, we had our blind spots. A big one—and the one this book is about—had to do in the simplest sense with those pesky unspoken body parts. At its most complex, it connected with our desire to raise a child who believed herself worthy of respect, love, and the biggest dreams she could dream. It was going to take living in another country to glimpse that missing piece, moving back to the United States to see why we needed to go beyond old-fashioned birds and bees, and a series of mind-blowing lessons to finally discover the joy of sex ed. Or at least the non-misery of it. Or at least the possibility of something like that.

Not long after Caroline dubbed my groin "Daddy," our little trio of a family said good-bye to our house in Minneapolis and boarded a plane for the Netherlands, where Dan's new job would begin. We had a new life to build in Amsterdam, where we would end up staying for the next year and a half.

We'd only had a couple of months to prepare for our move and very little time to ponder what to expect. But I had lived abroad before and traveled enough to know I could count on a honeymoon period followed by intense culture shock. Everything started out according to plan. We flew out of a stiff Midwestern winter and landed in sweet, supple springtime. We wandered the brick streets of our new city as indigo hyacinths and crimson tulips nodded from window boxes in perfect breezes. We learned our first Dutch words ordering fresh-squeezed orange juice for Caroline and milky *koffie verkeerd* ("wrong coffee" because proper is closer to black)—to go with our apple *pannenkoeken.* We gazed up at brick steeples piercing the bright blue sky and down into glossy wooden canal boats. We wandered blissfully into hordes of heavy black bikes, charmed by all the dinging bells and unaware they were meant for us. *Let op!* Out of the way, *toeristen!* Below our apartment windows on the broad, busy Prinsengracht, sooty gray coots squawked at swan families bossily airing their huge white wings. The swans parted to make way for long, glassed-in sightseeing boats flat enough to slide beneath low arched bridges that twinkled at night. Over and over Dan and I said to each other as we stared out the front windows, or wobbled through the park on our very own heavy black bikes, or just walked, pushing Caroline in her stroller: "Can you believe we *live* here?"

Our daily peregrinations soon went from car-seat-horror-screaming affairs to pleasant musical ones. Like everyone else in Amsterdam, we pedaled just about everywhere. Perched in a wooden box at the front of my secondhand *bakfiets* with her hair flying in the sun (or hood cinched in the rain), Caroline no longer fussed and certainly did not strain to escape. *Jingle bells, jingle bells*, she belted out everywhere we rode that first summer. "The wind gives me tears," she sweetly sighed on a breezy day. I loved this little firecracker of a girl beyond description. I loved the certainty with which she made up her mind, and the challenge of knowing she would not change it. She ordered for herself in cafés, paid tips to buskers, and fiercely insisted upon using public restrooms on her own. And the imagination behind those sparkling eyes: the dollhouse dramas she brought to life in our living room, the birdlike dances she timed to banjo music, the figures of her grandparents she lovingly crayoned like gangly four-tentacled squid. I treasured the glittering curious eyes that seemed so rarely to close and the tangled squirrel's nest we loosened from the back of her head each morning. That head: I loved it fiercely, desperately.

But I put no helmet on it.

"We believe helmets will make it more dangerous," our bike salesman said after refusing to order one for Caroline. "If the people look too safe, the drivers will stop being careful."

This is where I'm supposed to tell you that the honeymoon ended and a nasty bout of culture shock set in. But in reality, it just didn't go like that. Certainly, frustrating paradoxes like the helmet problem abounded—although I confess, we easily got used to riding with our heads exposed.

By and large, living in the Netherlands made life easier, not harder. Here, a relaxed but affectionate parenting style was the norm. Instead of hovering over their little climbers and sliders at the playground, Dutch parents opted to sit in the sun reading or chatting with friends, enjoying coffee (okay, or Prosecco and cigarettes). They were quick with hugs but unwilling to overreact to a skinned knee or a bumped nose. Yet they weren't teaching indifference, I realized after watching for a few months, and my horror shifted to admiration; they were teaching independence. Nobody appeared to think Dan and I were daredevils anymore when we let Caroline ride her scooter ahead to the street corners or climb a jungle gym out of arm's reach or walk into an ice cream shop to order for herself and pay "the monies" for her own scoop.

In a city as international as Amsterdam, the families we got to know certainly weren't all Dutch, but most seemed to embrace a typically Dutch mentality when it came to child rearing. Regularity, cleanliness, and plenty of time to play—not too much stress—were the goals of parents there, who wouldn't necessarily hesitate to leave a napping baby at home to run off to school to pick up a kindergartener. A little older, and kids walked or biked home on their own.

I didn't know it at the time, but social scientists and researchers, too, were finding things to love about Dutch social life. While we lived there in 2009 and 2010, Dutch children topped the charts as the happiest, healthiest, and best-educated kids on earth. Their parents, too, ranked as the most satisfied and least stressed anywhere. And the Netherlands consistently stood as one of the most gender-equal countries in the world. Living among them, I saw Dutch families thriving in ways that made me want to pay close attention and learn.

After a while, I assumed I had the Dutch secret sussed: these people were thriving on plenty of fresh air, exercise, nourishment, security, and opportunity. Their social safety net was strong. Universal health care, subsidized day care, flexible parental leave, and quality public education were biggies, but direct deposits from the government for things such as baby supplies, family vacations, school materials, and the general expense of raising kids were no small things either. And then there was this thing called *gezelligheid*, a uniquely Dutch concept of cozy-cute togetherness. *Gezellig* was an impromptu children's puppet show in the park, two old sailors cry-laughing over *biertjes* in a candlelit café, or the sight, when we glanced out the window on our way up to bed, of an open boat full of friends sharing woolen blankets and pouring wine beneath the stars. Biking, walking, talking, laughing, fresh air, flowers, balance, boats, and a bit of booze: I thought I knew the magic recipe, and I resolved to bring it home with me when, after a swift eighteen months, our time in the Netherlands came to an end. But I was still missing a crucial ingredient.

Libby arrived a few months after our return to the United States. It was early April 2011, and yellow Seattle sunlight flooded through the bedroom window. Libby and I reclined in bed, breastfeeding and sleeping. Just outside, the bright, inchworm-green leaves of an apple tree hid robins, raccoons, chickadees, and our neighborhood hummingbird, whose tin-can-telephone babble made a constant sweet comfort. Caroline came and went from the park smelling of wind and bark and clay. Newly glued to both of my daughters, I felt a bodily joy like I had never known.

But at night in the dark, I crashed. In my dreams I saw skydivers with tangled parachutes plummeting to their deaths. I clung to my daughters in the backseat of a van with no brakes, going downhill fast. I watched a jumbo jet take off over the ocean at night only to tilt and groan, a fatally injured colossus, into the ink-black sea. In the mornings my jaw was sore from clenching.

After the first few delicious postpartum days morphed into these surreal and scary nights, I had a new dream. Now I was pedaling quietly through the streets in Amsterdam, sometimes alone and sometimes with my daughters. The streets weren't real ones I could name, but the bricks, the gables, the bridges, the bike paths, and the canals told me where I was: underway, under my own power, and safe.

It didn't take a specialist in dream analysis to see: my fear had to do with raising daughters. The images in my dreams were telling me that despite arriving loaded with inherent potential, my children could very well become too hampered to take off, to fly, to soar, and to safely land. It was a pretty heavy metaphor, but I guess that's what it took to get through to a woman who was still hoping anatomical terms would somehow teach themselves to her preschooler. Now I felt more urgency. How would I teach my children? What knowledge would protect them? Was there any approach that wouldn't burn up their self-esteem? And why did the answer to my worries seem to reside in a place halfway across the globe?

As I nursed my new baby and tried not to fret, I began reflecting more deeply on what I had seen there. Living in Amsterdam, I had often been entertained by what I considered just a quirk of Dutch openness: a super-pragmatic approach to bodies and sex. In our host city of glowing brick bridges, jingling bike bells, and red-light alleyways, the locals always struck me as remarkably grounded: comfortable in their skin, coolheaded around other genders, libidos simultaneously intact and under control. Catcalling and street harassment were unheard of. As a woman in public, I never felt eyeballed. There was no lack of style in this cosmopolitan city, but compared to American life, a woman's appearance just didn't seem to carry so much importance, nor did girls and women seem to aim for a particular beauty standard. Some women wore makeup, and a great many didn't. Rainbow hair dye and trendy clothes were a shared province of young and old. And no matter where we went in the city, I never saw anybody go nuts about nudity. Little (and not so little) kids played naked in the public wading pool, and we had the occasional glimpse of a neighbor leaning out her window, bare breasts a-swinging, to drop a set of keys to the dog sitter. Regular families lived, worked, and sent children to day care in the red light district, walking to and fro without batting an eye—except to wave hello—at the legally protected, tax-paying, and barely clad workers in the neighborhood windows. Other things started coming back to me, too: fashions, especially for children, were gender-neutral and fluid. Normal body functions were seen as nonthreatening; at-home childbirth was typical. Caroline's preschool teachers used toilet teaching as an opportunity to send positive messages about body parts, and I heard parents using correct anatomical terms around their kids from babyhood on (but not exclusively—they weren't stuffy and used informal terms too, so a little boy's penis was just as likely to be called a *piemel*, akin to "willy"). I'd quickly recognized that none of the other mothers were running around with a "daddy" in *their* underpants. Pubic hair was just pubic hair, and kids seemed to know it as well as anyone. Crazy as it sounded, I had even heard that school sex education commenced at age four, and that many Dutch parents allowed their teenagers to have romantic sleepovers at home.

At the time, I had simply watched the families around me, amused and curious, yet not sure what it all added up to. But after I returned to the United States, those memories came back to me with new meaning. Now I wondered if the typical Dutch pragmatism about sex was a critical piece of the bigger picture of wellness and equality I had admired so much. For the first time, I saw commonalities between typical Dutch openness about sex and some of the other traits I had observed in Dutch culture, which were all similarly rooted in respect, tolerance, and an eye to the common good. I had felt those things myself, and they'd changed me. From my first days living in Amsterdam, I had felt physically welcome in a way that was unfamiliar to me as a woman who had grown up in the United States. I felt less concerned about my face, my hair, my clothes, my voice. No matter how I groomed, what I wore, or when I chose to speak, I simply felt *acceptable*. Day in and day out in my neighborhood as people lived by bike, skirts fluttered up, hair snarled, clothing smudged, and rear ends of every shape and size tipped skyward as their owners bent to untangle chain locks from racks and spokes. But no one stared, and no one snickered. In fact, no one but me seemed to notice at all. Over time, I realized this general acceptance of others, no more complicated than the golden rule, was the reason I felt so very okay in Amsterdam. It was a paradox, but when I felt no gaze, I felt more connected and attuned to the people around me. I relaxed, smiled, talked to strangers. I felt happier, more brightly curious, and vastly more creative. I had no doubt I could do more in the world.

After living in the Netherlands, I had naively expected to waltz back home a happier, freer version of my female self and that the future would be all rainbows and bluebirds and equal opportunity. But in the months after our return as I waited to give birth, Dan and I both experienced our native culture as profoundly more hostile than we'd noticed before. Ads, movies, music, pundits, and politicians relentlessly portrayed American women as sex objects, as inadequate mothers, as unreliable workers, as incompetent decision makers, even as "sluts" who deserved to be raped. Acceptable women, it seemed, were still stereotypes: either irresistible temptresses or old-fashioned household angels who knew their place.

As I noticed American culture peppering girls and women with unrealistic, contradictory demands, I started coming up with questions I hadn't asked before. Where had I gotten my ideas about gender, sex, and power? Why had I felt integral and confident living in Amsterdam, while at home (even in progressive-leaning Seattle) I felt discouraged, numb, and often voiceless? What and when and how on earth was I supposed to teach my kids about autonomy, freedom, pleasure, and desire? Was it even possible, in my culture, to uncouple bodies from shame?

The cultural lessons I'd learned as a girl about life in a female body hadn't fully served me, and judging by US data on poverty, male-on-female violence, rape, wage parity, and other signs of gender inequality, those lessons weren't doing much for my fellow citizens, either. I knew in my heart as well as my nightmares that if I stood aside, my two small daughters would receive the same messages. My friends raising boys had corollary concerns. How could they raise their sons to value everyone equally in a culture with a toxic definition of masculinity? How could they broaden the idea of manhood? I wondered if day by day, with quotidian simplicity, I could teach my children to expect equality. Could I teach them about sexuality in an honest, empowering way?

I knew I needed more than scary dreams and gut feelings to guide me. I had degrees in English and education, but now I wished I could go back to school for gender studies, history, economics. I wanted to become articulate about the deep-down concerns I had often felt but never knew how to explain, and there was no going back to the Netherlands. At least, not yet; we eventually began returning to Holland every other year for extended stays during which the kids attended school. But when Libby was a baby, I started where I could: in my own local bookshops and libraries, trying to discover what I needed to know about sexuality and what hope a stymied mom could have of raising children who foster—and expect—equality of all kinds.

By the time Libby was a year old, I had a house full of gender studies books and a (wishful) ban on Disney princesses. Dan was getting good at screening Monday night football commercials and working on how to explain why cheerleaders wore minimal clothing. The two of us soon shared an obstinate little penchant for gender neutrality. We made a family rule that no wardrobe would exceed 50 percent pink (ha). We tried to say "she" and "her" when we made up stories about squirrels and bees and truck drivers. If I was playing with figurines on the kitchen floor with Caroline, chances were good that a boy bunny was going to try on a tutu and the other bunnies might have to learn a lesson about freedom and acceptance. And if a stuffed kangaroo and a plush snake loved each other very much and wanted to get married, then we were getting out fake cake to celebrate regardless of genus, species, or pronouns.

Certainly some things were clearer to me now. But I had gotten as far as I could in my own backyard, and I was still having nightmares in which my children became birds with clipped wings. I still dreamed of comfortably pedaling a big sturdy bike through antiquated brick streets. I knew that living in Amsterdam had made me happier as a woman than I'd ever felt before. And I knew I wanted that same freedom—a whole uninterrupted, uncomplicated, unrestricted lifetime of it—for my daughters. But what was I supposed to do now? I felt increasingly resolved to do something substantively different. Something much more than avoiding too much pink and buying gender-neutral toys. I yearned to go back to the Netherlands to learn what that something might be.

Finally, in the fall of 2013, when Libby was two and Caroline six, our family returned to our old canal-ringed stomping grounds for an extended visit. We stayed in our former landlord's apartment, just below the flat we'd once called home. For me, the trip was part nostalgia and part mission. While my own children were still young enough to benefit, I needed to find out what the Dutch and other more gender-equal societies had been teaching that the typical American sexuality education—in households, classrooms, and the broader culture—left out.

One afternoon, Dan and I took the kids to NEMO, Amsterdam's science museum. Drifting together and apart among scores of other parents and kids, we spent the better part of a day exploring everything from kinetics to DNA. When we finally tumbled outside into the afternoon sunshine—one lucky stroke in an otherwise rain-soaked trip—Dan dug out water bottles and handed them to the kids as they climbed into the boxbike we'd borrowed. Then he turned to me, amazement on his face. "Could you believe that exhibit?" he asked.

"Which exhibit?"

Clearly I'd missed something.

"You need to go back in there," he said. "It's a huge display on the middle floor. Tons of pink and neon." He hopped onto the boxbike.

"Take your time," he said, humor in his hazel eyes. "See you when you get back."

A few minutes later I was posing for a selfie next to a long, luminous tube like a giant emergency glow stick mounted on the wall. Inside, gooey strings and globules stretched and swirled in a thick, moon-white mix. It was a little like a lava lamp, but also nothing like a lava lamp, because the liquid was meant to be semen. Fifty-three liters, to be exact: the average amount a man ejaculates in a lifetime. How had I missed this?

With their usual composure, the Dutch families milling around seemed to barely register the sex-and-puberty extravaganza, a permanent feature of the museum. To them, it was apparently no more remarkable than the brain-science display upstairs or the engineering experiments on the mezzanine. But after reading how many orgasms a woman can have in sixty minutes (134) compared to a man (16—oh, well), watching two giggling women arm wrestling with giant tongue puppets in a French-kissing diorama, and taking a computerized quiz that revealed my abysmal "sexual assertiveness" score (the onscreen game-show host actually laughed at me), I was admittedly a bit red in the face. There I stood, a married American mother in her mid-thirties, learning all manner of new sex facts from an exhibit designed for children. Despite all of my recent reading and my resolve to raise my kids with modern-minded openness, I could feel in my burning cheeks that my hang-ups were alive and well, especially when it came to female sexuality. But by a slight margin, my curiosity outweighed my discomfort, and I pressed on.

At the back of the exhibit stood a separate small hall with red velvet curtains and hot-pink neon: The PeepShow. A museum chaperone sized up my intentions and then handed me tokens to play the videos in each of three private viewing booths. On my way in, I noticed a black warning sign:

**THE PEEPSHOW CONTAINS INFORMATION ABOUT
SEX AND SEXUALITY NOT MEANT FOR YOUNG CHILDREN.
WE RECOMMEND ENTRY FOR CHILDREN 12 AND OVER.**

Just inside, I perused a glass display case filled with old-fashioned and newfangled birth control methods: cervical caps, sponges, diaphragms, and coils; a cascade of pill packs; animal-shaped condoms including a performing seal and a startled chicken; and a century-old "vaginal irrigator" that looked like a mini Ghostbusters proton pack (and was no doubt equally as useless against sperm).

Finally, I pushed aside the curtains to the video booths. The first film documented Dutch teen perspectives on virginity: different ideas about what that word means and how it feels to identify as one—for a girl in her teens, for example, or a man in his twenties. A second featured video blogger Hank Green breaking down the differences between sex (between the legs), gender (self-identity), sexual orientation (who you want to have sex with), sexual behavior (who you actually have sex with), and gender roles (socially constructed). And the last film was a montage of individual video portraits, from the neck up, of men and women climaxing. With a lot of arching necks, squeezed eyelids, lower-lip biting, and barely audible gasps, the premise was that nothing could be more erotic than a human face in a state of arousal. I couldn't deny it.

The PeepShow's final display case held an orgy at a standstill: fourteen pairs of wooden mannequins—the articulated, movable figurines artists use—glued together in various positions from the Kama Sutra.

I thought of the warning sign at the entrance—twelve and older, please, for decency's sake!—and had to laugh. I imagined how quickly an exhibit like Teen Facts, with its accurate body information, bill of sexual rights, acknowledgment of sexual diversity, and even kissing tips ("Don't bash teeth!") would leave an American science museum media-bombed and fund-slashed. Seattle's Pacific Science Center had recently installed a permanent exhibit on human health with a "sneeze wall," a floor-to-ceiling screen playing slow-motion video of faces going *ah-choo* while audiences receive a spray of mist. I could only imagine what NEMO might do with technology like that.

A closing announcement came over the loudspeakers, so with my last few minutes I sat down on a pink bench next to a boy of about eight to watch a giant-size cartoon projected on a high wall. The film, which I later dug up online, begins with two animated characters in their underpants, a boy and a girl, walking into separate cells within a time machine of sorts. The doors lock behind them. Throughout the film, a rising bar indicates their age: seven heading for sixteen. I put on headphones to hear the English voice-over.

"There they are. We can see two beautiful specimens—*homo sapiens*, young people," declares a fast-talking male narrator with a Dutch accent. "The girl goes first!" At age ten, the little character sprouts breasts—*pop! pop!* When she gets pubic hair at eleven, changes begin for the boy.

"He sees all kinds of things happening in his underpants... sometimes he also has an erection, just like that," the announcer says. And then a conspiratorial aside: "If we're lucky, we can catch a glimpse of that." And we do indeed: a bulge the little character tries to flatten.

The girl gets her first period—"That can be quite a shock the first time—yes indeed"—while the speaker points out the boy character getting restive. "If things go according to plan, then we'll get to see real-time his first ejaculation! Yes...yes...what a beauty! And it certainly won't be the last."

The kid next to me got bored and wandered off to join his mom, who was reading a display about acne. I turned back to the last few moments of animation. At fourteen, the boy finds itchy stubble on his chin. At fifteen, the girl giggles to find she can make her breasts bounce by bobbing her knees. When both characters hit sixteen, the lights in the machine zap out, the barrier between them disappears, and the two lean together in the dark.

"Great, isn't it?" the mad scientist asks. "It's fascinating to watch, every time you see it."

I was about to pull off the headphones and move on, but something about that last line left me momentarily pinned to my seat. The animation looped back to the beginning. Thinking of my own children as the confused little characters wandering into the cartoon puberty machine certainly did not give me a feeling of fascination. It gave me a feeling of dread. How come Dutch people didn't seem to feel that way?

By now I knew that Dutch teenagers had fewer problems with alcohol, drugs, unwanted pregnancy, STIs, and risky behaviors than their American peers, and there had to be more to it than fresh air and exercise. Something else deeply significant was going on here that left toddlers, school kids, teenagers, and grownups at ease in their bodies, equitable in their relationships, and ultimately healthier, safer, and more satisfied with life—including the sexuality that is an inextricable part of it.

As families flowed past me toward the exits, I realized I was standing smack in the middle of the key ingredient I had overlooked before when I tried to learn the Dutch recipe for a good life. What I'd missed was the *normalization* of sex. In other words, Dutch people weren't so open about bodies just for kicks. They were intentionally aiming for—and achieving—better outcomes. Tourist-trap red-light zones aside, I had seen proof that a place with lifted taboos didn't have to be a spring-break madhouse. It could also look like Holland: a little green-grass lowland of spinning windmills, fluffy sheep, tulips by the zillion, school sex ed for four-year-olds (it's true), intimate teen sleepovers under mom and dad's roof (*gulp*—also true), and some of the very lowest teen pregnancy and abortion rates in the world.

So did this mean that sex was missing from American culture? That didn't make much sense. Sex was splashed all over the place in the good old U.S. of A., and we'd proudly brought our trademark titillating mix of the puritanical and the promiscuous to the rest of the planet. But what was missing in my American life—in countless American lives—was an everyday place for conversations about sexuality. When it came to sex, we had *Do* and *Don't*, but almost no *hmm—let's think about that*. And definitely very little heartfelt *yippee puberty!* As I looked around NEMO that afternoon, I realized that if I wanted to raise the truly happy, healthy, independent kids I was envisioning, I couldn't assume plenty of good food and hugs and running around and bedtime stories were going to get us there. Nor would pushing back against gender stereotypes be enough. I would also need to give sex itself the breathing room to become a mundane, safe, everyday topic as normal as homework or soccer practice or weather.

This meant it was time to say good-bye to the awkward, all-American, old-fashioned fact-blurt about reproduction and protection. Instead of nursing dread about puberty, I needed to start thinking in the wildly different terms of *hopes* and *dreams* for my children in their sexual lives. I walked out of the museum and climbed onto my bike. Dodging tourists as I pedaled to meet up with Dan and the kids, I wondered: Could I learn to think like the mad scientist—*Great, isn't it?*—watching in wonder, observing with humor, guiding with trust? It was a daunting dream, but probably the answer to my nightmares.

2

Dropping the Fig Leaf

During that rainy September return to our old Amsterdam neighborhood, we managed to send Caroline off to first grade at the local public school—a chance for her to catch up on her Dutch, a chance for Dan and me to make new social connections. To that end, the two of us attended fall curriculum night, then tagged along for beers with some parents from Caroline's class. It was so hot and packed inside Café de Eland, a dingy brown bar across the canal from our apartment, that my glasses fogged up as we ordered *biertjes* and started introducing ourselves to other parents. Soon we were chatting with Tijn, the father of Lea, a third-grader in Caroline's mixed-age classroom. Tijn said he traveled frequently to the United States for work, so Dan asked him a favorite question as a conversation starter: What did he find bizarre about American culture?

Without hesitating, Tijn replied with a question of his own: "Do you remember seeing your parents naked?"

The heat of the café had already flushed my face, but I felt myself blush more as I laughed, shucking my down vest. "My mom, but not my dad," I answered. My mother had comfortably changed clothes in front of all three of us—me, my younger sister, and our little brother. As a child I knew the shape and feel of her body, from kissing her freckled forearms to soaping her back in the tub to irreverently patting her belly or buns. My father was relaxed too; he considered a bath towel or a pair of tighty whities—not exactly a suit of armor—to be decent enough around family.

Tijn's question, it was clear, pointed to American body shame—*adult* body shame. As soon as I answered him, I realized I didn't even know what Dan would say. He'd grown up with convention-bucking parents who could be fairly radical in their thinking. I turned to him, guessing he'd say he'd seen both of his parents naked as he grew up.

"Obviously I saw my dad," he said, "but I don't remember ever seeing my mom."

So I was wrong.

"That's what I thought," nodded Tijn, who told us he'd been familiar with *his* parents' naked bodies all his life—and he still was. When we asked about his own household, Tijn told us he and his wife made a point of keeping nudity normal around their three children. Certainly he bathed from time to time with his kids. Without a hint of shame, he described his daughter—the one in Caroline's class—prodding his penis in the shower, "to *learn* about it," he said, pausing for a sip of beer as he gauged our reaction. "It's not like we're having sex," he said. "But I think many Americans cannot tell the difference."

I tried to nod coolly as I stood there sweating. But I wasn't at all sure I did a very good job telling the difference myself. Or, to be more precise, what I *knew* didn't always match up with how I *felt*. I thought back to a year earlier, when five-year-old Caroline and I had hopped into the tub together for a little pre-bedtime soak. Facing each other, we soaped and chatted and relaxed. At one point, without saying anything, she'd reached toward my chest—not with total conviction, but not tentatively either—and grasped my right breast. She held it like a hamburger, squeezed it delicately, let go, and finally gave it a gentle poke. Then she looked at me with an expression that seemed to ask, *Was that okay?*

I looked at my breast, at her hand still in midair, and at her curious face. *Well*, I asked myself, *was it or wasn't it?* I was relieved she'd quickly let go, yet I wished I wasn't. I didn't want to be bothered by her curiosity, so it bothered me that I felt bothered by it. I wanted to send a positive message about breast and body. My silent discomfort unnerved me: Was it my own body shame I felt, and by reacting with anything other than acceptance, did I risk transferring that shame to her? Baffled as to the message I wanted to send, I said nothing. Instead, I gave a quick reassuring smile. The question in her eyes hung in the air. Since then, it had remained with me, and it had grown bigger.

Trying to unfluster myself with a gulp of beer, I thought about how calmly Tijn must have handled similar moments with his kids so as to keep from abashing them. In order to take those interactions in stride, he had to be unembarrassed and quite comfortable himself. Ever since living in Amsterdam, I had admired the Dutch for their comfort with the human body. In Holland, frank talk about the body began in very early childhood at home, where, from what I could tell, most parents were somewhat like Tijn and his wife: They didn't hide nakedness from their children, nor did they flinch from discussing parts and their purposes. Could I do more of that? *Should* I do more of that?

When we met Tijn, Libby was only two, Caroline just six. In our snug Seattle bungalow with a single bathroom to share, we all showered and bathed and dressed in a daily four-human weave of movement, sometimes washing together in a rush, or simply because bathing can be more convivial with company. Every once in a while, with what seemed to be a mix of curiosity and mischief, the kids clapped our bellies, patted our bums, squeezed and poked. Like Tijn, we knew we weren't doing anything sexually inappropriate with our kids when those things happened. Nevertheless, I wondered if I was doing the right thing to simply allow those moments to transpire without overblowing them by launching into discussions about privacy or "appropriateness" or other foreboding abstractions. I tended to keep my mouth shut in much the same bemused way I had in the bathtub with my inquisitive kindergartener.

That night in the bar, Tijn pointed out that even physical contact *without* nudity is suspected of being sexual in American social life. It seemed to him that American men "can't hug other people's kids to comfort them, even when they're crying," for fear of being labeled a pervert or a dirty old man. "But it's a natural human interaction," he said. "I think one of the most beautiful things is when a grandfather takes a young child's hand in the park."

Ah, the park. I remembered so well from our summers in Amsterdam how warm weather seemed to funnel all bikes into the Vondelpark. By noon, the sun warmed the giant wading pool, which overflowed with families. For two summers in a row, after preschool pickup at one o'clock, Caroline and I regularly met friends and spread our blankets on the field of grass surrounding the circular pool. After the first few afternoons, I almost stopped noticing that many of the children frolicked naked, even well into elementary ages. The dress code broke down approximately into thirds: some kids wore bathing suits, some simply stripped to underwear or diapers, and the rest went buck naked. Sometimes, Caroline joined the other children with her pale bare bottom reflecting patterns in the sun-charged water. Other times, when I managed to plan ahead, her swimsuit came along. Either way, I didn't hesitate to change her in the open. Parents didn't seem to think twice before sending their nude children out to play—and even the parents, grandparents, and babysitters resting on picnic blankets stripped to little bathing suits of their own, or they simply hiked up their skirts and shorts to capture more rays. While we expats jockeyed for a place under one of a few shade trees, many Dutch families did the opposite, ending the day with sunburnt shoulders and thighs.

I recalled sitting on our picnic blanket one afternoon, gazing out over the pool and spotting Caroline as she paddled at the water's edge with a little plastic boat. Around her splashed small bare bodies of every color with tangly hairstyles long and dark and wild and short and blond and curly. As children streaked everywhere, no sex categorization seemed possible without a glance at the groin. They squatted to pee in the grass, sprinkled the trunks of trees, tweaked themselves between the legs. *Savages!* I grinned delightedly to myself, trying to imagine the same scene in the staid city parks we'd left behind in the United States.

Watching the children swim and play had helped me remember— if not altogether rediscover—a time before shame, a long-gone sensation of absolute belonging in the world. I looked around at the full-grown bodies arrayed in the park, fleetingly certain that we belonged skin-to-grass no less than our children. Perhaps partly as a result of a glass of rosé in the woozy heat, I could see that we had the essentials in common: beating hearts, flowering brains, animal senses.

Everywhere around me, I saw a great deal of connection: parents, siblings, nannies, aunts, uncles, grandparents, and friends playing unselfconsciously with naked children, body to body, skin to skin, catching little ones when they slipped, hugging them if they cried. This was the connection Tijn was talking about. It relied, he insisted, on a lovingly cultivated familiarity with the squashy, curious, everyday wonder of naked human flesh. The result of which was that bodies are neither good nor bad. They just *are*. This physical habitude, Tijn suggested, allows people to be more relaxed in themselves and comfortably closer to one another.

As we said good-bye to Tijn and made our way out of the steamy bar that night, Dan and I held hands and softly laughed and shook our heads as we crossed the arched brick Berensluis, pausing to watch the reflection of the leaning Westertoren as its bells rang out the hour. It seemed to us that Tijn was right: American culture had confused the body with sexuality, sexuality with eroticism, eroticism with shame, shame with safekeeping. I wasn't about to advocate for some nutty nudist utopia—I'd never been one for nude beaches myself, even though I did opt to go naked at my neighborhood ladies-only spa. Instead, I simply began to wonder whether nonsexual nudity (that's what naturists call it) could even be conceivable in modern American culture. If so, could shame give way to more comfort, openness, and connection? Might we do less unwitting harm? Would I discover a better way to respond to my children's perfectly natural curiosity?

I had seen the Dutch tendency for body positivity even in the simplest picture books. True to life, babies, toddlers, and preschoolers were frequently illustrated naked—between changes of clothes, at bath time, after making mud pies, or just at random. This didn't only apply to books about bodies. It went for books about *kids*—so many examples I quickly lost count. Dutch picture books with baby characters often showed mothers nursing, and just as often gave a glimpse of brown in a diaper. Stories with sick characters could show vomit, and injured characters might be depicted in pain and even bloodied before getting better. In books about growing from baby to big kid, a page or two always hit toilet training. Genitals inevitably appeared. In many of the curiously vast number of Dutch books following children through a morning at preschool, potty time is mentioned as part of the routine. In one of my favorite illustrations, after the teacher has asked each preschooler to fetch his or her own little toilet from the cubbies, eight kids sit in a row on their plastic potties, each doing their own thing in the middle of the classroom rug. And then it's time to wipe, get those pants up, empty the potties, and wash hands. By contrast, the American Library Association (ALA) pointed out in 2017 how European illustrators who want their children's books released in the United States must appease American publishers by drawing clothes onto illustrated characters who appear nude in European versions of the same books.

Dutch television programs don't shy away from body functions, either. The first time I turned on an episode of *Sesamstraat*, the Dutch Sesame Street spin-off, the subject was noses, mucus, and hygiene. Despite a lot of snotting and guffawing, the episode lacked a sense of indignity or naughtiness. And even in Dutch social life, body functions are openly acknowledged in ways that can seem crude to visitors. Within two days of moving to the Netherlands, Dan and I had an appointment at the bank to set up a local checking account. When we arrived, we were greeted by a male banker even though we knew our appointment was with a woman. "My colleague is on the toilet," he apologized, so we'd need to wait. *What a jerk*, I thought, assuming she'd be furious if she knew he'd let on. But then our banker appeared. "Sorry!" she said brightly, reaching to shake our hands. "I was on the toilet!"

In 2013, Queen Beatrix abdicated the Dutch throne, and her son Willem-Alexander became king. In her continuing effort to keep her Seattle-based students up to date with Dutch kid culture, Caroline's Saturday language-school teacher emailed a link to a public television clip introducing children to the new royal family (the king and his wife, Máxima, had three young daughters at the time). The video was a catchy sing-along introducing everyone in the family, then taking pains to emphasize the most important thing: royals put on socks in the morning and poop in the toilet just like everyone else.

On that extended visit to Amsterdam when Caroline was six, she shocked us one day by coming home from school angry that we had sent her without a towel.

"Wait, what for?" I asked.

"For *gym*. After my *shower*. I was *freezing*, and I had to wait until my friend was done with *her* towel!"

It turned out that in Dutch public schools, quick showers are commonly required after gym class. "Then by the time they're older, they're used to it" in terms of both hygiene and normalizing body differences, Sandrine, a lower-elementary teacher, told me. Showering at school was a revelation for Caroline, who disliked the hassle of washing up at home but loved the social experience of the locker room at school.

Communal bathing seemed to work not only for schoolchildren in the Netherlands but also for the wider community. We had often taken Caroline to swim on Sunday mornings at Het Marnix, a public sports and recreation center close to our apartment in Amsterdam. It was a large, clean, modern complex with a vast—and unisex—locker room. This was typical of other public-pool facilities we saw in the Netherlands, offering rows of individual stalls for private changing (as long as changing in the stall next to someone of a different gender was private enough for you). Once in their bathing suits, all genders showered together next to the pool—less redundant when it came to building design, and less complicated for transgender people. At the Marnix, I saw how an all-gender, accessible locker room allows children and adults with disabilities who need support to remain with caregivers or companions regardless of gender differences. The Marnix also had separate communal changing rooms where families or swim teams could change together. There was even a colorful crib with waterproof padding in which a caregiver could corral a baby while changing.

Caroline looked forward to the locker room experience on our subsequent school-abroad trips to Holland—again when she was eight and once more at ten. But her head about popped off when I asked if she'd enjoy showering with her Seattle school friends: "Are you *crazy?* That would never work!"

The teachers and other professionals I spoke with in the Netherlands lamented that despite some national pride about comfort with nudity, body shame is creeping its insidious way through Dutch society, too. As late as the 1980s, elementary boys and girls up to age twelve showered in mixed-age locker rooms. "I never had a complaint from a parent," one longtime upper-elementary teacher told me. "Now parents call me, and some of the kids wear bathing suits even though boys and girls now shower separately."

Other people told me that topless sunbathing on Holland's beaches has all but ended with the current generation. "Now if a mother goes topless, her kids will tell her to cover up," the Dutch father of two sons told me, shaking his head. "That doesn't seem right."

The showers and sunbathing changes weren't the only evidence of change. Discussions about the march of body shame, fueled by internet harassment, web shaming, and slut shaming, as well as the everyday double standards parents hold for sons and daughters regarding nudity, have appeared with increasing frequency over the past few years in the Dutch media. But overall, from baby board books to anatomically correct dolls, television programs, preschool songs, and publicly funded royal videos, and even in the modern, gender-segregated version of elementary gym-class showers, the Dutch message was mostly that our human bodies *connect* us. Now that I was tuned in to this, I wanted to look for places in American culture where we normalize nudity for children's sake.

The first place I thought of was the public swimming pool—and its locker rooms, specifically. Just as in the Netherlands, I realized, locker rooms could offer a focused place—a petri dish of sorts—to observe our wider cultural attitudes about nudity and to judge whether they're doing us any good. Already at my own local pool in Seattle, I had noticed something odd. Each time I took the kids to their swimming lessons, my thoughts fixed for a few moments on the sign on the locker-room door:

ATTENTION: CHILDREN SIX (6) YEARS OF AGE AND OLDER MUST USE THE LOCKER ROOM APPROPRIATE TO THEIR GENDER.

It was just a standard plastic placard, but to me it seemed fraught—and not only because our community was just waking up to the concept that gender isn't always so clear-cut. What baffled me was the number. Who picked six? Why? Certainly many six-year-olds who visit the pool with a caregiver of another gender can shower and dress on their own in a separate locker room, but the sign's strong wording didn't carry the sentiment of encouraging independence. I wondered whose comfort the age limit was really about and what risks it was supposed to address. What did such a rule—even the fact of its existence—say about us as a society? Was my culture so busy sexualizing kids that even six-year-olds were somehow considered uncomfortably attractive? Or did we think children that age might themselves commit harmful leering? In particular, what did this rule say about us as adults and the germs of shame we carry and spread?

The everyday assumption that nudity represents eroticism is a profound entanglement sitting deep in the modern American psyche. It's why women don't go topless on our beaches (we are not there to have sex). It's why our wading pools require "appropriate swimming attire" for every age (we can't have tots attracting sexual attention). It's the reason Sally Mann's art photography of her children playing in the buff garners so much intellectual interest and so much scathing criticism (how can we not be appalled by our own minds when we look at kids and think of sex?). It explains why we are so uncertain about letting children, even very young ones, run naked in the yard. We hate to think of their wholesome bodies sexualized under the gaze of neighbors or passersby, so covering them up seems sensible—until we stop to think more about ritual coverings, particularly for girls and women: where concealment is the rule, objectification and gender inequality tend to be the worst.

Monica, a kindergarten teacher and fellow American expatriate parent who raised one toddler in Amsterdam and another after moving back home to Oregon, made a weary plea for advice to the broad mix of Dutch and international expats on the Amsterdam Mamas Facebook group one summer day in 2014. She'd been back in the United States for two years, and her older son was now four. She missed letting him play outside naked the way she had in the wading pools and beaches around Amsterdam. "The longer I live in the US," she wrote, "the less free I feel to let the kids be nude outside of a house. And I'm certainly more open to it than most parents I know—especially the parents of girls."

We Americans have had a tough row to hoe when it comes to dealing openly with having physical bodies. Our country was founded with a curious mix of progressive rebellion and puritanical reserve. It's not news that we still grapple mightily for the balance between notions of decency and the ideal of freedom. So even when I chose not to comment when my first-grade daughter and her second-grade friend stripped to their underpants to play outside in our Seattle yard on a hot day, I still wondered whether I owed the other girl's mother a text message. And would the message be informative—*Gorgeous day! Kids soaking it up in their undies!*—or would she want the chance to expressly permit or not permit her daughter to play outside undressed? *I think I trust,* I finally texted, *that you don't mind our girls doing water play in just underpants? Swim togs are available but they are more excited about nudity.* The message back reassured me: *Hell no I don't mind! I want them to be naked as long as they feel comfortable doing so.* At gut level, we both knew that our daughters calibrated their comfort against ours—and everyone else's. Keeping my mouth shut was essential in moments like this.

Meanwhile, that same spring, a four-year-old boy a few hundred miles to the north, in British Columbia, went running through the sprinkler, fully dressed, with his six-year-old brother while their dad washed the car. Afterward, uncomfortable in his sodden clothes, the younger boy undressed in the front yard. Two days later, while their father was out of town on business, a police officer arrived at the door and proceeded to question the children and their mother. An offended neighbor, it turned out, had called police on account of the nudity. There was no fine, but the officer warned the family not to repeat the offense. But what *was* that offense, exactly?

Caroline ran around outside our Seattle home in her skivvies (sometimes less) throughout her six-year-old spring and summer. By the following year, she still played outdoors in her underwear from time to time, but was more likely to keep an undershirt on or change (inside) into a bathing suit. Did she worry about what others would think if they saw her? Or how she would feel if seen? I wondered at that. I stewed about it. I read and reread that irksome sign at the pool.

I eventually called the aquatic center where I had taken winter lessons as a kid—and where posted rules now require children five and up to use the correct-gender locker room. Competitive team coach Erin Dunn answered the phone, and he was quick to be candid. "Locker-room etiquette is a never-ending issue," he said. As the father of a five-year-old boy and a two-year-old daughter, he admitted that when he was busy coaching, his son continued to use the women's locker room with his mother even though he'd technically aged out. The boy was capable of bathing and dressing on his own in the men's locker room, Dunn said, but the outdated shower buttons were too high and required a strong push. So his own son was a rule breaker in the ladies' room.

I asked Dunn to imagine a hypothetical meeting in which management and staff sit down to write the locker room rules about gender and nudity. What did he suppose were the risks they wanted to minimize?

He thought for a moment. "Let's say I had my daughter with me, and she was eight. In the men's locker room, I think that would be a little bit awkward. And I think it would be a little bit awkward for the people who are in there. What is that?" He made a quick calculation. "Third grade? She's not a little kid anymore. Kids are pretty smart at that point; they're pretty aware. They've got a long way to go, but they're not clueless. Maybe if we lived in a way more open society where people were like, 'I'll just change my clothes here on the street corner.' But that's just not how our society is."

Dunn was right. That's not how our society is *today*, but men, women, and children swam and bathed naked in public from prehistory into the Victorian era. Soon after that, in the United States at least, beachgoers in too-revealing suits could fear "swimsuit arrests." Since then, we've never given up trying to recover full rights to relax in the buff. After bathe-ins and other fleshly protests, American men won the right to go bare-chested in 1936. Postwar, bikinis were a fashion statement that rejected earlier decades' demands for female modesty. Today, activist groups in some states are still fighting—in both courtrooms and rather provocative protests—for topless freedom for women.

I told Coach Dunn about the Marnix pool locker room in Amsterdam. With private changing stalls and easier shower buttons, American locker rooms could simply be better designed for unisex, all-ages use. But layouts aside, I wondered if there wasn't more going on with American attitudes toward nakedness. When I first saw the Marnix locker room, I considered that while spas, beaches, and locker rooms in other parts of the world sometimes offer bathers ways to guard against being *seen* (private changing stalls), no one is entitled to protection from *seeing*. In other words, if you spot a topless sunbather or a man changing out of a sandy Speedo or your mom stepping out of the tub—examples of safe, well-intentioned, nonsexual nudity—even if you are a child, it's up to you to turn away from what makes you uncomfortable, not up to others to guess at your preferences or consider your line of sight.

Sifting through arguments about the appropriate age for children in locker rooms at this YMCA or that neighborhood pool, I started to wonder if I had it all backwards: Are adults the ones who feel most vulnerable, most violable? Is the child's gaze doing *us* some kind of harm? Then, reading the aquatics guide for the outdoor pool at Peter Kirk Park in Kirkland, Washington, where I occasionally swam outdoors in the summers of my childhood, I found it stated all too plainly: *Children 6 and older must use the locker room of their gender so that others are not offended.* How had it become so deeply shameful for an adult to be seen by a child? For an older child to be looked upon by a younger one? If humans learn by observing those who go before, then why not when it comes to living in our bodies?

As I searched, the most common complaint I encountered about locker-room rule breakers came from women who felt that children—particularly boys—"stare" at them. I thought about my own experiences as a girl in the women's locker room at the public pool, feeling quite certain that I did almost nothing but stare at the bodies around me. As an elementary school student, I discovered that my teenage neighbor had pubic hair—lots and lots of it! I noticed that old women's bodies could look papery and thin, or layered and poured like lava. I watched women with one breast, women with none. I saw that the bodies of children are not the bodies of adults, and I required more than my mother's sole example to expand my consciousness.

But a Fort Collins blogger wrote in a long 2013 post—one she herself called a rant—that "the women's locker room is…not a place where we teach anatomy lessons nor is it your home where your kids get to do whatever they want." A commenter agreed, saying that boys older than the age limit who can't use the men's locker room alone should—in all caps—STAY HOME. I pondered this. Why, I wondered, shouldn't it be the other way around? Shouldn't adults unwilling to be seen by children stay home instead?

Adult shame may be the driving force behind locker-room rules, but it's not the only one. In 2014, when the Palo Alto Family YMCA lowered the age limit for opposite-gender changing-room use to six after a crescendo of member complaints about the previous age limit of seven, it was reported by the *Palo Alto Weekly* that "some members said the problem is really about dedicating a separate space for family use where kids won't have to risk viewing naked men and women." But what was the perceived risk to the child who might see an uncloaked human body?

And yet there *are* risks—every caring adult has at some point been chilled to the bone by fears of child abuse. I certainly had. We know that children are vulnerable, and our fears of their exploitation are never far away. Pedophiles do exist, and abusers can lurk in children's own families and community circles. It's not a threat we imagine without basis, although it may be one we misunderstand. At the age of three, I had a babysitter—an adult woman—with a prurient interest in bathing and napping with me. This was no nonsexual nudity: she flashed me with her breasts and pressured me to show her parts of my body. When I told my parents, they whisked me from her care. I knew the situation was serious and scary, but I felt safe and protected because my parents reacted without doubting me. But this disturbed woman continued to make phone calls and harass my family despite the fact that my parents had involved the police, so my parents doubled down on their safety teaching with me. My mother went on to write a book and offer local lectures on child safety. She learned self-defense techniques and taught them to us three kids in the living room while my obliging father stood in for a perpetrator, wincingly covering his groin while we threw elbows. With a vocabulary for sexual crime and a repertoire of family rules and passwords for "suspicious" situations, I did feel I was better equipped than many of my peers in case of danger. But learning to live with a body on lockdown left me stymied about whether and how to enjoy it. The question for me as a mother—and surely for most caregivers—becomes how to balance freedom with protection. Perhaps doing so begins with knowing what we can and cannot control.

Contemplating this, I thought back to one of the summer days I'd spent with Caroline at the Vondelpark before we moved back to the United States. As the afternoon wound to a close, I gathered up our things and settled down on a poolside bench while my three-year-old finished up splashing. While I waited, a woman with a twist of thick blond hair and a bright blue uniform sat down next to me. Side-by-side, first in silence, we scanned the pool area. The day's horde had begun to thin.

"Which one is yours?" I asked.

"Here she is," she said in Dutch-accented English as a girl of seven walked over, still dressed from school.

"Hello," I said. The girl greeted me with a confident smile and told her mother she was heading across the lawn to the jungle gym. Her mother nodded, then turned to see me looking at her bright azure suit.

"I'm a flight attendant for KLM," she said. "I just got back from a trip in time to pick her up from school. So which one is yours?"

"There in the yellow swimsuit," I said. "I guess we weren't in the mood to go naked today."

"It's okay," she answered. "You know there are perverts here. It was just in the newspaper, men taking photos of the children. It happens every year."

My stomach clenched. "In the paper? Are they doing something about it?"

"What can be done? The police are aware, but there's not much you can do."

I scanned the lawn around us. At a glance into the patchwork of picnic blankets, I couldn't tell which solo adults were simply waiting for their children, like me, and which had come alone. Dozens of men and women lay with their heads propped on bags or towels, some with an ankle crossed over a knee, all tapping away on smartphones. It would be so easy to take pictures.

The flight attendant looked around also. "It's disgusting," she said.

I gestured at the crowd. "Do the parents know?" I asked.

"Of course. They all know," she said.

"But they're not covering their children?"

"Well, some do, I think," she said. "But that's not really fair to the children, is it? They should be free."

I agreed in theory, but I still felt quietly glad that Caroline wore her swimming suit that day. "Shouldn't they be free from creepy picture takers too?"

"Well yes, it's better if they are. But mostly they should be free from shame. It's not their fault."

"Is that why the parents don't do anything?"

"Maybe they don't cover their children, but they are all watching more closely."

I watched Caroline dump a bucket of water over her lap. "What happens if they see someone taking pictures?"

Now my neighbor looked sideways at me as if the answer should be obvious. "Well of course, they will walk over and talk to the person, and if they have taken pictures, they will tell them to delete them. Maybe they will call the police, and the police will do just the same."

The shrug of practicality—*What can you do?*—felt so Dutch to me. I thought of a story I'd heard about the central square in a neighboring village. An old town crank had gained a reputation for sitting on a public bench facing the cathedral doors. Whenever a pair of newlyweds emerged from the church, he would unbutton his pants and expose himself. The townspeople had a problem—and a quick, pragmatic solution: they moved the bench.

Caroline's wet feet slapped the concrete as she ran toward me, her suit bottom dripping. "I want to have a snack."

I toweled her down, scanning the crowd, knowing that now it was time to peel off her suit and dress her in the warm bright sun. I didn't go so far as to ask my neighbor, the flight attendant, to hold up a towel, but I did use Caroline's dress to keep her draped as I pulled up her underpants. Knowing I couldn't control what other people looked at or thought about, I wondered if what I was doing—unable, just yet, to *not* do—really helped at all. Or was I only sending a pernicious message to my child that her body was something we had to hide?

Almost every summer after that, from time to time I noticed parents making worried posts on the Amsterdam Mamas Facebook group about wading-pool leerers suspected of sneakily photographing kids at play. Sometimes the posts came with a photo of one suspicious character or another. The poster would plead on the forum for caregivers to stop letting kids swim naked—and then ask if they might be overreacting. Support, questions, and different perspectives would flood in from the community group. Few subjects on Amsterdam Mamas ever accrued more comments or more passion than those threads—and they all boiled down to two camps. One group, mostly foreign expats, insisted that covering kids protects them from exploitation—and what could be more important? The other group, with more Dutch voices, contended that telling kids they need to start covering up suggests it's their fault licentious photographers misbehave. This is the root of slut shaming and the ills of rape culture, they said, and worst of all, it replaces children's inherent freedom with shame. From following those discussions I learned that the most important thing to tell a child about the possibility of exploitation—even more important than strategies for self-protection—is that no matter what, being tricked or abused is never their fault.

In 2014, the judges of Texas's highest criminal court voted 8–1 to throw out the law that had brought them the case of a man charged with twenty-six counts of "improper photography" of children playing at a San Antonio water park. In the opinion, presiding judge Sharon Keller wrote that "protecting someone who appears in public"—except in bathrooms and private dressing rooms—"from being the object of sexual thoughts seems to be the sort of paternalistic interest in regulating the defendant's mind that the First Amendment was designed to protect against." Further along those lines, I would eventually hear from more Dutch parents who saw folly in thought policing: we just can't tell what another person is thinking or what motivates them. Sometimes, we can only try to work around them.

One late-summer afternoon in 2015, I saw a move-the-bench solution in action at the Vondelpark wading pool: safety volunteers in clearly marked T-shirts who passed the hours scanning not the wading pool but the ring of adults around it, watching for untoward behavior. At one point, two gray-haired volunteers—both grandmas, I guessed—approached a man reclining on the grass not far from where I sat. They confronted him, and he protested at first, but then he appeared to begin deleting photos from his phone. The grandmas gave him a final admonishment and then, to my surprise, left him alone.

Busy playing, the children themselves never noticed.

Living in Amsterdam, Dan and I had heard that covering one's windows in Holland is seen as a signal that you have something to hide, so we practiced getting used to leaving the drapes pushed wide open. It was nice; we didn't miss a minute of the canal winking at night under gothic iron streetlamps, or the seagulls wheeling over the water as sunrise peeked over the gable tops. And also that way, apparently, we didn't suggest to our neighbors that we had anything to be ashamed of. We just lived, making oatmeal in skimpy pajamas, taking the spiral stairs naked to the closet after a shower, changing at night with the lights on. Definitely once or twice I went skittering inside from the back terrace when a neighbor came out to shake a rug—we never totally got used to being so visibly bare—but over time I know we both had proud moments when we thought task first, clothing whenever. From our vantage point, we saw plenty: that dependable neighbor across the canal leaning from her attic window, this time scolding someone on the street, bare breasts quaking with her remonstrations; the gay couple straight across romancing shirtless over a candlelight dinner; even nudists boating past from time to time.

When we moved back to the United States, we stayed in a temporary apartment that stood just above street level. I was still jet-lagged and stung with culture shock when, one evening, I took a shower before dinner. As I toweled off and crossed the hall naked from the bathroom to the bedroom, I glanced out the open blinds. A city bus passed just then, its passengers seated at exact height for a full view. I shrank back in humiliation. Then my heart crashed to the bottom of my chest. I didn't at all want to censor the relaxed woman I'd become, but, it turned out, context was everything. In that moment, I found the American social expectation of modesty profoundly more powerful than my individual ability to feel free.

At the time, I didn't know that in many US states, it's against the law to go nude (genital area uncovered) not only in public but also inside one's own home if it's possible a neighbor or passerby could catch a glimpse. (I emphasize *nonsexual* nudity here. Indecent exposure, a threatening act with lewd intent, is rightly a crime in the United States and the Netherlands.)

Even though I was uncomfortable revealing my naked body to Metro bus riders, I technically didn't have to worry about legal ramifications if I happened to start making coffee on my way from the shower to the wardrobe. Indoors or out, in Washington State it is legal for a person of any gender to be nude. Every June, the Fremont Solstice Parade, right at the edge of my neighborhood, begins with one of the world's biggest naked bicycle rides. Dan and I have pedaled down (dressed) to watch, parking our bikes and hoisting our daughters high to see the exuberant sparkly spectacle of more than fifteen hundred

Solstice Cyclists, bright with body paint and waggling with flesh as they streak past. After twenty-five years, the Solstice Parade is a Seattle fixture, but every year a few citizens still call the police to report the nudity. In Washington State, to make an arrest for indecent exposure, the police must establish that the nudity was intended to be lewd and to cause fear or alarm in the victim. "What we'll say," Seattle police sergeant Sean Whitcomb explained to a reporter, "is 'What exactly about that nudity caused you concern?'"

It's a question to ponder. It was Tijn's question, too, in that steamed-up watering hole in Amsterdam. And it's the question that led Dan and me both to start telling our children that ideas about whether and when it's acceptable to be naked differ from place to place, family to family, and culture to culture. "It's a choice, not a rule," we tell them, using simple terms but hoping they'll begin to grasp the difference between social norms and moral absolutes. "Just because something isn't common doesn't make it wrong."

When I was a girl, I received plenty of well-meaning parental reminders to close my bedroom curtains while I changed in case a neighbor might glance in. We lived in a suburban neighborhood with big yards and big trees, but one never knew when a glimpse might fall through the window. By the time Caroline was eleven, I found myself occasionally fighting the urge—especially when she chose to undress smack in the window-filled living room on our densely populated Seattle street—to sweep the curtains closed, to tell her to change in her room, to ask her at least to go a little faster. But I've tried to hold my tongue, and Dan has done the same. As for the girl herself: she is not ignorant. She knows it is entirely possible that she might be seen, and she is pushing back in her own way, knowing that she could be freer, her body forgiven its existence.

Aside from the bodies of their child peers, Dan and I are likely to be the only ordinary nudes our growing children will know. Can our transient influence be enough? Like the bus full of commuters passing the apartment window, reminders are everywhere of social norms, of expectations, of limitations, of shame, shame, shame. Yet I want bodies to be so important and so revered in our house that we refuse to relegate them to the closet. Countless good parents spend so much fruitless effort trying to cheer their body-insecure kids: *The way you look doesn't matter! Your body is normal! You are perfectly acceptable just how you are!* Why doesn't it help much to say these things? In part because a lifetime of careful cloaking has already implied otherwise. In the end, it's almost impossibly simple. Real bodies become acceptable when they're part of everyday life.

For a time, my calm and sometimes nonreactions to both kids' impulses to reach for my chest every time I got out of the shower seemed only to lead to more frequent grabbing. So we made a rule that they needed to ask permission first, and that rule still stands.

"Okay, one poke," I laughed one recent bedtime as my ten-year-old, twice the age she'd been when she'd grasped my breast in the bath, asked permission as I sat on the edge of her mattress. "Then please go to sleep."

She smiled and gave a soft jab through my T-shirt and bra.

"It's so nice," she murmured. "Why don't *you* feel them all the time?"

"I do," I shrugged. "But maybe not as much as I used to—I've had them for a long time now."

"I can't wait," she sighed.

With those three words, joy on the edge of disbelief welled up in me. This girl *wanted* the body she had coming. It had been so different for me.

"I think you're going to love it," I said, kissing her good night.

3

Finding Words

My kids were still so little at the time, only six and two, but my visit to NEMO had left me with the feeling that I had some serious catching up to do. I could see that a key to the Dutch approach was to separate sex from fear. That meant I had to uncouple them in my own mind before I could teach my kids to do the same.

Back home in Seattle, I kept finding myself thinking back to a particular late-summer evening from a few years earlier when we still lived in Holland. The warm glow of a northern sunset lingered as I lay in bed, too hot, staring at the low attic ceiling. Music throbbed from passing party boats. Heavy chains clattered against bike frames, and loose fenders made tinny clanks as riders rattled past in the stretching dusk. Despite the dizzying hours of light, my mind roved to faraway dark corners, visiting one of my deepest fears: that my child, now three years old, would someday be sexually abused. *What if I don't protect her? What if I don't spot the threat?* My every ounce of reason told me that my child was safe and I needed to relax. But then, what was this worry in my gut? Deep down, I knew I needed to start giving her more information. But my mind was full of excuses: *Don't parents have enough to cover when it comes to raising and educating young kids? Why can't sexuality wait? Kids can't reproduce, so why do they need to know about these things? We don't teach them to drive when they're in preschool, do we?*

By the time true darkness finally settled over the city, Dan breathed evenly beside me, deep in sleep, his body barricading mine from the window just the way I loved. In her tiny bed across the attic, Caroline filled her small lungs and sighed. I had seen and admired Dutch openness, but I still dreaded telling her that my "daddy"—and her "bottom"—had proper names. She would need those words if she ever had to tell an adult about anything wrong—whether that was a stubborn itch or an inappropriate touch. Finally feeling sleepy again, I rehearsed a little: *And some children have a penis... Do you know how Daddy and I made you?... Secret touching from someone else is never okay.* I had words in my head. What made them so difficult to say out loud? And now that a few years had passed and six-year-old Caroline finally had some basics down, why did I avoid the subject? I still found it rather excruciating. Not precisely because I couldn't spit out the words, but more because I wasn't sure if I was choosing the right ones, or transmitting the correct knowledge, or getting the timing right, or even aiming where I ought to. After NEMO (and Tijn), I knew it was time to examine my discomfort.

More than half of American parents say they feel uncomfortable or only somewhat comfortable talking to their children about sex. In surveys, parents say feeling uncomfortable is the top barrier to having conversations about sexuality with elementary-age children. Sandy K. Wurtele, a psychology professor at the University of Colorado Colorado Springs, has found that only one in ten American kids between the ages of three and five can correctly name a penis, a vulva, a vagina, or breasts. Little kids know their *other* body parts, so it's clear the censor box is laser-focused on reproductive organs. As they get older, it doesn't get much better: A third of American teenagers say they've never heard from their parents about sex, and most sexually active American teenagers have not received any formal sex ed at all.

It turns out that sexuality educators have a go-to analogy to explain why talking about sex can't wait: What if we taught mathematics like sex ed, waiting until eighth grade and then diving in with algebra? Silly, of course. It takes years of practice, repetition, and foundation building to get to algebra—just as it takes years to develop sexual responsibility and independence. Same with driving, by the way: while the learner's permit comes later, skills such as concentration and spatial awareness—say, how to pay attention to signals, steer a scooter, and share the sidewalk—start developing in early childhood.

But even if we are certain it's necessary, we lack role models, practice, and support. Few of us feel adequately armed with information. Some of us feel uncomfortable about physical intimacy and confused when our own private emotions lag behind our fast-evolving social values. Many parents don't want to transmit fear-and-risk messages to their kids, but we aren't totally sure any other kind of message about sex is okay or safe. Questions of morality complicate and deepen our concerns. We fear crossing children's boundaries. We're often worried an informed child may offend others, especially other parents and teachers. And finally, yes, some voices in every community say it's corrupt to give children knowledge about sexuality. We hear them, and they give us pause. It's all enough to leave anyone mute. No wonder little kids tell researchers that the thing between their legs is a "pie," a "teapot," a "wing-wing," a "tally-whacker," "fat stuff," or just plain "yucky."

Back in Seattle, my new goal was to get more comfortable by reassuring myself that telling my kids all about bodies and reproduction was not only appropriate but also important. Americans may be famously reticent when it comes to teaching about sexuality, but it's not because we don't care about our kids, or because we're lazy, or because we're prudes, or because we're clueless (even though parenting has often made me feel that way). At some level, we *know* it's important to talk with kids about sex. We've heard the advice a million times: start talking to children early and often about bodies, reproduction, relationships, rights, self-awareness, and intimacy. That message comes from educators, doctors, psychologists, the American Academy of Pediatrics, the US Centers for Disease Control and Prevention, religious organizations, and name your respected institution here. No matter who's talking, they all want the same thing: to give youngsters the information, skills, and values they'll need for a healthy, secure life with plenty of opportunities for success. Accordingly, most American parents say they intend to follow this advice and inform their children early and openly about matters of sexuality. We parents consider ourselves primarily responsible for our children's sexuality education, and as a safety net, the vast majority of us—Republican and Democrat alike—say we want medically accurate, comprehensive sex ed backing us up in schools from at least middle school on up.

But…yakety yak. Knowing it's important and actually making it happen are very different things. When it comes to teaching kids about sexuality, there must be things that countless well-meaning parents dread even more than the risks of leaving kids in the dark. The fact is, transferring sexual knowledge from one generation to the next is *hard* for us. And while even a leading book by Sarina Brons-van der Wekken for Dutch parents on covering sex with kids is called *Blozen Mag* (*Blushing Allowed*), it's clear that most Americans have more than run-of-the-mill bashfulness to contend with. We struggle under a very unfair inheritance, generations-old, that taught us sexuality was dirty—or at least taboo—before we learned anything else about it. That lesson is harmful and difficult to unlearn, even for ambitious parents who want to try something new.

Another problem for parents teaching children about sexuality is that the responsibility either feels (a) incredibly heavy or (b) like someone else's. Studies show (and chagrined parenting coaches report) that mothers assume most of the responsibility for talking to their children—daughters and sons—about bodies and sexuality.

For the first few years of parenthood, Dan and I had an unspoken arrangement: we wouldn't actually *talk* about how we planned to talk about bodies with Caroline, and I'd pretty much keep the whole affair in my department. Like most American dads with a female coparent, he followed my lead, and that seemed to work until it slowly dawned on both of us that our kid was missing out on a *whole entire role model* in the sexuality department.

That was just a waste. Dan is bright and willing and smart and insightful. His relationship with each of our daughters belongs uniquely to them. A gag order—or even just a cautious silence—on one of the most important parts of their lives was simply not going to do. I stepped back, and he stepped up.

Part of the difficulty in getting there is that some moms *want* to keep sex talks in their department. And there's an equal and opposite problem of dads not exactly begging to be involved.

"David won't take Matthew to the puberty class," a divorced mother told me in reference to Great Conversations, a two-night course for adolescents and their parents that is popular in Seattle. Rachel had already taken her daughter and hoped to leave it to her ex-husband to attend with their son, but he preferred that she take the boy. Around the time Rachel told me that, I happened to watch a mini documentary about sex ed in the Netherlands. One scene showed a school meeting in which parents received information about upcoming lessons for their elementary-age children on relationships and sexuality. After the meeting, the filmmaker interviewed a few parents. "We treat sexuality in a very down-to-earth manner," shrugged Jan, a father with round blue eyes, tidy hair, and a sport coat over a T-shirt, about the approach he and his wife used with their two children, ages eight and ten. "We're bringing our children up in an open-minded way, so yes, we've dealt with most of the questions…at home already." He shrugged again, as if to say the subject of sexuality was not on his list of challenging parental responsibilities.

Accordingly, the Dutch dads I've asked are remarkably comfortable talking with their children about bodies—and as I researched this book, I noticed they seemed comfortable talking with *me* about their children's sexuality as well. On short notice one Saturday morning at our children's Seattle-based Dutch-language school, a Dutch father canceled his morning plans and stayed after drop-off to participate in a focus group I'd organized comparing Dutch and American approaches to sex ed. Another Dutch father had a commitment, but he asked for my email address and later reached out to see if we could set up another time to discuss, in his words, "this important topic." That morning I heard from a well-balanced cross-cultural group of fathers and mothers. By contrast, when I hosted a similar discussion for a group of sixteen American parents in my Seattle neighborhood, Dan was the only father to attend (hopefully not under spousal duress).

The following week when I was out of town, Dan took nine-year-old Caroline to the second meeting of the Great Conversations class for girls, offered at our local children's hospital. In an auditorium of more than a hundred parents and daughters, he was the only father in the room.

Although I think he's extraordinary, my husband is in many ways a typical guy who probably never pictured himself sitting in that scenario. He has needed to push his comfort zone just the way I have, and just the way many of us do. He didn't beg to go to puberty class with Caroline, but he wasn't reluctant about it either. To him, the reward of staying connected with his growing daughter was more important than the risk of awkwardness. After their duo stuck out in the crowd that night, Dan and Caroline called, laughing, to tell me their story.

"I was proud," she said. But I get ahead of myself.

Like so many caregivers in our generation, both Dan and I knew early on that sex shouldn't be considered filthy or shameful, but there was still a part of me that cringed to think of going into it with a preschooler or kindergartener. I felt stuck wondering how Dan and I could give our child what she needed for safety and empowerment without spoiling her trust in the world or disturbing her happy harmony with her body. And what if we did the job *too* well? In American society, where sexual knowledge is considered illicit for children, did we really want to have the best-informed kid in the neighborhood?

For a while when Caroline had been younger, I'd even thought (hoped?) that leaving sexuality unspoken would lend the subject gravity, sanctity, and importance. But one Dutch woman suggested quite the opposite: What if parents who don't talk much about sex but who are open and honest on other charged subjects—health, faith, addiction, mortality—inadvertently send the message that sex is a *less* important part of life? Something to get around to learning later, like water polo or how to truss a chicken? And is that why, she wondered, the smart, well-rounded female college students we read about in books such as Peggy Orenstein's *Girls & Sex* see a blow job as a reasonable exit strategy from a bad date? And why kids who, as my friend put it, "trade sex for chewing gum" don't value that part of their lives more highly? She had a point; I wanted to find the balance, and that had to start with finding words.

If sex education progresses like math education, then learning anatomical terms is like learning to count to ten. In other words, as a good many parents and educators will testify, body parts are the easiest part. But it's all relative; that doesn't mean teaching them is *actually* easy. It may be baby-level information, but terminology alone, I knew, can be surprisingly difficult and even contentious.

Until college, I only sort of knew the word for clitoris. I knew I had one, and I probably could have gotten the word if it came up on a quiz (I actually did take a health class in college, but all I remember is that one of my classmates impregnated the teacher that semester). Perhaps I was belatedly curious, but for whatever reason, looking up the actual *name* of that spot between my legs didn't happen until some time around my junior year, when I was twenty. So then I could spell it, but I still had pronunciation to contend with. "Clytoris"? "CLIT-oris"? "Cli-TOR-is"? *Bleh.* It didn't exactly roll off the tongue. "Penis" isn't any better. It reads like *pen*-is and sounds like it's named after urine or a legume. But at least we all pretty much agree on what a penis *is.* It was bad enough to be a clit-illiterate college woman, but worse was waiting until I had *two daughters* to hunker down with some diagrams and finally put to rest my vague, long-held confusion about the difference between a vulva and a vagina. *Vulva*: the female external genital area. Includes the outer and inner labia, the clitoris, the opening to the urethra (pee!), and the opening to the vagina. *Vagina*: the word millions of people use when they mean vulva, including a *New York Times* health blog post in 2016 urging parents to teach kids correct terminology. More specifically: a vagina is the internal muscular, tubal canal connecting the vulva to the uterus. Even in basic anatomy descriptions, it can be hard to find a non-penis-oriented description for these parts. I have seen the vulva, labia, and vaginal opening called the "entrance" to the vagina. For whom? Probably not the woman who lives more or less on the other end of things, and certainly not to menstrual blood or the baby traveling one way only. We might just as easily define the anus as the "entrance to the rectum" or the male urethral opening as the "entrance to the penis."

People have strong opinions about whether it's necessary to always use correct anatomical terms with very young children. The debate tends to be an always versus never argument, but I can imagine something effective in between. We want kids to know the correct names of their parts so they can stay empowered, safe, and healthy. So we have to use them often enough for kids to have the words on recall. I think that can happen in a family that still says "bottom," and one whose members "toot" just the same as they pass gas. The trick—and the challenge—is to teach correct terms *before* their informal substitutes and to use accurate language every time it's called for—and oftentimes when it's not. After all, kids learn "toes" before "tootsies," "head" before "noggin," "eyes" before "peepers." Why? Because primacy conveys significance. Even when we name a child, we announce the full name first. Diminutives and nicknames come later.

Some people battle terminology problems by going the other direction, trying to make the whole game more appealing. *Snippa*, a new word to mean "vulva" invented by a Swedish social worker in the 1990s, has been adopted in Sweden so that girls and women can have an everyday analogue to the common but unscientific term *snopp* for penis.

A sexual development brochure on kids ages zero to six distributed by the Dutch youth health service advises parents to choose words "that you think are nice, and that you can use easily." Then to explain to children that just as with noses and feet, genitals can have other names, and to give examples.

In our house, Dan and I had followed the lead my parents had set, starting our babies off by using "bottom" for the entire genital-anal area, buttocks too. When more precision was needed, we went along the lines of "Does it sting closer to where your pee comes out or where your poop comes out?" Alas, not every child can distinguish. So after a few miscommunications when she was a toddler, we encouraged Caroline to go by feel and apply any necessary ointment herself.

But precise language has its rewards, I learned when I started reading expert advice, which seemed to be what my gut had been telling me on that sleepless night years earlier in Amsterdam. Toddlers and preschoolers empowered with the correct terminology for their body parts are more likely to start out with a healthy, positive self-regard instead of negativity or shame about their bodies. They are considered safer from predators, who are thought to choose victims who seem unaware of their bodies and their rights. Children equipped with accurate anatomical language may stay healthier, given their ability to communicate clearly with caregivers and doctors in case of concerns.

With that in mind, I wished I had used correct anatomical terms much earlier and a lot more often. I didn't stop using more general words such as "bottom," although "front bottom" and "back bottom" got the bum's rush. While I still could, I even made the shift from "wipe your bottom" to "wipe your vulva, from your clitoris to your anus."

No joke.

I know. It's a lot. But looking back, I know that both of my children were frustrated at times by our lack of precise language. It is hard enough for a very young child to differentiate types of pain: *Does it ache, does it itch, does it burn, or does it sting? Now please say exactly where the feeling is located on this handy unlabeled map.*

Laying down terminology is a challenging enough start, and I've learned the hard way that repetition is the key after that. When she was almost four, Caroline, who had been born in a hospital via cesarean section, witnessed the at-home birth of her little sister and cut the cord herself. We had done our best to prepare her for that moment with plenty of birth videos and conversations, including information about how the baby got started in the first place—in our case, the most common way—which, on one festive occasion, Caroline had enthusiastically outlined for her grandparents. So imagine my chagrin when, soon after her sister's birth, Caroline paused in conversation one morning to search for the right word for her father's genitals. "His, you know," she paused, "his...dangly bottom?"

His *what*? Had we not been over this? Clearly, Dan and I had been letting the conversation drop for way too long between opportunities.

We were learning—and would keep learning—that in order to make things natural, we would need to repeat ourselves way more often than felt... natural. Too many times, I'd dusted off my hands, thinking *Whew! Done!*, after giving names for body parts, facts about reproduction, explanations for those ear-perking candy-wrapper-like sounds coming from the bathroom during my period, even calm replies on the surprise occasions when subjects like birth control or abortion came up in public—only to find myself a few months or a year later faced with a child insisting she's never heard any of it before.

It took a lot of practice for Dan and me to simply learn to act normal—to keep from making faces or using helium voices—when sex-related subjects came up around the kids, and we still have to push ourselves to take up the subject when opportunities knock. And knock. And knock.

One evening—always playing catch-up—I reexplained the words "penis" and "vulva" to three-year-old Libby just before she plopped into the bathtub with her big sister.

"So, what does Mommy have?" I asked.

"A vulva!"

"Yes, and what about Daddy?"

"A peeen...?"

"Yes, penis."

"It sounds like peanut," she said, sounding a little disappointed.

"It really does. So what does your sister have?"

"A vulva!"

"Yes!"

I had done it! Information! Repetition! I felt awfully proud of myself as I went downstairs to rotate the laundry. Little did I know I'd barely gotten her started. Seven-year-old Caroline knew that my idea of effective repetition was still too close to a three-year-old's idea of never-before-mentioned. When I came back upstairs, I heard her picking up my slack, asking Libby which genitals certain friends possessed. Then she moved on to neighbors, relatives, teachers, and the various pets on our street, including our two goldfish and the dead and buried cat. Libby loved this game.

"Okay," I heard Caroline say. "Ready for another one?"

"Yes!"

"What does Santa Claus have?"

"VULVA!" No need to think about that one.

"No, penis," Caroline corrected her.

"NO! VULVA!"

"He's a boy, so it's a penis."

"No, it's not."

"Okay," Caroline said. "Next one. What does *Sinterklaas* have?"

"Vulva. Next one."

We would soon discuss that not everybody identifying as a boy has a penis and not everyone presenting as a girl has a vulva. But for now, I had to hand it to the little one. American Santa, Dutch Santa—who really knows what's inside those magical pants?

Around that same age, Libby demanded a greater role in mealtime table chatter. Relevancy was not a feature of her developing conversation skills. Over one autumn breakfast, she discussed horses, a nonspecific boat ride, and a memory of going to the aquarium with her babysitter Carly. And then she said, "Mommy, when I was little, I was on your tummy and on your back." She may well have been talking about the baby carrier I used to wear. But never mind; I forced myself to grab that ambiguous bull by the horns.

"Yes!" I said. "Before you came out, you grew in my uterus"—I patted my abdomen—"and then you came out of my vagina."

"Oh," she said slowly, except it sounded more like "ehhhw." She gathered her thoughts and then said, "I came out of your tummy, and Caroline came out of Daddy's tummy."

"No, Libby," Caroline interjected. "Actually, Daddy can't have a baby come out of his tummy or his penis."

"But Daddy helped make you both," I said.

"How did that work again?" Caroline asked as Libby, satisfied, tucked into her oatmeal.

"That's when the mom and dad have intercourse," I reminded her, "or sometimes we call it sex, where the penis and the vagina join together."

"*Oh*, yeah."

I paused, waiting to hear if she'd ask more. But she looked bored.

"Will you look at this?" Caroline said a moment later, picking at the chipped white enamel on the windowsill. "It was green once, and pink before that!"

"This house was pretty much all pink inside once, actually," I said.

"Hard to believe," she said, shaking her head.

The human reproduction stuff would require more repetitions—and some alternative routes to parenthood such as insemination, in vitro fertilization, adoption, and even surrogacy—before things would really start to stick. With practice, it did get easier. No lesson came across as scary or shameful as long as I didn't feel—or seem—scared or ashamed myself (thank you, junior high drama class). And over time, I felt more and more convinced: even life's most important lessons can be so unspectacular as to be forgettable. But rest assured that no one ever lost sight of the truly shocking: that the old lady who once owned our house painted the whole doggone thing pink.

4

Innocence

When I first practiced talking about reproduction with my kids, I found it far easier to start with the biological and leave out the relational. I could explain the egg-and-sperm connection like a champ, but found myself blushing as I glossed over genitals uniting—and almost never breathed a word about what grown-ups might think and feel and say when they want to have sex. On a purely clinical level, describing most sex acts can be done in a fairly straightforward way, just as one puts a fork in one's mouth or shakes someone's hand. But it's much harder to talk about lovemaking. I'll admit it: the word "lovemaking" itself makes me cringe, and it seems I am not alone.

One evening over wine with girlfriends, my friend Tina shared that she'd had no trouble answering when her five-year-old daughter—a classmate of Libby's—asked, "What happens when you have a baby? Does it hurt?" All of us mothers leaned in. What had she answered?

"'Well,' I told her, 'the vagina gets bigger and the baby comes out.'"

It had been that easy, Tina said, to explain how a woman's body can stretch open. All in all, she reassured her daughter, it wasn't too bad. But sometime later, when the two of them were looking at a body book together at home, Tina said they turned to a page about intercourse. "And for some reason, I just couldn't tell her about *that*. Why was I so uncomfortable? My kid is a super question asker." It was plain to see that Tina was proud of this and wanted to meet her daughter halfway. "But I think I'm just not ready to go that deep with her. When we talk about it here [among adults], it's such a simple thing. But when I'm talking to my five-year-old, I'm embarrassed."

Our friend Megan, a therapist and the mother of a second-grade son and a preschool daughter, nodded about that. "I think it's because that's the emotional part. The one part that's more psychological and not simply mechanical. It's confusing for us."

"The intimacy part of it is hard," nodded my sister, the fifth-grade teacher, who was by then the mother of a two-year-old. "We have the pedophilia fear, and the fear of crossing the boundary of a child's comfort level without really knowing what that comfort level is, or how it serves the child. But I guess we have to go back to counting on our relationship or trust with that particular kid."

A term that comes up often in sex ed is "age-appropriate." But what does that mean? As parents and educators, we are constantly trying to determine boundaries—not just how far we can go, but also how far is too far. And it's no wonder we find this so confusing when it comes to teaching kids about sex. As Americans, we have such contradictory boundaries, and therefore mixed messages, when it comes to physical contact and intimacy: hugging weirds a lot of us out, but many of us do it compulsively even with near strangers. At the same time, we ask teachers and professional caregivers to keep their hugs with children to a one-arm embrace. Kids are taught to be wary of intimate contact but aren't always given a choice about whether to kiss grandma and grandpa. And while nonsexual nudity will get a movie an R rating, it's perfectly acceptable for the strip club near my house in Seattle to advertise with a photo banner on the sidewalk. On a moral map like this, it's no wonder so many loving parents worry about crossing invisible lines with their children. What if we tell them too much? Can information be harmful? What if I accidentally molest my child's mind?

I asked Elsbeth Reitzema, a sexuality education consultant with Rutgers, a fifty-year-old international center of expertise on sexual and reproductive health and rights in the Netherlands, about this problem. She explained that when Dutch parents and teachers tell very young children about intercourse, "It's the same as explaining how milk comes out of a cow. Or when you have an itch in your ear and you put your finger in it. When a baby is made, the man puts his penis inside the vagina. To the child, that's the same as putting a finger in your ear."

I was beginning to see, as I listened to Reitzema, how hard it was for me as an adult to separate sex from feelings of eroticism. But a child's conception of sex could be both nonerotic and entirely accurate.

"I think that some parents look at children thinking that *telling* them is the same as what we have *experienced* as adults," Reitzema explained. "We know how it feels to have sex. When we talk to kids about it, we take that emotion and knowledge with us. But the children are different."

Seattle's own sex-talk guru Amy Lang, founder of Birds & Bees & Kids, agreed, explaining to me in an email that children "have a different lens, one that's more theoretical and science based. They don't personalize the information like adults do. It's just info to them, like learning about how ice cream is made, how to read maps, etc."

Reassured by Reitzema, Lang, and other experts that children don't interpret sexual information in the erotically and emotionally connected way of adults until they reach puberty, I realized my task was to learn how to explain the hows and whys of sex to my kids without fearing I was doing something harmful or wrong.

According to a Rutgers guide on teaching young children about their bodies, toddlers and preschoolers "are not too young to talk about love and sex. In fact, this is a good age to talk about it. At this age a child feels very strongly bonded with their parents. He is sensitive to any information you give him. Furthermore, children are very curious. Make use of that. Don't be afraid you'll say too much: a child grasps only what they're ready for." In some parts of the world, caregivers simply aren't given to wondering if teaching about sex might be abusive. But to answer these questions for myself, I had to learn to think in clear, separate categories about the parts of human experience that are sexually reproductive, such as childbirth, breastfeeding, and puberty; the parts that can be erotic, such as physical attraction, acts of lovemaking, and pornography; and other parts of life that are none of the above and simply human-animal and biological, such as nakedness, toileting, and mammograms. Considering these differences helped with the worry that communicating with my young kids about sexuality might be transgressive. Was it harmful? In the categories of sexual reproduction and body functions: no, just as breastfeeding a baby and cleaning his genitals are not the same as molesting him. When it came to depicting the intimate side of sexuality, Reitzema reassured me it should be fine to explain feelings, emotions, and acts—as long as the grown-up isn't attempting to get off on the conversation. But unequivocally, "porn-watching is damaging for kids," she said. It was a relief to hear my gut was right on that one. The boundaries were getting clearer, and I saw plenty of untrodden territory just waiting to be covered.

Children's books can offer the easiest ways in to conversation. Indirectly, they can also reveal a great deal about grown-up qualms. Sex educator Lang knows it, imploring parents around the Pacific Northwest to plop down with a kid, grab a body book, and "just read it. No one will die. No one will throw up."

When Caroline was five and Libby was one and a half, I spotted a picture book on the American Library Association's 2011 list of the year's most frequently challenged books: Dori Hillestad Butler's *My Mom's Having a Baby!*, first published in 2005 and after that challenged by library users in at least nine states. Intended for ages four and up, the book appeared inviting and sweet with its bright, wavering watercolors by Carol Thompson. Curious, I put in my order—and read it with Caroline as soon as it arrived.

In the story, Elizabeth, whose character is about five years old, narrates the lessons she learns from her parents about how a baby develops, how this particular one got inside of her mom in the first place, and how he eventually gets out.

"How do Dad's sperm and your egg get together?" Elizabeth asks her mom.

"That's EXACTLY what I was just wondering!" Caroline screamed when we got to that line.

As we read through the book, Caroline got happier and happier—and I scanned for reasons the book had been challenged. Maybe the objections had to do with the illustrations. Thompson's paintings depict anatomically correct versions of Elizabeth's cheerfully naked mom and dad, and on the following page a vignette of the two adults in bed under the sheets, kissing, with red hearts floating in the air. There, Butler writes that all of the hugging and kissing feels so nice that "the man and woman want to get even closer to each other." The penis and vagina do their part next in an act that goes unnamed. On another page, Elizabeth cuddles with her mom in pajamas. Jumbled with them on the bed are books about birth and babies, as well as a charmingly frumpy pink bra. Eventually, Elizabeth's mother's water breaks, and she goes into labor at home. She unbuttons her maternity jeans to accommodate her contractions. When she sits on a stool, the small illustration shows a hint of pubic hair. At the hospital, baby Michael emerges headfirst from between his mother's legs. He's depicted on the next page lying in a hospital bassinet, arms and legs thrown wide like a starfish, penis uncircumcised, with an expression of wide-awake newborn surprise. On the page after that, his mother nurses him, and Elizabeth prepares to give her new sibling a gift of rainbow booties and a matching cap.

As we finished the book, Caroline wrapped both of her arms around my arm and squeezed. "I'm going to have a baby someday," she gushed.

"Yes, you could," I said. "If you decide you want to be a mother."

"I *do*," she said.

It had been a small mission of mine to teach my kids that not every woman is a mommy, so just to make sure, I said, "But do you know there are some women who decide they want to *not* have any babies and be a grown-up without children?"

She looked concerned. My little snuggler—I should have guessed why. "But then, what about when they want to get close?" she asked.

"Oh," I paused. Had my kindergartener just asked about birth control? Indeed it appeared she had.

"So," I said. "Grown-ups actually have figured out good ways to get that close together without making babies. Like one way"—was this really necessary?—"is with something called a condom. It covers the penis and catches the sperm so it doesn't go into the vagina."

She looked relieved, but the conversation wasn't over. "How do animals do it?" she asked. "How do they get close?"

We talked about scenarios—horses, birds.

"One thing I know for sure is kittens just cuddle up together," she said, nodding to herself. Looking at the thoughtful little face beside me, I saw the peace that comes from knowing the truth—and clearly not a truth that's scary or gross.

A few years later on a visit to the Netherlands, I picked up one of the country's most popular children's books about bodies and sex, Sanderijn van der Doef's *Ik vind jou lief* (*I Like You*), intended for ages two and up. The cover illustration had two round-bellied tots sharing a smooch in the playground sandbox, and inside, much like *My Mom's Having a Baby!*, the Dutch book featured winsome illustrations of bodies, families (including same-sex parents), and a sweetly smiling man and woman in bed (on top of the sheets instead of beneath them, although still discreet). But this book for a much younger audience surprised me by anticipating a child's questions—and answering them—in the exact order Caroline had asked hers. On the page with a man and a woman having sex, the description was much the same as Butler's, including the mention of good feelings and pleasure. But *Ik vind jou lief* included a key detail: "Sometimes people don't want any more babies. Then the woman takes a pill, or the man puts something over his penis." And the next page was all about how animals do it. Cats too, although they did more yowling than cuddling up.

Over the years, Butler's book—as well as *Ik vind jou lief* and other books like them—submerged in our home library and resurfaced from time to time. One evening when Dan was in charge of bedtime, the kids picked stories and snuggled up with him to read. From the kitchen, I heard his steady voice recounting familiar lines: "Hi, I'm Elizabeth. This is my mom and dad. You can't tell by looking at my mom, but there's a baby growing inside her." Libby was now four, old enough to understand Butler's book, and with a little smile, I paused my tapping at the computer to listen. Dan read the book with warm intonation, just as he would any other bedtime story. I could hear the girls asking questions now and then, and although I couldn't quite make out the specifics, I could hear Dan's voice answering plainly and simply. He sounded comfortable. Gratitude washed over me. What was so wrong with this book again?

Still half-eavesdropping on story time, I pulled up the ALA report from a few years earlier, which listed four reasons parents had challenged *My Mom's Having a Baby!*: "nudity; sex education; sexually explicit; unsuited to age group." All of that despite positive recommendations from children's librarians. Curious, I clicked over to Amazon and started reading the customer reviews and comments, which were equal in number positive and negative.

"Way too much detail for a 4 and 7 year old!" came the first comment, giving me pause, as those were the precise ages of the munchkins in jammies having story time with their dad in the next room. "If this book ever finds its way into my kindergartener's hands.... It'll be a pile of ashes in my back yard," commented 58chevy348. Another parent wrote, "I am shocked that our 8 year old daughter was able to check this book out of the school library.... If my wife and I want our kids to know the information in this book only we should be able to give them this book, when we feel they are ready!"

Similarly, E Jayman wrote: "When my 7 year-old said 'what does s-p-e-r-m spell', I immediately took the book from her. She is not ready for that kind of information."

While most of the one-star reviews used phrases along those lines—*not ready, only when they're ready*—the ages of the kids in question got higher and higher.

"My daughter is 13 and we have started discussing 'how a baby is made' just recently," wrote S. Bolliger. "Sure she was curious when she was younger, even fascinated, with pregnancy," but that was not the time to get "graphic."

"This book would maybe be okay for a teenager," another reviewer agreed. "I was planning on giving it to my eight-year-old, and it was way too graphic and almost too much information for anybody but an adult."

A few voices among the reader reviews for *My Mom's Having a Baby!* pointed out that societies in which sexuality education begins early count fewer teenage pregnancies, abortions, and STIs. Still, there was little hoping that data could overcome what seems powerfully intuitive to many parents: that kids will promptly try anything they're taught, so we can't teach them about sex until they're at the age for it (which remains undefined). Therefore some secrecy and obfuscation is essential to their loving care.

As story time ended in the next room, I read the last of the negative reviews and nearly overlooked a simple line from S. Dunk: "Childhood and innocence is [sic] so very precious," said the one-star review. "I don't believe most children are ready for these graphic explanations."

Innocence. Here was the heart of the matter. As a culture, we Americans cherish children. We say we revere the "sanctity of childhood." And despite the fact that even in America things used to be more open, sex education over the past half century has gained a sinister reputation: it is nothing less than the elimination of childhood, an irreversible darkening of the soul. If a child who learns about sex can no longer be called a child, of course we'll want to guard them from that knowledge.

Perhaps no one hears this concern more than the fundamentalist organization Focus on the Family, whose parenting guide and website seek to offer clear reassurance: "Giving a child facts about reproduction, including details about intercourse, does not rob him of innocence." But the idea that a child who is educated about sexuality is no longer a child is a tenacious concept—and a peculiarly American one. While "innocent" and "child" can be used as synonyms in English, this is not always the case in other languages, including Dutch.

Butler herself understood this well when she appeared on *Fox & Friends* to defend her book from would-be censors. She was interviewed alongside a Texas babysitter who had been shocked at what one of her charges had been able to find in the children's section of the local library. The girl, who was old enough to select, borrow, and read her own books, quietly lost herself in *My Mom's Having a Baby!* on the way home in the backseat of the car—then reportedly told the babysitter it "disgustified" her. The babysitter went to her local Fox news station to complain.

"These people don't see themselves as 'censors,'" the author Butler later blogged. "They see themselves as 'protectors.' Not only do they want to 'protect' their own children, they want to 'protect' everyone else's, too. They just have a different definition of 'protection' than I do."

In 2007 when then Senator Barack Obama spoke at a Planned Parenthood convention in 2007, he said that providing age-appropriate, science-based sex ed in schools—even for kindergarteners—is "the right thing to do." The media picked up on it, and within a few days the Reverend Dr. Debra Haffner, a Unitarian minister and author of several books about sexuality for children and adults, appeared on Fox's *The O'Reilly Factor*. Host Bill O'Reilly asked Haffner what a kindergarten teacher could say if a child were to ask where babies come from. In a school where a comprehensive sexuality curriculum has already been established, she said, "you might say, 'In a special place inside a woman there's a uterus, and inside the uterus—'"

"No—" O'Reilly interrupted.

"—the baby begins to grow."

"Here we diverge," O'Reilly said. "Five-year-olds, I don't want 'uterus.' They don't need to know that."

"Does that sound like a scary word to you, Bill?"

"They're not qualified to know it. It's beyond their capacity to understand."

"It's a three-syllable word."

"Here's why I object to the uterus," he said. "There's nothing wrong with the word 'uterus,' okay? There's nothing wrong with it. But here's why I object to it, and I object to any kind of specificity in this area for five-year-olds. You're blasting them out of their childhood.... I want children to remain children as long as possible."

"And I want them to remain children," Haffner rejoined, "but be educated and informed by trained people, by caring adults and by caring religious leaders."

However, as long as innocence was defined as freedom from "explicit...sophisticated biological terms," as O'Reilly put it, his guest had an obtuse argument to rebut.

Comparing at a glance—the clothes they wear, the toys they play with, the picture books marketed for adolescents—I think many observers would consider Dutch children more "innocent" than average American kids. Instead of shielding kids from sexual knowledge, Dutch parents focus on preserving different markers of childlikeness: carefreeness and play.

In his book *The Embarrassment of Riches: An Interpretation of Dutch Culture in the Golden Age*, historian Simon Schama meticulously reveals that the Dutch have been a child-centered people for centuries. A full two hundred years before parents in other European countries such as Italy and France stopped abandoning thousands of babies to foundling homes and rural wet nurses, Dutch art depicts families making toys for their children, taking them for walks, and patiently teaching them. Babies and children appear in engravings and paintings as symbols of virtue—as well as makers of morally instructive mischief. In other words, childlikeness was not defined in terms of purity. This positive regard for children and childhood continues to flourish in the Netherlands. In its Innocenti Report Card series, begun in 2002, UNICEF publishes data about the welfare of children around the world. With the Netherlands topping twenty-eight other rich countries by comparison in 2012 and again in 2016, the report showed that Dutch girls and boys benefit from a combination of some of the best material, educational, health-related, and emotional well-being in the world. When researchers ask them directly, Dutch children self-report being just as happy as the data suggests. If it's safe to say that Dutch people love kids and revere childhood, then surely it follows that they wouldn't teach young people about sex if doing so were harmful.

Not long ago Dan and I took the kids out for pizza to celebrate our wedding anniversary. To suit the occasion, the two of us smooched a few times at the table while we waited for food. Both kids laughed out loud, delighted by the public display of affection. Then six-year-old Libby said with great pride, "I know how a baby is made."

"Yes?"

And in her clear bell voice: "First the penis and the vagina join together. Sperm comes out of the penis and goes into the vagina to find an egg. And then a baby grows!"

"Super," I said.

The people at the next table didn't even cover their kids' ears—Seattle.

"And," Libby continued, not too pleased I'd interrupted, "If someone doesn't want to make a baby with a man, she can go to the doctor to get sperm."

I looked at Dan. Neither one of us had been doing the repetitions lately, but I'd seen the books lying around, and Caroline had been going over things with her sister.

"Perfect," I said to Libby.

"Very impressive," said Dan.

The pizza arrived. We ate a ton and walked home through a hot haze—summer forest fires were filling the city with smoke. Libby rode along on her scooter, stopping to pet every cat who would hold still. At home with a little time left before bed, she and Caroline went down to the cool basement and returned to their imaginary game of Playmobil—farmers corralling horses, explorers driving around looking for food, tiny plastic kids playing in a tiny plastic pool. Through the floor I could hear them playing—chirpy voices conjuring worlds— and I had no reason to think they were anything but children still.

The old-fashioned American birds-and-bees talk is often called traumatic—sometimes laughingly, sometimes not. So why don't Dutch kids—or very young kids—seem traumatized by accurate information about human sexuality? Maybe, some suggest, it's because they aren't given time to build up false illusions that must later be toppled. In other words, maybe the trauma of "the talk" is really the trauma of undoing the familiar, imagined stories a child has relied on to answer their own questions—those famous suppositions such as babies being born through belly buttons that comfort kids in the absence of facts. Or maybe on another level, the trauma comes not from upended notions of biology but from deeper confusion about morality.

My friend Lindsey is the warm, creative mother of three quite different children. I've always learned from watching how she responds to each of them uniquely, and I love the way she tells heartfelt stories about her parenting—the victories and the challenges. She had long felt certain that her oldest child, a daughter who met easily with anxiety, should receive the facts of life on delay and only in small doses. To stall, Lindsey had always told Kendall that babies come from "a special kiss between a mommy and a daddy." But one day when Kendall was ten, she heard something at school that sent her home with a frown and some big questions.

"Okay honey, sit down," Lindsey told her daughter. She explained intercourse. She produced a book and told Kendall she could choose whether to look at it and could ask whatever she wanted. Things seemed okay until Lindsey began explaining sex as something adults can enjoy together whether they want to make a baby or not. Here Lindsey saw her daughter's resigned face turn crestfallen.

"You and Daddy do that?" she cried. "Not to make babies, just to *do* it?"

"Yes," Lindsey said.

Shaking her head, Kendall burst into tears. "But you're good people," she cried.

It was heartbreaking for Lindsey to discover that in her daughter's mind, being a good person and having sex had evolved into opposing notions. I got goose bumps when Lindsey shared this story with me. How frighteningly easy it had been for the harmful idea of sex as filth to take root in the unfilled space around that well-intended "special kiss."

I thought about the unlearning Kendall needed to do then. It wasn't so much that the truth from her mother had crossed her boundaries, but that the wrong boundaries had drawn themselves to begin with. Now she had new questions to grapple with at the very sensitive beginning of adolescence: Where does a person's essential goodness and virtue and lovability reside? How does sexuality fit in?

In Lindsey's story, which she generously shared with me because she knew I was working on this book, there is an interesting background character: the child at school who spilled the beans. Almost as much as we worry about raising an ignorant kid, we worry about creating that notorious overinformed one.

One evening when Libby was almost six, her aunt, uncle, and toddler cousin came over for dinner. We sat around the table passing guacamole and fish, chatting about their new baby, soon to be born. Libby beckoned to Dan and whispered in his ear. He whispered back, and then he said so we all could hear, "It would be fun to ask Mommy that, too."

She paused and looked across the table at me with her big, clear brown eyes.

"Can I tell Mommy the question?" he asked her.

She nodded.

He lowered his voice a bit and said, "Libby wants to know how you *know* when it's time to put the sperm into the mommy."

"Oh!" I said. "Well, for one thing, you have to be grown up."

"That's what I said," Dan said.

"And both of the grownups have to decide together that it's a good idea."

"That's what I said too," Dan said.

Libby nodded. And that was that. Bless my sister and her husband; everybody just went on with their burritos and their table chatter. But it could have been different.

In 2014, Jezebel blogger Tracy Moore wrote about the day she heard from the preschool teacher that her four-year-old daughter had told classmates that babies come out of vaginas: "First, I was so proud. Then I realized she was asking me to make her stop." The teacher told the little girl she could only talk about such things at home with her parents, Moore wrote, which made her daughter feel she was in trouble.

To be honest, when I worry about my informed children offending someone outside the home, it's not because I'm afraid of what another kid might learn; if the information is accurate, it's likely to be helpful. Instead, I'm afraid of the social repercussions: I would hate for my child to be punished or humiliated, as Moore's daughter was, for possessing basic sexual knowledge. And as an adult in the equation, I'm loath to step on any other parents' childrearing toes. It's a delicate dance. I've spoken to so many parents who say they *want* to be open with their kids, but they don't know how other adults in their lives— family and friends—will take it. Or I'll hear from parents who say they are very open with their kids at home, but their kids have been duly warned not to share the facts of life with anyone else.

"Seriously: Vagina is the Santa Claus of kid intel?" Moore wrote about the preschool debacle. "Once the vagina is out of the box, hearts will be broken and childhoods destroyed?...Later on when my daughter is older she can call her vagina Puff the Magic Dragon for all I care. But for now: Vagina. I'm not going to make my kid not say vagina, and it seems weirdly restrictive to then tell her to never mention it to others."

Just as countless older children have the sensitivity not to ruin Santa for the little ones, they seem to me remarkably well able to judge when a younger child's ignorance is safe and sweet and when it calls for immediate correction. Older kids don't always do right by the little ones, but at least they seem to know when they're transgressing. And when they follow their conscience, it's a beautiful thing. I have loved the gift of my older daughter chiming in, allowing me to clam up and listen while she tells her little sister about how there was *some* blood when she was born, but not too much, and how the doctor says we had better not use soap on our vulvas, and how boys can wear dresses if they want because it's just a choice. On the other hand, realities differ. I know one mother whose elementary-age son is a premier athlete who travels with middle school and high school boys to participate in competitive events. She told me that ever since her son started team travel at age five, she's been diligently coaching him not to listen to things the older boys say. Lately she has begun to wonder if she should just front-end it all by delivering an accurate, holistic story about sexuality to her son. He might be the youngest, but that doesn't mean he can't know best.

Most of the time, we can't even anticipate who will be bothered, or how, or when, by our children's knowledge and our family values. Janine, an American mother who runs a Dutch imports store with her Netherlands-born husband, told me about the culture shock of moving from Australia, where the neighborhood kids would all be "naked in the sand and mud, running in the backyards," to a Pacific Northwest island with a conservative Protestant tradition. When her six-year-old son had a playdate with a same-age girl from another family, the kids were a mess after playing outside all afternoon and Janine thought nothing of putting them in the tub together for a bath. But when the other mother found out, she was livid. Her daughter's soak in the tub with a boy was beyond the pale.

Similarly, Ilse, a Dutch artist and mother who lives outside Seattle, told me about a time when her family hosted American friends for dinner. All evening kids from the two families ran around inside, swooping through the house and her art studio, where she kept a large-format book of artist nudes resting open on a table. After the guests had gone, she walked into her studio and noticed that someone had flipped the huge book face-down to hide the pages. She shrugged and turned it back. "It wasn't *my* problem," she laughed when she told me the story.

Taboos about what we can say in public can make normalizing body talk difficult for parents. So although it makes perfect sense to talk with a child about nutrition in a bakery or about conservation at the beach, we often wait for body-talk opportunities to present themselves in perfect private moments. Some parents justifiably choose to ignore this convention, like the single mom I know who patiently answered when her little boy demanded full information about the provenance of babies in the middle of the grocery store.

But then there's also that edgy moment when you're in the dairy aisle to grab milk and a woman blocking the path with her cart is telling her friend, the stockboy, all about how her preschool son proudly presented his genitals at the birthday party and said, "I HAVE A PENIS"—*didn't you, honey?*—and how it was *so* awesome. She knows everyone can hear her, and I get it: she wants to help *all* of us to normalize. But it's a hard balance to strike.

When my American friend Mary went out to dinner one night with her three daughters ranging in age from two to eight, the kids chose that moment to pin her down on the finer points of the facts of life. From their expat home in Luxembourg, they had taken an all-girls vacation to Stockholm, and the restaurant happened to be a hushed, fancy place. The Swedish diners sitting closest to her table (who clearly understood English) occasionally caught Mary's eye and raised their wine glasses as she repeated all the basics and then worked through in vitro fertilization, adoption, different kinds of childbirth, and the answers to questions such as this one, from her oldest daughter: "Do you have to be in love to have a baby?" By the time she paid the bill, Mary knew the story had legs. So she took a straightforward approach and posted about it on Facebook. "Just a heads-up to my kids' friends: my children are very well-informed on this matter. You're welcome."

I remember the winter afternoon in Seattle when I realized our house had become *that* house: the one with the Books. In English, in Dutch, or just in black-and-white art photography, you could get your human-body manuals here. That day, Caroline had invited a classmate over to play. As fourth-graders, they were smack at the age when an average American kid might know all about sexuality while plenty of their peers still know next to nothing. Together with little sister Libby, the older girls set up a make-believe library in the hallway next to the bookshelves. It was a pretty strict institution: for every book you checked out, you had to record the title, pay some fake money, commit to reading a certain number of pages, and leave your signature. When you returned a book, you had to provide a written review, which was then thoroughly rubber-stamped with green reindeer. When I happened to give the library records a glance, I noticed that someone—one of the older kids, by the looks of things—had checked out Cory Silverberg's *Sex Is a Funny Word*. "I loved it and like it," the patron had written in orange ballpoint pen. "I learned all about

SEX!" Except that last word had a slight problem. *Wow,* I thought, *sex-positive when you still get your s backward!*

Holding those sweet homemade library records in my hand, I realized that a small miracle had come to pass. After starting with my "daddy" and Dan's "dangly bottom," our home had become a place where full-disclosure body books mingled with baby board books on the easiest-to-reach shelves. But I'll admit, I did cringe a little. It was possible that our guest had acquired new knowledge her parents would have preferred to convey. Yet I did not believe that information could hurt her.

I was more concerned with a bigger question—one that had been niggling for a while: When we stop trying to limit how much kids know about their bodies, how much do we rightfully control what they *do* with them?

5

Privileging Pleasure

One sunny winter morning I was puttering around the house with my two-and-a-half-year-old, both of us enjoying the bright rays streaming in. After breakfast, she went into the living room to play with a new jigsaw puzzle—a weird-looking turtle whose shell was made of plasticky, checker-sized pieces marked with letters of the alphabet and numerals zero to nine. The pieces were all similar, and they didn't fit together very well. It was perhaps a toy whose intended use wasn't the best one.

I went to the kitchen to fix another cup of coffee and soon noticed that my daughter had gone rather quiet. I glanced into the living room. *Huh.* There sat my lovebug, her curls in a topknot, bare-bottomed on the floor with her pants around her ankles. She was still trying to do the puzzle, sort of, but given that the pieces just didn't fit very well, she was also branching out, looking for, ahem, better places to put them. She was concentrating very hard as she rotated through the pieces, trying one after another. Observing her utter absorption, I thought of Naomi Wolf's book *Vagina*, in which she makes the fascinating claim that a woman's genitals connect directly with her creativity.

So there was that, but there was also a slightly panicked *What do I do? Say something? Say nothing? Stop her? Ignore her?* My confusion tied with everything known and unknown, valued and devalued, appreciated and overlooked about female reproductive parts. I didn't want to mess this moment up.

According to a recent UK survey, only half of adult women can identify the cervix or vagina on a diagram of female reproductive parts. Even fewer can point to the vulva (the external genitals one can see). Sixty-five percent say they're uncomfortable using correct terminology for their genitals and prefer code words. A similar survey showed that only half of men—who have a disproportionately strong influence on women's health care policy—could correctly label the vagina.

But both men and women do just fine when it comes to identifying the penis, foreskin, and testes. Sure, those male parts are all external and easier to see, but the invisibility defense doesn't stop adults or even young children from understanding that human bodies possess brains, hearts, bones, and stomachs. There's something else going on when it comes to female reproductive anatomy.

As a mom who fit the statistics perfectly and comes late to identifying her own parts—I only took the time to memorize them in detail when I had a pair of daughters to raise—I've wondered why we have so much trouble with female anatomy: how to name it, first of all, but after that how to talk about, think about it, and interact with it. Why was it especially embarrassing to explain the unique capacity of female genitals to produce pleasurable feelings? Since we aren't sure how, or whether, to talk about the part of sexuality that feels good, many parents just don't mention it, and kids learn not to ask too many questions. This can set up the idea that those unnamed parts—female ones in particular—are unwholesome, or unimportant, or just plain bad. Some women literally die of this embarrassment, which was the rhetorical point of the UK survey, commissioned by a gynecological cancer awareness nonprofit called The Eve Appeal: a lack of familiarity with their reproductive parts and the five cancers they're susceptible to—uterine, ovarian, cervical, vaginal, and vulvar—prevents too many women from telling doctors about problems or even noticing them at all. Without a doubt, that's the worst-case scenario. But psychologists have long observed that body shame can lead to the inability to enjoy sex. So if it's true that we're so unused to ourselves, and that the lack of familiarity is tied to shame, what about the quiet loss, for millions upon millions more women, of pleasure?

As a parent, I had puzzled about this. How does the idea of sexual pleasure, for girls especially, get quashed at an early age? What would it take to improve the message? To teach a child not only to identify her parts but actually to prize them?

I certainly did not want to shame my daughter as she played with her turtle puzzle—I wanted her to know she had the right to freely enjoy her body—but in the moment, my whirring mind couldn't quite let it go. I convinced myself I was looking at a teachable moment for *something*. Like, let's see... Okay, what if the toy was different? Really poky? Or toxic? Or super messy? I thought of a friend who once found herself picking glitter from between her daughter's legs.

I decided to walk quietly into the living room, so as not to interrupt her flow too much.

"Are you playing?" I softly asked.

"Yeah," she said, keeping her focus.

"Does it tickle?"

"No."

"Does it hurt?"

"No."

I paused. "Does it feel good?"

"Yes."

I took a deep breath. Now what?

"We should be careful about putting things in our vulva because that might hurt," I said. *Here we go; enter adult hang-ups.* "Maybe," I ventured, "we shouldn't put toys there." *Lies.*

"But I want to," she said matter-of-factly, without looking up. *Conversation over.*

"Okay," I said, forcing myself to turn with my coffee and walk away. Something told me I had better find something different to obsess about. At the same time, I had a fleeting wish to be as connected as my child seemed to be, so naturally and unself-consciously finding pleasure at her center.

At that point, I hadn't yet seen any advice about this kind of thing. It certainly didn't occur to me to ask my daughter to move her puzzle project somewhere else. Soon, though, I would begin hearing a pretty standard line: that kids should not be told to stop behaviors an observer might interpret as self-pleasuring—but should be instructed to take the activity to a private space such as the bathroom or bedroom.

I chafed at that advice every time I heard it, but I didn't stop to think about why until one morning a few years later, when I opened my email to find a thought-provoking question in sex educator Amy Lang's twice-monthly newsletter, which reaches thousands of subscribers. That morning's Q & A presented the case of a three-year-old girl who had discovered car-seat "rubbing."

"I DO NOT want to shame her," the girl's concerned mother had written, "but also want to dialogue about privacy and having special time alone in her room or the bathroom." The problem was that the girl's object of choice for rubbing was tied to the car. So much for hauling off to the bedroom or bathroom.

Lang suggested the mother offer her child some new car toys as distractions. If that didn't work, without getting dramatic, the mother could try saying she sees what her daughter is doing, and while that might feel good, it's something to do in private. And then she could ask the child to stop because it makes her (the mother) uncomfortable.

This was definitely the prevailing advice on what to do about kids touching themselves. With so many parents rightly becoming concerned about the ways we instill sexual shame, giving permission by saying, "It's okay in private" is a big step forward. But when I read about the car-seat rubber, I had to wonder if we weren't still missing the mark.

Ever since the puzzle affair, my reservations had only increased about adults telling kids—especially girls and very young children—to go be alone with their genitals. On the surface it sounded like reasonable enough advice, but still, I found it problematic.

First of all, young kids don't necessarily understand the concept of privacy—which any parent of a toddler or preschooler already knows. In a departure from the standard viewpoint, author and sex educator Deborah Roffman acknowledges this in her sex-and-parenting guide *Talk to Me First*. Specifically in reference to very little kids, she writes: "Most adults today know it's normal for young children to soothe themselves by stroking their genitals whenever they feel anxious or sleepy or bored. But do they have to do it in church? Well, yes." She says it's best to ignore those behaviors until kids begin grasping concepts of privacy and personal space around age five or six. In some cases older children, too, may be best served when adults ignore or avoid overreacting to the behavior.

"Go do it in private" may be the accepted answer these days, but is there any other activity that we tell young kids is acceptable only as long as no one else sees? Where does that land on the list of Most Shameful Things? I also wondered if, since a little boy with his hand down his pants is more likely to be seen as doing something inevitable, our "when-and-where" vigilance might apply unfairly to girls, whose pleasure has been both taboo and misunderstood for centuries. It was hard to imagine the upside of telling my kid that her fiddling between the legs made me uncomfortable. *Your sexuality, which is new and feels good to you, is somewhat offensive…so that's confusing and maybe embarrassing, but don't be ashamed.* I was starting to see how adult discomfort can affect kids' clarity about who owns their sexuality and on what terms they may enjoy it.

"My belief," Lang told me later, "is that tone carries far more weight than the actual words." That sounded right to me, since tone often flows directly from our values. And when it comes to children's relationship with their genitals, those values are complicated.

As the primary organ of female orgasm, "the clitoris' only role is for pleasure, and because pleasure is not talked about, the clitoris is often not talked about," British sex educator Justin Hancock told a UK education reporter in 2016. Over the centuries the clitoris (pronounced "*clit*-er-is") has been regularly omitted from medical and scientific texts. It appeared in *Gray's Anatomy* a century ago, but its label was removed from the 1948 edition, possibly over "hygiene" and morality concerns. It's not difficult to find modern resources omitting the clitoris or giving only cursory mention without including it on diagrams or describing its function. In his guide for parents called *The Talk: 7 Lessons to Introduce Your Child to Biblical Sexuality*, popular lifestyle blogger Luke Gilkerson provides a short glossary that makes room for "penis," "testicles," "scrotum," "erection," "ejaculation," "semen," and "sperm" without naming any visible female genitals aside from "vagina," which is technically internal. There is no "vulva," no "labia" (outer or inner), and certainly no "clitoris" in the glossary or anywhere else in the book. Talk about failing to acknowledge female pleasure. (Although, to be fair, "orgasm" isn't positively acknowledged in the book at all. A man's penis only "does something called ejaculation.") It might seem unfair to pick on a single book this way, but as a guide for parents on how to instruct their children, it's one crystalline example of the general erasure of female pleasure in American life—whether from trusted medical texts, school curricula, children's books, parenting guides, movies, music, and even erotica and pornography, which, for better or worse, do influence our collective ideas about sex, reciprocity, and equality.

In my house, I decided, it was time to bring the clitoris out of the dark. When I looked up the word in 2017, the *Oxford English Dictionary* defined *clitoris* as "a homologue of the male penis," whereas "penis" was defined as "the male genital organ" and certainly not as a homologue of the female clitoris. The OED also described the clitoris as "a rudimentary organ," compared, presumably, to the more highly evolved penis. *Merriam-Webster's* defined the clitoris as "small" (compared to what?), while never mentioning size in its definition of "penis." Annoyed, I kept researching. I found myself briefly envious of the simple German word *Kitzler*—tickler—which leaves no ambiguity about the point of a clitoris. Eventually I turned to the Online Etymology Dictionary, an extraordinary collection of more than fifty thousand words maintained by a Pennsylvania historian and newspaper reporter named Douglas Harper, who was good enough to define the clitoris as the "erectile organ of female mammals." It was unclear, he wrote, what Greek root the coiners intended: to sheathe? to shut? Or perhaps "little hill"? Harper noted that an Italian anatomist claimed to have discovered it in the sixteenth century: "He called it *amor Veneris, ver dulcedo*"—the love or sweetness of Venus. But, Harper winningly added, "it had been known earlier to women."

It seems that throughout history, whenever the clitoris was "discovered" by a male scout, it would soon enough (conveniently?) be forgotten. During witch hunts in Europe and early America, any sign of female lust—including the possession of a clitoris, which was considered a physical abnormality and called the "devil's teat"—could be the kiss of death for a girl or a woman. Today, having a clitoris isn't grounds for execution, but it does make girls and women vulnerable to mutilation. It's estimated that more than two hundred million girls and women worldwide have endured some form of female circumcision—the complete or partial removal of the clitorial head and/or hood, also called "clitoridectomy" or "female genital mutilation" (FGM). It's another kind of erasure, literal and bloody.

In the United States, FGM has been used across the centuries to get girls to stop touching themselves. Beginning in the late nineteenth century, clitoridectomy was used "primarily for three objectives: to stop masturbation, to enhance female capacity for orgasm within heterosexual vaginal intercourse, and to 'correct' homosexuality or hypersexuality," writes Sarah B. Rodriguez, a medical history scholar who has studied the trajectory of female circumcision and clitoridectomy in the United States. She ventures that these procedures have been more common in this country than we realize. "Because of the relative ease in performing these procedures, they were often accomplished in a physician's office in a short amount of time: they were quick procedures that provided women and girls in the United States a surgical method for sexual acceptability." A friend of mine recently learned that her grandmother, a youngster in 1930s Ohio, would have been a car-seat rubber in her own time. Her concerned parents called the doctor, who stopped by and removed the child's clitoris as she lay on the kitchen table. Circumcision for girls under eighteen became illegal in the United States in 1997.

Certainly when the clitoris is altered or cut away, there is the possible destruction of a girl's capacity for sexual pleasure. But it may be even more destructive in the sense of how central, how integral, this part of a female body is. Losing it would be like losing the head of one's penis. Naomi Wolf has posited that the way a woman feels about herself—and the rest of the world—mirrors the way she feels about her genitals. It's a wild claim, but I sense truth in it.

Although self-pleasuring doesn't have the bad rap it used to in the United States, it was only during the Clinton administration that US Attorney General Joycelyn Elders was briskly fired by the president for agreeing at a 1994 United Nations conference on AIDS that teaching children about masturbation might reduce unsafe sex—and she hadn't breathed a word about pleasure. We still live in a time when well-meaning parents—at least one I happened to hear of—will buy their kids a fully accurate and up-to-date book about human sexuality but razor out the page mentioning masturbation.

Not every culture has traditionally effaced female pleasure. In a French-inspired sex manual so popular among Dutch readers that it went into seven printings between the years 1687 and 1715, "the external anatomy was objectively described with the clitoris clearly understood as an organ of pleasure," writes Simon Schama in his book about Dutch culture in the Golden Age. Similarly, in today's most popular Dutch sex-ed curriculum, *Kriebels in je buik*, a digital lesson for fourth-graders states: "The clitoris is a very sensitive place. Touching it can give a nice feeling." The lesson plan's clitoris illustration was revised in 2017 to be larger and more accurately depicted as a four-inch-long organ in a double-wishbone shape, most of which is internal. The idea, Elsbeth Reitzema, who is one of the authors, told me, is to show that a clitoris is not in fact pea-sized, as it is often described, but in fact comparable in size to the penis. That "pea" is only the head, the tip of the iceberg. The implicit message of the revised drawing, she explained, is to visually represent for young learners that the organs are comparable not only in size but also in their capacity for pleasure. (In fact, although the curriculum doesn't go into such detail, the glans clitoris has twice as many nerve endings as the glans penis.)

The World Health Organization takes the position that every person has the right not only to sexual health care and education, reproductive freedom, and sexual autonomy but also to "pursue a satisfying, safe and pleasurable sexual life." Accordingly, instead of ladling out pitfalls and warnings, experts tell Dutch parents to let their babies feel their own bodies and likewise not to forbid older children from touching themselves. They say there's just no need to freak if your daughter "breastfeeds" her doll or if your four-year-old son furnishes his penis in class—he'll eventually learn that some things are better kept to himself. Again and again, the Dutch *dos* are for kids and the *don't*s are for grown-ups.

In a way, the hands-off (for parents) Dutch advice makes teaching kids about bodies and sexuality sound almost pleasantly mischievous, the way hiding cauliflower in the mac and cheese is a lighthearted bit of subterfuge. You know you're doing them good, and they don't even catch what's happening. I have to think a lot of our stress as American parents about how to "deal with" early childhood sexual behaviors comes from the pressure we feel—at least I know I've felt it—to use those teachable moments to tell kids what *not* to do, try, say, feel, or permit with their bodies.

Imagine getting into the mindset of my friend in Amsterdam who had a window repairman come to her house one afternoon. She laughingly told me the story: as he worked on fixing the window in her three-year-old daughter's room, the girl sat half-undressed and splay-legged on a little chaise with a hand between her legs.

"I didn't know what to do," her mother laughed when she told me about it.

"Did you stop her?"

"Well, no, not at all!" She said her daughter had every right to masturbate—she didn't avoid that word—particularly in her own bedroom, and it was up to the worker to keep his composure and ignore it. Which, it's worth noting, he did.

My sister, delivering spring sex-ed lessons to her fifth-graders at a private school outside Seattle in 2017, noticed that even though the thoroughly modern curriculum she was using called the clitoris "very sensitive," it stopped short of naming any function for the organ. "But what is it *for*?" the girls kept asking.

"Well," she said, treading thoughtfully off-script, "Some people would say it feels good. It can be for pleasure."

She told me she was struck in that moment to see a "visible relief in the room." She saw the girls' shoulders drop, their nervousness dissipate. They'd been confused, thinking, "*Well, what's the* point *of that thing?* And once there was an explanation, it felt better."

I wondered if the relief might also come from an inkling of permission to know and use one's body. Your urethra is there to pee; therefore you can safely assume it's okay to pee. Your clitoral function is pleasure; therefore it's reasonable to enjoy it.

And so, in addition to the three available options for the car-seat rubber and the turtle-puzzle worker—"distract her," "tell her to do it somewhere else," and "ignore it"—I would now add another possible approach: Option four—are we ready for this?—would be to go ahead and encourage it. I'm thinking along the lines of a nodding, smiling "Doesn't *that* feel nice?," and then carrying on with whatever was going on before. I still planned to mention that lots of people like to have those moments in private, but I wasn't going to make it a household rule. I was encouraged by the Dutch advice to trust that my kids would self-regulate eventually—and meanwhile might make a tiny dose of progress in a sexist world.

So if the name of the game was to avoid making a fuss, I had to keep picking away at my complexes. A conundrum for me had always been whether to prevail on my kids to wash their hands after they happened to touch their genitals. On the surface, it seemed like a perfectly reasonable and hygienic request—and I enforced it after the kids used the toilet. But when it came to hand washing after they touched between their legs for whatever other reason, was I sending an unintended message? If I wanted to normalize all body parts and didn't remind the kids to wash their hands after covering a yawn or clipping their toenails, what was the difference with a vulva? When my sister told me she'd been wondering about the same thing for her three-year-old, I got curious. Like any body part, of course, genitals have microbes—often quite necessary ones. But are genitals *particularly* germy, or was that just in my head?

Healthy vaginas and penises are self-cleaning with their own microbiomes, which is why doctors say not to douche or use soap on those areas. More so than genitals, mouths, belly buttons, and fore-arms are among the main contenders for Germiest Body Part. With those things in mind, I started doing quick cost-benefit analyses on whether I needed to tell a child who has touched her vulva to wash her hands. How contaminated did I think her hands really were? What did anybody stand to catch? The answers were usually *not very* and *nothing*. By letting it go, I liked to think I left open the rare possibil-ity of two female humans growing up *without* the notion that their genitals are inherently dirty. Without a hand-washing rule, the risk of the kids spreading anything serious was probably no greater than if they happened to touch some other body part. But the cumulative risk of acquiring the idea that genitals are "yucky" could be much more serious. A sense of one's genitals as offensive may produce feelings of shame, which can have a lifelong negative effect on a person's sexual pleasure and even function.

I saw real-life examples of this at the 2016 opening, at an Am-sterdam art gallery, of Wipsite, a sex-ed website for adults created by sex educator Belle Barbé and visual artist Marilyn Sonneveld. The opening showed Sonneveld's original pieces: sculptures, including a pink-dyed tampon pyramid, as well as colorful, abstract drawings depicting everything from bacteria to sex positions. But the exhibit also offered interactive pieces meant to reveal the need for tasteful, respectful adult sex ed. (Yes, even in the Netherlands plenty of peo-ple deal with sexual shame.) For an exhibit on "cunt shaming," the artists made a "punanie" sculpture of pink fabric and a white hairy fringe around an opening that made the whole thing look like a gi-ant sugar Easter egg one could peek inside. Little scraps of paper and pens sat nearby. The invitation was to write down the specifics of your own genital shame, then place the paper inside. Guests could then remove a piece of paper from within the sculpture and pin it to a cork board on the wall, symbolically making someone else's shame public, ostensibly on everyone's behalf. It moved me to read such core humiliations written on little square papers in the neat, blue-ballpoint handwriting of mature adults: *I'm ashamed I farted during cunnilingus. I'm ashamed that I have a hemorrhoid on my ass.*

I'm ashamed that my children know I have sex. I'm ashamed to have anal sex because I think my butt smells poopy. I'm ashamed I called out the wrong name for a partner. I'm ashamed of vaginal secretions in my underwear.

To really root out shame, the exhibit reminded me as one after another embarrassing but deeply human moment came to light on the pin board, truth and pleasure needed to become more important, and more discussed, than secrecy and privacy.

When she was four, my youngest made a discovery. It appeared to be a hole, and she was ecstatic about it. It turned out to be not exactly a hole, just the tiny space between the clitoral glans and hood—but it looked like a hole, and that made her very proud indeed. I remembered seeing the same thing and considering it a hole when I was a little girl.

My hole, my hole, my precious teeny hole! she would sing as she got ready for a bath.

After a few days of this, I realized I had forgotten something.

"Do you know what you can do?" I asked her.

She shook her head.

"You can always use a mirror to see *all* of your parts. Any time you want! Would you like to do that?"

Did she ever. I offered her a handheld mirror.

As the bath filled up, I explained she could just plop down on the floor mat and use the mirror to see all of her vulva and everything in it. As she did so, I watched her expression change. She became momentarily speechless, brimming with a mix of pride, joy, and total astonishment.

"Mommy," she said when she caught her breath. "I can see So. Many. HOLES!"

"Isn't it *wonderful*?" I said, taking my cue from her flushed and happy expression. "Now you can see what you *have*! And you can do that anytime."

And so she did.

"MOM! Come here! I think I found something!" she shouted from the bathroom a few weeks later. She was getting better at this: she'd used her purple hiking shoe to prop up the mirror, leaving both hands free.

"Look!" she cried as I dropped to my knees next to her. "There! What's that?"

"That opening there?" I asked.

"Yes!" It was more than she'd quite noticed before.

"That is the opening to your vagina!"

"Vagina," she repeated.

"That is where you could have a baby come out someday."

"Ohhh!" she squealed.

Just then, Caroline came through the front door.

"CAROLINE! COME SEE!" Libby yelled.

With no idea what she was walking into, she followed the sound of her sister's voice into the bathroom where the shoe-propped mirror told the whole story.

"LOOK! MY VAGINA!"

I saw my older daughter take a breath and put on a spiders-aren't-scary face. She bent to have a look and nodded. "That's interesting!" Apparently Dan and I weren't the only ones in the house challenging ourselves to normalize sexuality.

"How was choir?" I asked Caroline a few moments later in the kitchen.

"Fine," she said. "But you never told *me* that."

"Told you what?" I asked.

"About using a mirror to see." She was angry.

I had been feeling neglectful for not catching Libby sooner with this information—had I really left my elementary schooler in the dark entirely?

"I didn't?"

"Nope," she said, turning on her heel.

I thought of that challenging question: *What are my hopes and dreams for my children in their sexual lives?*

"I definitely should have," I told her. "But it's not too late."

She shrugged. *Yes it is.* I imagined for a moment what it would be like for a person not to discover their penis and testicles until fourth grade. Full physical awareness clearly counts for a part in healthy, happy human development. According to social scientists, girls' and women's lack of knowledge and ownership of their own genitals— their vulnerability to having their reproductive parts characterized, defined, and used by others—contributes to gender inequality. Nurse and educator Julie Metzger describes how, in her popular Great Conversations puberty classes for kids ages ten to twelve, which can attract 150 attendees per meeting, she shows a "picture of girls' anatomy, looking at their perineum. So, between their legs. And I say to the girls—who of course kind of reel back when they look at that at first—but I say, 'First of all, you just now have learned something that hundreds and hundreds of millions of girls will never know in their entire lifetime.' And that it's their job to advocate for those girls for the rest of their lives because they just now learned something that most girls on the planet actually do not know."

I thought about the second-wave feminist workshops in which women gathered with mirrors to get to know and appreciate themselves better, which have all but faded out. Now, though, there's the internet, with personal-tour offerings such as the impressively thorough, if clinical-sounding, "Self-Exam: Vulva and Vagina" from ourbodiesourselves.org.

When my first daughter was very little, behind my motivation to teach her about her body had been the fear of sexual abuse. If she knew some basics, then I could get to the safety guidelines. I never thought body knowledge was important in its own right, a way to sow confidence, positivity, and even happiness. But over time I learned I could step back and trust that as normal childhood behaviors came up, I would not need to embarrass my kids with corrections or feel embarrassed by a child's normal behaviors.

One summer evening when Libby was six, Dan and I lingered at the dinner table. She had just come back in her horsey nightgown to finish her slice of Dan's birthday cake. As she climbed up to sit on my lap, she asked for a reminder.

"Mom, what's that tickly part in my bottom called again?"

"Oh, that's your clitoris," I said.

"Clitoris," she repeated, her brow studious.

Just then, a birthday call came in for Dan from his parents. Libby and I kept chatting.

"Do you know what your clitoris is for?" I asked.

"No," she said. "Is it yucky?"

"It's not yucky," I said. "It's for feeling good!"

"That's it?"

"That's it!"

"It's lucky to have something like that," she decided. Then a worry crossed her face. "Mom, are any kids born without clitorises?"

"Yes," I said. "Kids who are born with penises don't have clitorises."

"That's sad," she said. "I love my clitoris."

I squeezed her as our conversation went on. Eventually Dan said good-bye to his parents and hung up.

"What are we talking about?" he asked.

"Clitorises," I said.

He smiled. "Still?"

"Yep," chirped Libby.

There was just that much to say.

6

The Doctor Is In

I have a secret, and I don't have to tell anybody," Libby sang, sidling out of the kitchen and down the basement stairs. Most of the time her voice, like so many in her preschool tribe, blared at top volume. But this announcement came in a softer, more mysterious tone. I would say my alarm bells went off, except they already had. I knew her secret. I'd known it for a week, and I had no idea how to talk to her about it—or if I even should. She was four at the time, and I'd been in the process of waking up to the idea that my kids should be perfectly familiar with their body parts for the purposes of safety as *well* as comfort and function. But this was a new conundrum: What about when other kids got involved?

We'd just returned from a hot and colorful family trip to Costa Rica, where, in a remote lodge surrounded by trees that flashed with violet hummingbirds, yellow-striped toucan bills, and crimson macaw feathers, our daughters had befriended two Swiss girls, the only other children in the camp. Libby, who was almost five, and Giulia, six, quickly bonded despite a language barrier bridged only by the occasional word from Libby's small Dutch vocabulary to match Giulia's German: *papegaai, Papagai,* parrot. The girls hiked side by side, shared a snorkel, made little twists in each other's hair as our families shared dinner in the evenings. One night when Giulia dropped into an exhausted sleep on a cane bench after the evening meal, Libby crouched beside her, absorbed in her friend's dreaming face. The next night, the roles reversed.

Giulia and her family left the lodge a day before we did, but the eight of us met up one more time a few days later in the tiny surf hamlet of Dominical. Dan and I settled down at a table with Thomas and Marina, a firefighter and a nurse, to hear more stories about their home in Basel and to laugh about the odd parts of our stay in the jungle, including the lodge manager's string of pot-suffused booty calls. With a sweet river breeze churned by a fan above our outdoor table, we talked for three hours, ordering coffees, then smoothies, and eventually lunch. The four girls made chalk designs on the café walls, took turns on the wood-and-rope swings at the counter, and gained confidence to wander farther. When we finally went to the counter to settle our bills, Marina, whose combined sense of humor and earnestness I liked very much, disappeared around the corner to check on the kids. When she returned, she playfully clutched my arm and whispered, "They showed their butts to each other."

"Who?"

"These two," she said, indicating the younger pair, Libby and Giulia, who had just scampered out into the open. "I don't know if it was just the backside or what."

"Good for them," I laughed, trying to play it cool. I immediately felt like an idiot, wondering if I seemed to care too little while I feared I actually cared too much.

"I think it's okay," Marina said. "But I thought I should tell you." Fortunately, the two of us had some context for this: on a hike a few days earlier, we'd shared a long conversation about girls and bodies and trying to raise children without sexual shame.

I thanked her. "I'll talk to Libby," I said.

But a week had passed. We were back home in Seattle, and I still hadn't said a word—despite the fact that Libby, with her musical cues floating up from the basement as she rummaged through the toy area, was all but begging for a conversation. I was afraid that if I said the wrong thing—if I hinted, even accidentally, that Libby had done something out of line—then this very body-curious and body-positive child might feel ashamed and driven to secrecy. But then there was my other fear: if I said nothing, then Libby might get into trouble— perhaps a misunderstanding with a friend, a scolding from another parent, or even an upsetting correction at school.

Knowing I would come to a plan, I wasn't concerned that my temporary silence made my daughter necessarily more vulnerable to abuse. Protecting my children—all children—from harm is my deepest drive as a parent. I knew too well from my own childhood experience with a twisted adult babysitter that the risks were real. But however intuitive the idea seemed, I resisted making the leap that young friends playing willingly together would want to play in the same manner with adults. That seemed illogical: predators make the overtures to their victims, not the other way around, and children don't *like* to be molested they way they like to play with friends. No, instead, I saw social humiliation as the more immediate peril of letting Libby go on doing her thing. But the only ways I could think of interfering would almost guarantee the same outcomes. So even though it seemed brazen to keep waiting, I decided not to say anything until I found a message I liked.

Then Libby popped back up the stairs hauling her red plastic play doctor kit, complete with stethoscope, bandages, syringe, and name badge.

"Can I have a playdate?" she asked.

In American culture, "playing doctor" is more than just a game. It is as much a rite of passage as a source of discomfiture, and most of us use the euphemism the same way: referring to instances when young children, dressed or undressed in the course of their play, look at or touch one another's genitals. Similar bare-bottom games are "mommies and daddies," "doctors and nurses," "boyfriends and girlfriends," and even the up-and-coming "midwives." When it's normal and healthy, this type of child-to-child sexual exploration takes place between playmates of similar ages (usually not more than four years apart). It's playful, mutual, good-humored, and common. It arises in seemingly limitless bizarre forms as wild and unpredictable as children's imaginations. But one thing is consistent: it's positively confounding to adults. The moment Marina had told me about the girls "showing their butts to each other" at the café in Costa Rica, I registered a deep conflict between what my culture says to do—*make it stop!*—and the potential illogic of that.

One day after school when I was about six—this was in the mid-1980s—my mother walked me over to the house of a neighborhood boy from my class at school and dropped me off to play. Patrick and I stood around in his bedroom upstairs while his mother remained downstairs. It was a dull interval. Finally, Patrick had the idea that we could take off our underpants, and with no compunctions I followed him to the bathroom. He pushed the door closed until only a thin crack of the day's blue light diffused into the dark room. Naked from the waist down, I straddled the edge of the bathtub while he dropped his briefs to his ankles—and his mother opened the door. In no time at all she'd whisked us back into our clothes, called my mother, and sent me home to have a Very Important Talk. I don't recall the talk, but I do remember that no one blamed me except to say that I should not have gone along with the boy's idea. I decided to keep secret that it had never occurred to me to resist the plan. The two of us wanted equally to see one another's body parts. It had seemed a perfectly reasonable trade, and I'd sensed no risk. By the end of the day, however, I felt icky and kept cringing about the whole thing. I understood that Patrick was in big trouble, I wouldn't be playing at his house again, and that was that. It was an unforgettable incident, but not a particularly instructive one. Wasn't there something more useful that my playmate and I could have learned? Now that I was a parent, my childhood embarrassment had ripened into confusion.

My uncertainty aligned with that of countless other parents, caregivers, and teachers who have for decades sought sound advice on how to address early childhood sexual exploration. In the 1980s, with the number of US dual-earner households steadily rising, day cares and preschools boomed, and caregivers and teachers began seeking professional guidance on how, or whether, to address the sexual behaviors of their young charges: genital self-soothing at naptime, for example, or pants around the ankles in the playhouse. At a 1993

Colorado symposium on child-to-child sexual behavior in schools, educators concluded that they found "little agreement as to what constitutes developmentally appropriate sexual behaviors...little scientific research to help guide practices and policies...[and] almost no information on cultural differences in expectations of appropriateness of young children's sexual behavior." Furthermore, they concluded, "the subject is so influenced with assumptions about what is 'right' and 'wrong' or 'good' and 'bad,' that it is difficult to be objective and helpful to practitioners."

After the symposium, Mayo Clinic child abuse researcher and psychologist William N. Friedrich set out to define the boundary between healthy childhood sexual exploration and the extreme behaviors that may indicate a history of abuse. In 1998, he published a landmark paper in *Pediatrics* describing normal sex behavior in more than a thousand American children who had not been abused. The story quickly hit the *New York Times*, no doubt to the relief of countless parents. As reported by their primary female caregivers, kids between the ages of two and five displayed the most sexual behaviors. Friedrich found very few differences between the frequency of boys' and girls' sexual behaviors at any age. For the youngest set, the most common behaviors turned out to be "standing too close," touching their own genitals at home or in public, touching (or trying to touch) women's breasts, and looking at (or trying to look at) nude or undressing people. Six percent of caregivers for boys and girls ages two to nine reported having chanced upon their children touching other children's sex parts. Even acts such as putting mouths on genitals and inserting objects into the vagina or rectum appeared in nonabused children's behavior without, Friedrich concluded, automatic reason for concern.

Meanwhile, other surveys asking adults to recall their childhood sexual behaviors revealed that the numbers fly upward when a study counts firsthand experiences. In a 1988 survey of more than 1,000 American students, 42 percent recalled some kind of sexual experience with another child before puberty. A few years later, a similar survey found that 85 percent of college-age women remembered participating in some kind of sexual play with a childhood friend. By

2002, a Swedish psychologist surveying young adults had similarly found that 83 percent recalled some form of childhood sex play with one or more friends.

Experts say that kids play this way with same-gender as well as other-gender friends, which has no bearing on future sexual orientation. One of the hardest things for adults to understand about young children's sexual play is that children's exploration is not rooted in adult ideas of sexuality. The play may be fun and feel good, but it is curiosity-driven and lacks the emotional, intellectual, and relational eroticism of adult sexuality. Knowing this seems to allow some adults to put fear aside: In a 1996 survey of American professionals who work with children, 65 percent of teachers responded that four-year-old children showing their genitals to one another was "acceptable" (although presumably not at school). Ninety-three percent of therapists felt the same.

The final report of the Colorado symposium stressed that early childhood educators needed to keep two critical and equally important goals at heart: protecting children from abuse and offering positive support so that all children could thrive in their sexuality. "The tendency of our society to concentrate on problematic sexual behaviors constrains our ability to determine and support healthy sexual milestones," the summary said.

But of those two objectives, the prevention of child sex abuse was the only one that stuck. That goal—and fear—was already in the 1980s American zeitgeist as a result of increasing awareness of the prevalence of child sexual abuse and expanding child protection services across the United States. Over the next thirty-plus years, abuse prevention became the central communication about sexuality for young children in America, and it remains widespread in children's books, parenting guides, and advice from sexuality educators.

While the safety message is undeniably critical, its original complement—the idea that adults must acknowledge and nurture children's sexual development alongside their social, emotional, intellectual, and physical growth—has yet to see light. This interested me as I considered what I might say to Libby. I saw a new wave of parents getting hungry for nuance, willing to wade into gray areas, and inclined to weigh old social norms against a more positive regard for body and sex. In other words, if there was a way for me to talk to my daughter about playing doctor without embarrassing her, I was going to get to the bottom of it.

At the library, I began plowing through children's literature and parenting guides. Most of the widely circulated picture books on touch and the body focus squarely on safety with an unmistakable message: keep "private parts" private. "Mom taught us that our private parts are very special parts of our bodies," says the young character in *No Trespassing—This Is MY Body* by Pattie Fitzgerald. "She said there is a very important rule about private parts. 'No one should look at or touch our private parts, or try to play a private parts game with our bodies.'" Cornelia Spelman instructs readers in *Your Body Belongs to You* that "some places on your body should never be touched by other people—except when you need help in the bathroom or getting dressed or when you go to the doctor. These are the places on your body covered by a bathing suit. They are called your 'private parts.'"

My Body Is Private, a still-in-print and widely circulated picture book from 1984, when professionals and parents were beginning to grasp the threat of child sexual abuse, offers this rule: "My mom says that everything covered by my bathing suit—my breasts, my vagina, and my bottom—is very private. Nobody should touch me in those places unless there's a very good reason. A boy's penis and bottom are very private, too."

One children's book struck me as particularly scary. Kimberly King wrote *I Said No!* with her son Zack after he had a traumatic sleepover with his best friend next door. As the story goes, Zack was five when his six-year-old friend wanted him to do *something*—it's never clear what—at bedtime. Zack had read *Your Body Belongs to You* with his mom, and he became terrified, certain his friend had done something "very bad."

Unable to convince his friend's mother of this, Zack spent the night hiding behind the bathroom door. According to King's afterword, her son spent the next six months in therapy to process the terror he'd experienced.

If playing or asking to play in a sexual way is labeled plain *bad*, I wondered how the story might strike the millions of kids who had done so, like the brown-pigtailed girl who'd been all but crowing about it in my house. I identified more with the parent next door who is vilified in King's picture book.

The unequivocal rule, repeated throughout many more books, certainly gave me pause—and not just because my kids' rash-guard swimsuits covered them from neck to knees. The thing was, I simply hadn't felt the impulse to dead-stop Libby from exchanging naked looks, or even touches, with another young friend. I felt caution, certainly, but I was looking for a more nuanced approach.

I was not finding one. From the American Academy of Pediatrics to Dr. Spock to Dr. Sears to the best-selling authors of *What to Expect: The Toddler Years*, American medical authorities, parenting experts, and educational professionals appeared to agree: early childhood sexual exploration in the form of "show-me" games, such as that fraught game we call "doctor," is normal, expected, perfectly healthy, and must not be permitted. Their advice ran along remarkably uniform lines: When you discover children playing a nude or touching game such as "doctors and nurses" or "mommies and daddies," first take a deep breath and calm down. Remember that children who are traumatized by childhood sexual play are usually damaged not by the game itself but by adult reactions to it. Then, with your best poker face, ask some evenhanded questions to make sure the play was cheerful and mutual—and promptly redirect the kids to another activity.

Most of the parenting guides I read shared a single noble goal on this subject: to prevent child sexual abuse. What I found largely missing were messages *supporting* children in their sexuality. I wanted to know if it was possible for a book, or any message at all, to accomplish both. Even when American authors made an effort to empower children with a sense of control over their bodies, as Robie Harris does in her enormously popular body books *It's Not the Stork* (for ages four and up) and *It's So Amazing* (for ages seven and up), the message often wound up mixed: *Your body belongs to you, and you decide how and when you want to be touched. Also be sure to keep your genitals private.*

Just as I was finishing up with body books, a friend brought me a brochure that her daughter—along with all of the other students in her large district—had received at school. Produced by the University of Washington's Harborview Center for Sexual Assault and Traumatic Stress, the excellent packet offered one bit of reasoning so perfectly circular I had to scratch my head: "It's not okay to touch other people's private parts, or to show people your private parts. That's because these parts are private."

I wasn't getting anywhere. How was I supposed to nurture and support my child's budding sexual development by contending that her natural curiosity and healthy instincts made her misbehave? And as a parent in a situation like that, what was I really supposed to be afraid of? I wanted to know what exactly stood at risk.

When I sought out advice on *why* the games had to be interrupted—after all, many of us recall harmlessly playing that way—I found very little. One of the few possible reasons I heard was that telling kids to stop gives them a chance to practice keeping boundaries. More sinister was the suggestion that children who play bare-bottom games and aren't corrected may risk becoming sex criminals. And just as scary was this analogy: If children play show-me games with same-age peers, what's to stop them from engaging in similar play with a pedophile?

I could see the place for those serious and scary concerns, but at the same time I wondered how credible they were. As for boundaries, most parents know that children can learn limits from any clear set of rules, even with gray areas and exceptions. For example, the (fanciful) guidelines for sugar at my house: *We may eat sweets, but not too many, and never right before dinner except on special occasions.*

While it is rare but possible for children to be abused by other children, I found no research indicating that playing doctor can *condition* children to become perpetrators or victims of sexual assault. According to the US Centers for Disease Control and Prevention (CDC), the real risk factors for perpetration of sexual violence include alcohol and drug use; general aggressiveness and acceptance of violence; hostility toward women, conformity with traditional gender role norms, hypermasculinity, weak laws and policies connected to sexual violence and gender equity; and social norms that support sexual violence, male superiority, and sexual entitlement while reinforcing women's inferiority and sexual submissiveness. Protective factors, on the other hand, are the kind that well-regulated childhood games of "doctor" could actually teach. They include the use of reasoning to resolve conflicts and "empathy and concern for how one's actions affect others."

Finally, as alarming as the analogy sounded, it seemed a fallacy to believe that young children who have been allowed to play naked with their peers would find a pedophile's advances anything but terrifying. It's just not normal for an adult to "play" like that—which is something we can, of course, explain to children, doubling the layer of protection their own gut may well provide, and empowering them to say something if any such strange thing were ever to happen.

Eventually, I turned to a booklet that professionals use called *Understanding Children's Sexual Behaviors* by clinical psychologist and school consultant Toni Cavanagh Johnson, whose private practice is based in California. But even in that publication, I still didn't find what I was looking for. Although Johnson offers various scripts for stopping sexual exploration between young children, the booklet doesn't address the question of why, outside of reinforcing social norms, caregivers ought to do so.

The only American expert I found with a wide audience who even hinted that it might be acceptable for children to play naked was the Reverend Dr. Debra Haffner, the one who defended the word "uterus" to Bill O'Reilly. As the author of several parenting guides, including *From Diapers to Dating: A Parent's Guide to Raising Sexually Healthy Children from Infancy to Middle School*, Haffner writes that "some sexologists even believe that early childhood sex play teaches children some important skills." Those scientists, Haffner explains, point to primate studies showing that sex play among immature monkeys prepares them for successful adult mating. "And although I certainly do not believe that children *need* this type of behavior to become sexually healthy adults," Haffner says, "I agree with those professionals who say that most of it is harmless."

She counsels parents to teach their children that people's bodies are their own and that children "have the right to decide if another child may touch your body during a game or any other time." Daringly, she adds that "there is no 100 percent foolproof way to protect your children" from sexual abuse, and children cannot protect themselves either, suggesting that we might be overinsulating, unnecessarily panicking, and even sexually stunting our young. She approaches a disturbing question: What if teaching children to reject sexual behavior in order to protect them actually does nothing of the sort?

Still, Haffner's final advice is unambiguous: while understanding that "show-me" games are normal and possibly even beneficial to children, caregivers should always calmly stop the behavior and perhaps offer other ways of learning about bodies, such as with a book.

Among the children's books I explored, two surprised me as Haffner's did by circling the idea, without necessarily landing, that children might conceivably be free to choose who touches them, when, and how. In *Sex Is a Funny Word,* an award-winning 2015 book for children in second grade and older, Cory Silverberg carefully avoids making any prohibitions or permissions:

> Keeping something private means it's just for you. You might choose to share it with people you trust, but if it is private, it should be your choice....Our bodies are private too....Which parts we show and which parts we keep private depends on many things like our communities and families, how old we are, and who we are sharing with....Everyone has times when they want to be touched and other times when they do not want to be touched. And everyone has times when they change their minds.

If they know their mind in the first place, I thought as I read. I'd been wondering how children trained to always say no can develop a healthy relationship with yes.

In *What's the Big Secret? Talking About Sex with Girls and Boys*, Laurie Krasny Brown and Marc Brown write for an audience of four- to eight-year-olds: "It's natural to be interested in your own body and how it works. . . . You may be curious about how other bodies look—other boys' or girls' or even your parents'—especially the parts usually covered up by clothes." The text is followed by an illustration of a preschool boy plastered with bandages saying, "I'll show you mine," to his playmate, a girl in a lab coat with a toy stethoscope around her neck. She replies confidently with her hands on her hips, "Let's see."

In the midst of my conundrum, I left Seattle for a research trip to the Netherlands. It had been three weeks since Libby's "secret" exhibition with Giulia, and although I had been carefully observing, I continued to hold back from saying anything. I simply hadn't been satisfied with the advice I'd found. In Holland, meanwhile, it was mid-March and time for the *Week van de Lentekriebels* (Spring Fever Week) when a number of Dutch schools simultaneously teach the relationships and sexuality lessons required by law for children ages four and up. (In the Netherlands, children generally start primary school as soon as they turn four, while most American kindergarteners enter at five.)

Spring Fever Week ties to a single curriculum for four- to twelve-year-olds developed by Rutgers, the international sexuality research, health, and outreach center with a long history in Holland. When I walked into the Rutgers headquarters in Utrecht to learn more, I was struck by the stylish space. Banks of large windows looked out over the fourth-largest city in the country as gray morning clouds broke apart in a blue afternoon sky. I passed a wall of glossy in-house publications, scholarly journals, and sexuality-related consumer magazines. A sculpture made of female condoms graced one of two large sitting areas. The space exuded ease and confidence. This was no renegade upstart organization scrambling for spare change. It was an established and influential NGO.

In a conference room over tea, I first met Elsbeth Reitzema, the project leader for Spring Fever Week who would go on to support me in the writing of this book with key information and helpful interpretations of the Dutch approach. With a degree in psychology, she had worked for Rutgers for ten years and helped to design the curriculum I would soon get to know. She was also the mother of a boy about Libby's age. I pictured him like her: strawberry hair, freckles, and blue eyes that glittered when they narrowed. When I asked if it was a busy week for her, she glanced over at her phone and smiled. It was only Tuesday, she explained. She was still waiting for her phone to start ringing with questions from teachers or complaints from parents. We talked for a long time about the curriculum and culturally different attitudes toward sexuality between our two countries but also within the Netherlands, where, although Amsterdam is often regarded as the most free and tolerant city in the world, other regions are defined by intense religious conservatism. Those areas in particular, Reitzema said, don't use the Rutgers curriculum. "They can't find themselves in this," she said, tapping the booklets Rutgers used until the curriculum went all-digital in 2017. "It's too liberal."

Instead, they offer other lessons to comply with Dutch requirements that all schools must address sexuality at every grade level. "We think it's negative," Reitzema said, describing one competing curriculum's message as "You have to be afraid. Don't touch your body. It's a sin. Being homosexual is okay as long as you don't practice it." But she said she'd seen one small victory, at least: the authors of one alternative lesson plan had recently removed a sentence that called being gay or lesbian a disease. This brought them one step closer to complying with the national education mandate regarding sexuality, which includes the specific aim of reducing homophobia.

"Can I ask you a question from my personal life?" I asked Reitzema as our time wound to a close. "It's about my daughter." I explained the show-and-tell from Costa Rica and admitted I hadn't brought it up with Libby yet. "Now she wants to play doctor when her friends come over. I'm sure I should talk to her, but I honestly don't know what to say."

Reitzema smiled. "We call it *doktertje spelen*"—playing doctor— she said. "We have rules for that game: Only do it when everybody wants it. Don't hurt each other. And nothing goes into any orifice." She reached into the swag bag of materials I'd received at the front desk, swishing through giveaways such as heart-shaped blinky bike lights and a translucent bar of soap with a condom in the middle to find a booklet for parents about the sexual development of children from zero to eighteen. She turned to the page focusing on four- to six-year-olds and gave the caveat that it might just as well say two to seven since there is no precise range for normal childhood sexual experimentation. With a mounting feeling that I might finally get my answers, I looked at a little illustration in the booklet: a boy with a stethoscope listening to the exposed tummy of a laughing girl in a T-shirt and tights. Just beneath the illustration came a question from a mother about her son who, she said, played doctor frequently with his friend, another little boy: "Should I condone it?" she asked. And sure enough, the answer was different from anything I'd seen before: "Playing doctor can do no harm; it's totally normal for children to do so. Teach your child some rules." And there they were again, written out in a bulleted list: "Don't play unless you want to, don't do anything against another person's will, don't stick anything in body openings (mouth, ear, nose, vagina, anus), and do no pain."

"*Doktertje spelen* at school can have different rules," Reitzema added as I closed the pamphlet. For example, she said, teachers might require children to keep their underpants on in the classroom.

"Wait," I said, incredulous. "Children are allowed to play doctor at *school*?"

"Of course," she slowly said, her intonation making the words sound like a question as she tilted her face at my reaction. In my delighted shock, I had pitched back in my chair and thrown both hands above my head. "After all," Reitzema cautiously continued, "children of this age go to school." I could see her wondering if her interviewer had gone nuts, but after all of the dissonance at home—*It's okay, but don't do it*—finally something made logical sense, even if it was a shock to the sensibilities. This was how it looked for parents and teachers to say, *It's okay, but we must teach you how to play mutually, respectfully, and safely.* There was an unmistakable ring of the future to it: *consent, fairness, prevention.*

Right in front of me on the table, the curriculum for four- and five-year-olds being taught around the Netherlands that very week laid out clear recommendations for teachers: make sure children know the rules of engagement for *doktertje spelen*, including what's typical and what is allowed. Faced with kids undressing together or touching each other's genitals, teachers are advised to remain calm, remind children of the rules and social expectations, and check biases before deciding whether the behavior is tolerable. The same curriculum counsels teachers to ask the children "What would you do… if a friend wants to play doctor but you don't want to? What can you say to that friend?"

Still flabbergasted, I joked to Reitzema that kids might be arrested for touching one another's genitals at school in the United States. It was an exaggeration, meant to emphasize different social norms; I had no idea I was on to something real. In 2011, a Madison, Wisconsin, prosecutor charged a six-year-old boy with first-degree sexual assault for "playing doctor" with two five-year-olds, a boy and a girl. The district attorney bypassed the boy's parents to deliver him a summons threatening jail time for failure to appear in court. In 2006, school administrators in Waco, Texas, suspended a four-year-old boy after he hugged a teacher's aide and rubbed his face in her chest. In both cases, parents dreaded the legal ramifications for their children, and rightly so, according to a Human Rights Watch white paper that says branding young children as sex offenders is a harmful criminal justice practice that follows children throughout their lives, needlessly destroying futures.

To say that Dutch parents and teachers accept and support childhood sexual games doesn't necessarily mean they're particularly fond of them. It's an uncomfortable area that they navigate with questions and concerns just as American adults do. In a Q & A on the Dutch parenting website Ouders Online, for example, a Dutch mother wondered in 2010 how much *doktertje spelen* was too much; her five-year-old daughter had said she didn't like being poked in the "pee pee" while playing doctors and nurses. The psychologist who responded congratulated the parent on having the fortitude to allow the children to play, but reminded her to teach her daughter the rules: no pain, no poking, and not to play unless she wants to.

Reitzema stressed that not every Dutch preschool and primary school tolerates child-to-child sexual exploration, so I wondered if the permissive ones might be few and far between. But the more I looked, the more widespread it appeared for teachers in the Netherlands to tolerate some sexual behaviors. Even in the professional journal of the Algemene Onderwijsbond, the largest teachers' union in the Netherlands, a 2010 article about how schools can handle "fiddling in the doll corner" doesn't advise prohibiting child-to-child sexual behaviors. Reitzema explained that Rutgers curriculum trainers educate teachers about the rules, but individual schools are responsible for making their own additions—how much undressing will be permitted, for example—and communicating their stance to children and parents.

Just like their American counterparts, Dutch parents and professionals learn to observe and assess whether a behavior seems normal or indicative of a problem. Teachers in Holland aren't immune to overreacting, Reitzema said. "We have some incidents when teachers don't know it's normal behavior. Then an expert comes in to teach everyone the rules. To tell them it's not okay to [break the rules], but it is okay to have this kind of experience."

"As adults, we almost can't help but to look upon children frolicking naked as sexualized behavior…but a child is oblivious," Dutch parenting expert Marina van der Wal told readers of *De Telegraaf*, the largest newspaper in the Netherlands, following such a controversy. "Don't deprive your children of this exploration, but set boundaries, keep an eye on things, and follow your gut."

Reitzema expressed something similar. "If they know the rules and it's been discussed, it's much easier for kids to come to you when there's a problem or they don't like it," she said. Then she stated what I'd heard no American dare to suggest about preschoolers: "We want them to have a good and nice sex life." She meant later in life, but implied that it's necessary to teach key lessons early. "You want, when they are ready to have sex, that they will have it when they *want* it, fully consented and protected."

I thought of a recent conversation with my former landlord in Amsterdam, Anne Marie, a documentary filmmaker who had grown up in a large family in The Hague in the 1960s and '70s. We sat perched over the busy Prinsengracht canal at the little marble-topped table in her front window. When I told her I was interested in how children can explore their bodies without acquiring shame, she told me she'd had "a lot of little boyfriends" as a girl before she got older and became interested in women. Most of the time she and her childhood friends played rough-and-tumble sports in the street, but even as a child, she said, "I loved *seks*." She meant this in a broader sense of exploring bodies and sensuality, not in the narrow American definition of intercourse. "I *loved* it," she said again, smiling with nostalgia before going on. One day, when she was around seven or eight years old, she was in her bedroom with the door closed with two friends, both boys her own age. They were undressed and exploring. Anne Marie's older brother, who was about sixteen at the time, had his ear to the door. Eventually, he went to tell their mother. "And my mother punished *him*, not me," Anne Marie said. "She told him it is normal and it is safe with friends my own age. And she told me later what happened, so I would know. And that," Anne Marie said, straightening up in her lambskin-draped chair, "*that* made me even happier, even more in love with life. It taught me that I was all right and it was good to have a body."

Before we parted, Reitzema recommended a series of children's books on sexuality by Dutch psychologist and sexologist Sanderijn van der Doef. The books were so popular, she said, that I'd be able to find them in just about any bookstore. Indeed, I found all four titles I wanted in the first shop I tried.

In *NEE!*, a picture book for children four and older about how to say (and hear) yes and no, Van der Doef covers the usual child-predator scenarios: the stranger at the park offering a lollipop, the visitor who wants to put you on his lap, and which adults may and may not help you with your *billen* (bottom). But she is careful, ultimately, to leave discretion with the child: aside from helpers, "no one may touch your bottom or your body if you don't want them to."

In *Ben jij ook op mij?* (*Do You Like Me Too?*), a subsequent book intended for ages six to eleven, Van der Doef goes beyond anything available for an American audience of the same age group: "Did you think sex was only for grown-ups?" she asks youngsters in the book's opening. "Sex is for everyone.... For old people and for young people, like you." Like Anne Marie, Van der Doef keeps the definition of *seks* broader than we tend to allow in English, saying it's a good and luscious feeling that can come from many experiences: when you touch yourself, if you receive a Valentine covered in hearts, when you are struck a certain way to see your friend in the nude, if you hold someone's hand, if you touch the hidden parts of one another's bodies, or when someone in your class says they really like you. If you caress and tickle each other, she writes, it's only fun if you both want it. She writes that it's wrong to do something to another person's body that they don't want, and no one has the right to do that to you, either. The message is similar to the American one, but gives the child more autonomy: *Your body is yours, it is special, and only you can decide.*

The popular Dutch books by Sanderijn van der Doef include safety messages, but they hold positive sexual development as their main mission. Child abuse prevention is treated as one part of a much bigger picture. At the end of *NEE!*, I found the rules for playing doctor once more: mutual consent, no pain, no inserting anything anywhere. It seemed Dutch kids were going to learn the rules one way or another, whether from a parent, a teacher, a friend, or a bedtime story. All I could think about was getting home to Libby and finally getting it all out in the open.

My moment came on a sunny Saturday morning later that month. My jet lag had started to wear off, and the girls and I had just looked at photos from my trip. I was still unpacking my bags and pulled out Van der Doef's colorful books. Both girls wanted to hear them, so we started with *NEE!*. When it came to touching, I paused. "Libby," I said, "did you know that when I was a little girl and playing with my friends, sometimes we wanted to look at each other's bottoms?"

Her face lit up. "I do that too!" The secret was out.

"We called it playing doctor," I went on. "And did you know there are rules for that game?"

She wrapped both arms around my knee, and locked her wide brown eyes on my face, desperate for the details. Caroline, nearly nine, had stopped clambering on the back of the couch behind me. She sat still, listening.

"WHAT ARE THEY?" Libby belted. She'd been waiting long enough.

"First of all, everybody has to want to play. If somebody doesn't want to, then you choose a different game."

She nodded.

"And you never hurt each other, and we don't put anything into any holes," I said, wishing I'd said "openings" instead. But I went on. "Not nostrils, or ears, or vagina, or mouth, or any place like that."

As she took in the rules, a rare expression came over Libby's face. I recognized it from the day she'd realized she could read her first words. Her cheeks went pink, and she seemed momentarily speechless and deeply pleased. This was how empowerment looked on her little face: a mix of choice, freedom, and clear boundaries on her part, and trust, encouragement, and clear expectations on mine.

"And Libby," I added, trying to hedge her expectations, "some families might have different rules, so it might be good for other kids to ask their parents first. I'm pretty sure school has different rules too." And then I told her that in some places, teachers *do* allow children to play that way. "It has to do with where you live and what your community finds important," I said, knowing Libby had tuned out but Caroline was still listening.

Libby spent most of that day playing outside with the kids next door: two girls and a boy, ages seven, six, and almost four. They had been her most frequent playmates for years already. At one point in midafternoon, she bolted in through the front door, grabbed her doctor kit, and shot out the back. Then she came clattering back to shout through the door: "Don't worry, Mom! I remember the rules!"

I knew that our neighbors had different rules about modesty in their house, so I felt more than a bit curious as the kids set up their doctor's office. They arranged everything in plain view in the sunny expanse of grass between our two houses. I heard them talking, and I waited.

"Mom!" Libby burst through the front door again. "We made a plan!" She said the neighbors didn't want *their* bottoms checked, "but *I* didn't mind, so they're just going to check mine!" Breathless, she sprinted back outside. I puttered in the kitchen, drifted into the bedroom to fold a few shirts, glanced out the window a few times. They listened to a bad elbow with the stethoscope. They vaccinated each other's heads. I unpacked the rest of my suitcase. And then I heard Libby wail. I tracked her howl as she ran around to the front porch and banged through the door into my arms. "Now they say they *won't* check my bottom," she nearly screamed between sobs. "They don't *want* to. That was the only reason I wanted to *playyy*," she wailed.

My heart, my love. I had sort of suspected it would go this way. I hugged her harder. I felt all the disappointment in her shaking shoulders and thundering chest. At the same time, I felt a thrill of discovery like the one I'd had in conversation with Reitzema. Here was my almost-kindergartener running to me with her biggest feelings about having a body and wanting to explore it. They were early feelings, of course, but entirely real and, I could see now, foundational. She knew she had to respect her friends' decisions about what was right for them.

Once Libby recovered, the playdate resumed without fanfare. The next time I glanced out the window, a doll was the patient. Later, when the medical toys sat once again on the shelf, the kids lay asleep, and the sun exhaled a last rosy glow through the bathroom window, I thought about Libby's afternoon game. The entire interaction had been a small-beans trial run for the more consequential ways Dan and I hoped to be involved with our daughters' adolescent and teenage lives. It was exactly as Reitzema had said: Once she knew the rules, Libby would find it easy to come to us for help. The lines of communication were wide open for business. By contrast, the poor kid had eaten a perfectly harmless dandelion off the lawn the previous day, and it had taken her all day to work up the courage to ask me if she was going to be all right. But keeping me posted about her plans and crying out her heartbreak over a game of doctor, well—she had no hesitations about that. I knew I hadn't solved the riddle of the parenting universe; we still had plenty of unanswered questions and challenges to come. But for the moment, I felt good. It had turned out to be so easy. Child's play, really.

PART TWO

FLY

7

What (In)Equality Is Made Of

What are little boys made of?
What are little boys made of?
Frogs and snails and puppy-dog's tails,
And that are little boys made of.

What are little girls made of?
What are little girls made of?
Sugar and spice and all that's nice,
And that are little girls made of.

What are young men made of?
What are young men made of?
Sighs and leers and crocodile tears,
And that are young men made of.

What are young women made of?
What are young women made of?
Ribbons and laces, and sweet pretty faces.
And that are young women made of.

—Walter Crane, "Natural History," from
The Baby's Opera, 1877

The summer Caroline was ten and Libby was six, Dan and I sent them off to a weeklong day camp for girls focusing on spatial thinking and engineering. Lessons on everything from paper-airplane flight to 3-D printing design positively lit them up—they were exuberant every afternoon. Except, on the last day, they seemed to come home with little rain clouds over both of their heads. Just before dinner, Caroline told me what they'd learned that day.

"Our teacher told us," she said, hesitating with some discomfort, "that girls are naturally better at social skills. But boys are born a certain percent more physical, and like to play with cars and stuff. So the boys get more into things like engineering."

I could tell it was hard for Caroline to say the words, as if she were confessing to a flaw. Libby looked at her big sister, nodding.

"That's why they were wanting us to really try hard to be engineers," Caroline went on. "So the boys won't get all the jobs."

As my kids explained it, I could tell the teachers were making a well-intended effort at transparency with the girls: there *is* a gender gap for women in tech, engineering, and other STEM-related jobs. As educators concerned with girls' progress, they weren't going to deny that. They wanted to motivate the kids by encouraging them to compete.

"I thought boys and girls are born the same," Libby said, hanging her head a little. "But they're not." Neither of my children looked happy.

But I was.

I was thrilled, in fact, because I knew on the spot what to tell my kids. Only a few months earlier, I wouldn't have been so sure. All of my adult life, I had fallen under the sway of pop psychology books such as John Gray's *Men Are from Mars, Women Are from Venus* and Louann Brizendine's best-selling *The Female Brain* and *The Male Brain*—not to mention the steady stream of magazine articles and news spots about studies pointing out behavioral and cognitive differences between men and women, boys and girls. I had believed, as some writers and theorists still insist, that those differences are innate. Biological. Immutable. And I had felt ashamed of them, because no matter how beneficial "social skills" and "empathy" and "nurturing" can be made to sound, all the real-world advantages appeared to go to boys and men.

But that year, I'd turned to better literature. It was out there—a lot of it—but quieter by default, because it is so much less splashy than articles with bias-confirming "proof" that nature gives the human sexes different brains and divergent ways of using them. *The Truth About Girls and Boys* by Caryl Rivers, a journalist, and Rosalind C. Barnett, a social scientist and psychologist, was the first of several books I had waited much too long to discover: a detailed, expert rebuttal of the major recent books and articles feeding our cultural obsession with sex-difference findings. Eye-opening books by scientists including Lise Eliot (*Pink Brain, Blue Brain*), Cordelia Fine (*Delusions of Gender* and *Testosterone Rex*), and Rebecca Jordan-Young (*Brain Storm*) also helped wipe away my old assumptions about inherent sex differences in cognition and abilities.

As I read about the impact of media-darling gender theorists Michael Gurian and Leonard Sax, who boosted their careers starting around the turn of the millennium by asserting that boys and girls have naturally different learning styles, there again were the perennial ideas that girls' brains are innately suited for caring and empathy while boys' brains are built for problem solving and leadership. Peddling such ideas, Gurian and Sax, I learned, had powerfully influenced public education by promoting gender-segregated schooling, which is illegal in most of Europe but has ballooned in the United States since 2000.

Whether we characterize the idea as an excuse, an explanation, or an obstacle to gender equality, I had been among the many to accept without much questioning that nature gives boys and girls different brains. I'd taken it (grudgingly) as a given for so long that at first I had a hard time embracing the reality that no scientist has credibly demonstrated any cognitive differences between male and female newborns. The more I learned about the lack of evidence for any biological gap, the more telling it seemed that for centuries there's been such a hot clamor to identify one. Why aren't scientists—or the rest of us—so feverishly invested in proving that male and female bodies digest food differently, say, or bend at the elbow in sex-specific ways? Because an argument about intelligence comes down to power: who gets access to it and how they get to use it.

Perhaps the most irritating "finding" that won't go away is a 2000 study by Simon Baron-Cohen and colleagues in which he "demonstrate[s] beyond reasonable doubt" that newborns choose what to look at based on their sex. Brizendine relied on this study, and many other books and articles continue to invoke this supposed landmark finding: a dubious inquiry conducted with a small number of babies, the results of which no one, not even Baron-Cohen himself, has managed to replicate. To be clear, Baron-Cohen's conclusion that newborn male babies prefer to look at a mobile while newborn girls choose to look at human faces—a sensational claim that is still often cited—turned out to be false, just as any mother of a newborn boy could have told us.

Dr. Elizabeth S. Spelke, the Harvard-based cognitive psychologist who pioneered infant-gaze studies, clarified the point a few years later when her university's president, Lawrence H. Summers, publicly suggested that a shortage of women in science could be due to their innate lack of math ability. "My position is that the null hypothesis is correct," she said after scouring the baby data. "There is no cognitive difference and nothing to say about it." The facts about male-female brain differences turn out to be a lot of that same nope, nada, zilch. But it's just not click bait. Since consumers are thought to want information about gender *difference*, the many excellent studies that search for them and find none simply languish off the airwaves. As Emily Bazelon put it in a review of *The Male Brain*, "Would Brizendine have gotten this kind of pop for a single book called 'The Male and Female Brain: Mostly One and the Same'? Not a chance."

The unspectacular truth is that female and male babies are not born "hardwired" to learn, think, and behave differently. That doesn't mean that parents at the park and social science researchers who point out gender differences in children and adults aren't seeing real phenomena. The problem is mistaking learned behaviors for inborn, immutable ones. In *Misconceptions*, Naomi Wolf breaks this down: "You don't have to be a genius, at the age of three, to figure out that if you're a girl, you'd better act in ways that the grown-ups identify as girl-like, and vice versa." In fact, researchers have shown that young babies are already scanning their environment for clues about gender roles and developing their own gender stereotypes by eighteen months of age.

Here are the most important lessons I learned from my reading: At any age, male and female brains—and behavior—overlap far more than they diverge. As casual observers of gender, even when we think we're being objective, we tend to exaggerate gender differences and minimize similarities. Adults treat boys and girls differently even when we think we're treating them the same. Over time, as the world influences us, observable behavioral differences *do* emerge between men and women. The magnitude of those differences depend on where and how our lives are lived. In some cultures the gap is large, and in others it's negligible. This is strong evidence that gender roles come with practice, not birth. "Simply put, your brain is what you do with it," Eliot writes in *Pink Brain, Blue Brain*. "Nature exerts its pull at all ages, but what is most important is how children *spend their time*." It is not by biological fate but with repetition, reinforcement, and, with any luck, the chance to follow our own individual interests that we build the tendencies and abilities that over time become identity. When we are raised in full freedom, where we land on the gender spectrum is the result—not the cause—of who we are.

So on that summer day after engineering camp, I had an upbeat response for my girls. "I'm so glad you told me what your teacher said. Because guess what!"

"What?" they asked in unison.

"Scientists know better now! We've learned that boys and girls are *not* born with different brains. Getting good at something has to do with what you practice most," I said. "So for that part, your teacher was right."

Caroline exhaled and stood up straighter.

"I like that better," Libby said. Suddenly energized to play, she bolted out the open front door. "I knew it wasn't true anyway," she called over her shoulder.

It was a good moment, but one that drove home the dangers of stereotypes and the ways generalizations can become self-fulfilling prophecies. Gender is a touchy subject, particularly with so many people uncomfortably credulous, as my girls and I had been, that male and female babies are born cognitively different. But if, as researchers tell us, gender roles are drawn out by influence and practice, then the questions change: What exactly are girls and boys rehearsing? How are we unwittingly using language and games to mold girls and boys in ways that reinforce sexism and inequality? What if we could see, in the ways children and adults play, how the groundwork is laid for the eventual discrepancies in attitudes, status, opportunities, influence, and body sovereignty that characterize our American gender gap and foster a rape culture in which a pussy-grabbing candidate is electable for president? For one thing, it would be overwhelming, and we'd understandably want to cover our ears. But also, we'd be looking at a genuine opportunity to create, from the roots up, a culture in which people of different genders are conditioned to unite rather than compete for power.

Priscilla Long, a writer I admire, has an easy but effective approach to change. When something needs addressing, she doesn't tell her students (or herself) to go fix it. She only asks for a 5 percent improvement: the first step in a better direction. With that in mind, I started looking more closely at the gender lessons hidden in the simple everyday games we play. And I wondered: In our great responsibility to teach equality, what if we could do just 5 percent better? I went looking for ways to do that, especially around how we socialize young people with regard to status, looks, smarts, caring, roles, and consent.

Separate Recipes, Disparate Status

Janine, the American mom I met through our kids' Dutch-language program in Seattle who runs a Dutch imports store, lived in several countries, including her husband's native Holland, before her family settled in the Pacific Northwest. She'd quickly learned that each country had its own rules, but they all had norms that were different for girls and boys. When her family lived in Brisbane, her preschool-age son wanted pink sneakers with a glitter swoosh. "I knew in Australia that wasn't going to go down very well." In Holland, "it was more okay for boys to wear more what Americans would consider feminine clothes," but Dutch dress still had subtle gender distinctions: girls might wear leather fashion boots, for example, whereas boys would sooner go for leather high-tops. By the time Janine's son was ready for kindergarten, her family had moved to the United States. When they went to pick out his backpack, the boy, who had not yet internalized the local gender code, fixated on a glittery pink one featuring a giant tube of lipstick.

"I didn't want him to go to school and get made fun of, but I didn't want to be like, *no*, because I don't want him to think he can't have it. How far do you go when he's in kindergarten?"

Or, really, at any age?

"Developmental psychologists describe young children as 'gender detectives,'" writes social scientist Fine in *Testosterone Rex: Myths of Sex, Science, and Society*. "Children see that the category of sex is the primary way that we carve up the social world, and are driven to learn what it means to be male or female. Then once they come to understand their own sex, at about two to three years of age, this information takes on a motivational element: kids begin to 'self-socialize' (sometimes to the chagrin of feminist parents)." I knew what she meant: that black-hole period in preschool when it seems just about every girl gets sucked into princesses and fairies while boys swirl off into superhero and "bad-guy" games.

It seems to come out of nowhere, but in fact the stage is set for them. The first gender idea we begin practicing with boys and girls, whether we intend to or not, is that the sexes are meaningfully different. This might seem like an obvious and even important thing to teach, but not everyone believes that's a healthy idea. Once difference is established, status becomes the next question. "The big mistake is to confuse the persistence of the status quo with the dictates of testosterone," Fine writes. As she puts it, "gender is a hierarchy," which is why, even though boys and girls are limited by the roles prescribed for them, we still concern ourselves mostly with the limitations experienced by girls: in the United States and around the world, girls and women are the ones with measurably less safety, opportunity, influence, and autonomy.

When there's a power and status differential between two groups of people, no matter how you couch it, talking about what's "naturally" different between those groups has the ring of justifying the status quo—which is the prerequisite for shrugging off a boy's aggressive tendencies, for example, or a middle-school girl's sudden aversion to math. So instead of hearing, "Geez, look what Marco picked up from *Star Wars*," or "Jordan has totally lost her confidence in algebra—I wonder why?", instead we hear, "That's just the way it is," and "Can't do much about it," and the great exonerator, "They're just born that way."

As a culture we shape gender to suit our values by offering children things we think they should like and by specifying how much crossover will be tolerated—which necessarily leaves certain opportunities outside the consideration set. I thought of this recently at the school playground, when a father came pushing a stroller toward the field where Caroline's fourth-grade class played a game of Ultimate. Their white disc whizzed back and forth. The man looked into the stroller at his infant. "You *like* shiny things that go fast, don't you?" he said, making winky reference to sports cars in an approving tone to the baby, whose little head was still so wobbly I frankly couldn't tell *what* he was looking at. Maybe the dad would have said the same thing to a daughter. But if he did, he'd have been actively busting stereotypes.

Even when comparisons are equally positive or equally negative—boys are industrious, and girls are caring, for example, or girls are overly emotional, but boys are destructive—we're still in problematic territory, where the act of comparing and contrasting is considered valid. This leads to the eventual acceptance of gendered ideas about power and sets up children to become each other's adversaries instead of champions.

Up to three-quarters of women recall being "tomboys" in middle childhood—a strategic childhood shift, some scholars argue, that comes with awareness of boys' higher social status. Being "one of the guys" is considered a positive attribute for girls and young women, while there's no similar prestige for the boy who wants to be "one of the girls"—or even for girls who are especially "girly."

For parents striving to be open-minded, it's a delicate problem. Janine's solution to the lipstick-backpack conundrum was to pique her son's interest in a few additional backpacks, then to purchase all of them so they could decide at home. Eventually, the boy did settle on something else, and his mom returned the runners-up to the store.

After Janine shared this story, I could see that Dan, who heard it too, was troubled. "The idea that pink isn't for boys—that's a problem we adults create," he said. "It's about how we set up feminine things to be bully-worthy."

"It's too scary to put a boy in pink," a friend once confided to me. She recognized that while "boy" colors on her daughter came across as assertive and aspirational, putting pink on a boy was like slumming— a foray into a lower social realm. She said even if she chose to do so with her baby, her husband and other family members would disapprove. And in public, it would just cause confusion—something I knew to be true. When Libby was a newborn and our family took a trip, I dressed her in sapphire blue pajamas. "Oh, how old is he?" gushed an older woman at the airport, tugging her husband's arm to have a look at the baby.

"She just turned six weeks," I smiled.

"She?" the woman said, glaring at me, suddenly angry. "Why would you dress her like that?" The mistake embarrassed her, and it was my fault for breaking the social code. I could only imagine the blowback for traveling with a newborn boy dressed in fuchsia. We could hardly begin delineating the narrow rules of masculinity any younger.

Later in a group discussion I arranged about Dutch and American perspectives on sexuality and gender, I heard something interesting from Candice, an American mom raising kids with a Dutch husband. She told the group about her two-and-a-half-year-old son, Lex: "My little guy has lots of blond curls," which her extended family only seemed willing to tolerate to a point. Recently the adoring comments had changed to "Okay, it's time to cut that." But the message was shifting right at the developmental moment when Lex himself began to *identify* with his curls. "No, this is my hair, this is *me*," Candice said, describing her son's reaction to the proposition of a haircut. "These are my curls. I need these curls because this is Lex."

What stood out to me in that moment was that Candice's sensitivity to how her son felt about his own image outweighed her concerns about how the boy's appearance made her other relatives feel. Patric, a Dutch father in the room, nodded along with Candice's story and then described his own teenage son, saying "he has long blond hair, but he feels very masculine." Appearances may be superficial, but looks clearly send messages. Even though we were only talking about hair, I knew these parents were describing concrete endeavors to raise children with modern and expansive views of masculinity.

We all know that "girly" is used dismissively while "boyish" can be a compliment. "Quit talking in your little girl voice. Talk in your boy voice!" snapped a mom on the ferry when her six-year-old, a stout, blond fellow with a cowlick, ran ahead and begged her to hurry as he pointed outside at the sunny, windy bow. I'd heard him myself, and it never occurred to me that he sounded like a girl, "little" or otherwise. He only sounded like a kid in the throes of excitement. But for many American parents, love for a child means it's never too soon to teach manliness, or at least anti-girlishness—even if that child is female.

The truth is that Dan and I would have worked just as hard as Janine to keep the glitter-lipstick backpack out of our daughters' hands. Harder, in a way: both of us would have been more willing to simply tell our daughters, "No, you can't have it." I hope we would at least explain why: not because it was for the "wrong" gender, but because it was just *too* gendered in a landscape with too many partitions already.

Sweet Pretty Faces: Looks and Self-Esteem

Dan brought a story home one day when our girls were in kindergarten and fourth grade. He'd been catching up with some former co-workers at happy hour and found himself listening as two of them, both mothers, chatted lightheartedly about compliments they pay their daughters that they'd never bother giving their sons.

"You know," Dan said, oblivious to what was coming, "I think I can honestly say that I have never told my daughters that they look pretty."

His incredulous friends promptly informed him that he was the worst dad ever.

"You *have* to!" they said. It's the Most Important Thing to tell women and girls, especially as their father, they insisted. These moms explained to Dan that his daughters would reach adolescence and discover they were being socially evaluated on their looks—and he was about to send them into the fray without any money in the bank. In short order, they prophesied, Caroline and Libby would start feeling terrible about themselves. These women weren't likely to be wrong: half of preschool girls are dissatisfied with their bodies, and almost all girls report feeling that way by adolescence. But does this really mean girls don't hear *enough* about their looks?

"I get it," Dan told his colleagues. "Looks are social capital. They're going to have people tell them about their looks eventually. But for now, I tell them they're fast and smart and strong."

The women rolled their eyes. "Go home and tell them they're beautiful," they said.

We all see the setup in which a girl's looks are so scrutinized and so picked apart that they become either her number-one asset or her number-one problem—which can be seriously limiting in either case. Dan's coworkers took a practical approach with their kids: if female happiness was riding on self-image, then no doubt we should do everything possible to send them off with confidence in their appearance. Arguably Dan and I have taken a more idealistic and riskier approach: teach them that the world will judge them by their looks, but that we think it's a harmful standard and therefore reject the game.

The deeper problem is that our culture teaches girls that their attractiveness—their worth—will be determined by other people. In other words, the Most Important Thing for their self-esteem is beyond their own control. When Libby was three and climbed into the dentist's chair, he gushed about her clothes and her smile. "That's such a pretty headband," he finally said, tapping the rainbow parade of Mexican worry dolls holding back her hair. "How did you know those were all my favorite colors?" At the next visit he said to second-grade Caroline, "I bet your boyfriend really loves that dress." (We soon changed dentists.) These creepy but commonplace remarks are the beginning of sexual objectification. When a girl learns to think about her appearance not as she sees and values it but as she guesses others will like, she begins separating from her authentic self. That also happens to be the precursor to our famously lopsided American manner of male-female intimacy: one partner thinking about how he feels, while the other thinks about how she is supposed to be making him feel.

Although Dan was just going with his gut on not praising his daughters' looks, it turns out research supported his claim that girls' self-esteem needn't ride on feedback about their appearance. For better health and emotional wellness, experts say it matters less what we tell kids and more what they take away: that they are loved and safe. This is what every caring parent—whether they tell their daughters they are beautiful every day or almost never—is doing absolutely right. Ultimately too, though, part of keeping girls loved and safe is protecting them from early sexualization. Staking self-esteem on one's looks can lead to mental health problems such as eating disorders, low self-esteem, and depression, the American Psychological Association stated in a major 2007 report. The authors concluded that "when parents...communicate the message that other characteristics are more important than sexuality, they help to counteract the strong and prevalent message that it is only girls' sexuality that makes them interesting, desirable, or valuable."

When American girls as young as six are asked to choose a paper doll like themselves, they overwhelmingly select the most sexily dressed image. The psychologists who designed the study concluded that "mothers who find it important to teach values and help their daughters apply these values in real life situations, such as when watching TV, may be more effective buffers against their daughters' self-sexualization by preparing them to successfully navigate the onslaught of sexualizing messages out in the world." Talking to girls about what they'll face in the wider world is more work than just telling them they're pretty, but the more I read, the more it became clear that this is how to build a more durable self-esteem.

At a 2012 public lecture in Seattle, Peggy Orenstein, who examined the early sexualization of girls in her book *Cinderella Ate My Daughter*, offered up the surprising relief of absolute permission to shelter my kids like an abbess from mainstream messages about sex roles. As parents, she said, we ought to "limit the culture box" for as long as possible. Here was a liberal-minded journalist telling us to go ahead and shield our kids from commercials, magazines, and movies as long as we possibly could—even for kids getting into their elementary years. This gives us time, she said, to teach children media literacy and critical analysis: how to decode sexist advertising and be wary of stereotypical or harmful male-female narratives—including the insidious message that girls are valued above all for their looks.

There came a day in my pregnancy with Libby when a longtime acquaintance looked me appraisingly from head to toe and then complimented the tolerable size to which I had expanded. We had just settled in Seattle, and that afternoon we were walking to the neighborhood bakery with our kids. In a moment of clarity after going so long without experiencing the "male gaze," I realized I was tired of being sized up by this guy. It occurred to me that I could ask him not to comment on my body again, whether I was pregnant or not. So with my heart in my throat—no one likes a scold—I did that. And as part of the bargain I silently pledged to follow my own advice. No more words about other people's shapes, sizes, changes, haircuts, makeup, faces, fashion—*especially* not with children. It was time to get creative and find some other ways to greet old friends (no more "you look great!") and say hi to kids (instead of "Cute T-shirt!" why not "Whatcha up to today?"). That's when Dan and I hit upon a handy new phrase. From that point on, whenever one of our daughters emerged from a bedroom or the dress-up bin, whether she was decorated in leggings, lingerie, or a lampshade, we aimed to say something along the lines of "Well! You sure look ready." It seemed to be all the feedback they needed, and perhaps we were overthinking it, but we liked the way "ready" implied the kid was going to go *do* something rather than simply *look* like something.

While an incessant focus on girls' looks creates the negative opportunity for them to learn and reinforce self-objectification, it also may create a corollary positive opportunity for boys to get ahead—to literally spend more time in a day focused on more beneficial activities such as studying, extracurriculars, tinkering, and play. When my daughters have ask for pierced ears or manicures and pedicures, for example, or when they think about whether they will someday shave, I try to remind them how much *time* it takes to deal with a beauty routine. I want them to grasp the opportunity cost.

Time will tell, but as far as we know, our kids are doing fine so far without extra praise for their looks. When comments about pretty faces and nice dresses come her way, our oldest will smile, then glance at her dad or me, and, with a grin, roll her eyes—her kid version of a wink. She gets the picture.

My friend Jenny, a Los Angeles financial advisor and mother of two, recently gave me a perfect example of the disparity between how boys and girls are valued. When her oldest child, with the support of a team of clinicians, socially transitioned from living as a girl to identifying as a boy just before starting kindergarten, the way he was treated (by adults in particular) changed overnight. He had the exact same face and body as when people considered him a girl, but with a shorter haircut and "boy" wardrobe, people commented on his looks far less often than before.

When he was younger and still presented as a girl, adults had frequently exclaimed over the child's striking looks: dark hair contrasting with pale skin and shimmering, downturned blue eyes. As a girl, "he would get a lot of comments about how beautiful he is," Jenny told me, laughing about how hard it had become to switch to old pronouns. "He gets none of those now." Jenny mentioned a little "beauty mark" right above his lip. Before he cut his hair short and changed his wardrobe, she said, "people would comment on the beauty mark. He still has it, but people don't notice it anymore." On a recent vacation, a tourist commented that the boy had a remarkable face and compared him to Keanu Reeves. Jenny and her husband both noticed the comment and talked about it later because it was the first time in months that they'd heard anyone breathe a word about their child's attractiveness. More often by that time, Jenny said, he was praised for being brave and quick to solve problems.

Frogs and Snails and STEM-Success Tales

When our girls were young, Dan worried they weren't getting good enough at throwing and catching. He instituted Twenty Catches, a daily rule: each kid needed to make twenty catches by bedtime, whether that was in the yard with a football or in the tub with a bar of soap. I rolled my eyes at my sports-star mate and insinuated he was forcing an interest in sports where there was none to be had. When it was time for our family to choose a long-term neighborhood in Seattle, we decided to start by picking a school. On our tours I tended to ask administrators all kinds of predictable things, while Dan had one essential question: "Where are the balls?" If the school didn't have a ball closet, or if it wasn't easily accessible or well-enough stocked, Dan took note. He often followed up by asking how many days a week kids had physical education opportunities. Those questions embarrassed me at first—I was afraid they sounded unacademic—but as the years passed, I started to see the connections: now he tactfully challenged teachers to redouble their efforts with our daughters in mathematics even when they appeared to be doing just fine. Somehow he already sensed what I learned only later: that the spatial lessons of sports and physical activity parlay into STEM success, and that parents and teachers underestimate girls' math abilities in comparison to boys', which may be the actual reason behind girls' math interest waning in middle school despite their equal performance with boys at that age. When I learned that researchers have found that adults practice spatial thinking (such as sports) more with boys than girls, I was sorry I'd ever questioned Twenty Catches, a practice that was fun, first of all, and also bound to give both kids better reflexes, hand-eye coordination, spatial sense, confidence, and even opportunities.

"Better make it forty catches," I told Dan when I finally caught on.

These days our yard is littered with little pieces of asphalt roofing. It's brittle up there and due for replacement. But while the occasional windstorm makes things a little worse, Ball-On-Roof is the real culprit. It's a game Dan invented to keep the Twenty Catches rule fun and to teach kids to move their feet and get underneath the ball to make a catch. He launches a rubber playground ball way up high so that it bounces—*thoink!*—almost straight up off the low pitch, then plummets down toward the kids. Like a version of flyers-up, it can be played with a group—Caroline's friends find this game riotous—or played alone. They play before and after dinner, sometimes all afternoon on weekends. Occasionally it's my job to be the launcher. Over time, I have seen a daughter whom I assumed wouldn't take much interest in sports become one to make spectacular catches look easy. At home as I work my way around scattered Lego structures thanks to Dan adding them to the kids' birthday and Christmas lists, I think of the ten-year study of thousands of children and parents showing that sons are offered more problem-solving activities than daughters—such as building sets, which can give any child an early edge in developing spatial skills. When girls do excel in problem-solving and spatial tasks, studies show that adults are more likely to say the girls had been "hardworking" in contrast to the "natural talent" they ascribe to boys.

In other words, even when boys practiced more, only the girls' practice was recognized. This connects with the truly chilling result of a study published in *Science* in 2017 showing that boys and girls internalize stereotypes by the time they are six years old about which gender is more brilliant: boys. At that same age, girls in the study—but not boys—began avoiding activities described as being for "really, really smart" kids. The girls were more inclined to choose a game in which they were told they would have to "try really, really hard."

"These studies speak to the early acquisition of cultural ideas about brilliance and gender, as well as to the immediate effect that these stereotyped notions have on children's interests," the authors wrote. So much for any lingering idea that young children freely follow their innate interests without social cues about gender interfering.

One busy morning at home, the four of us were all hustling around trying to finish up breakfast and get out the door. None of us noticed that five-year-old Libby was still at the table struggling to close a cereal box top. Her frustration finally boiled over, and she got all of our attention when she blew up and shouted, "I need a *lesson* on this!"

Dan promptly walked over and demonstrated how to slip the cardboard tab into the corresponding slot on the opposite flap. She tried again. When the tab finally popped into place she let out a laugh. "*Now* I see!"

Observing this scene, I was struck by what my daughter had *not* said: "I can't do this." She only said nobody had taught her *how*—and clearly she resented the omission. She was so alive to her ability—to her *right*—to learn. We still had some time left before those things risked fading away.

Sugar and Spice and All That's Nice About Nurturing

Years ago, I walked into a coffee shop with three-year-old Libby, who was pleased as punch to line up behind a baby in a car carrier. His mother had set the bucket on the floor to give her arm a rest.

"Oh! Baby!" Libby exclaimed, putting her hands on her knees and crouching to peer at the tiny face inside. Impossible delight! A human even littler that she was!

"Oh," sighed the mom as she turned around. "That is so sweet."

I smiled at her, wondering why she looked sad.

"I have two boys now," she said, gesturing at the carrier. "The other one's three, and we're not having more kids. And I'll just—" suddenly her eyes filled with tears. "I'll just never experience this as a parent."

"Experience what?" I asked, genuinely baffled, hoping I wouldn't make her cry harder. It was almost time for her to put in her espresso order.

"*This*," she said, gesturing at Libby, who was bugging her eyes and talking nonsense to the baby. "Boys just don't *care* about babies."

Even if that were true of her three-year-old, I knew it wasn't true of the general population. Still, she wasn't wrong that a divide opens up between girls and boys, who aren't equally *expected* to care about, or for, vulnerable others. While grown-ups practice empathy, nurturing, and communication with girls by doing things such as involving them in child care and talking through complex feelings, it turns out that boys are given fewer opportunities to cultivate these life skills. It's a practice—or a lack thereof—that begins early and plays out dramatically later. Researchers have shown that American parents treat infant girls as more fragile than infant boys. They more readily soothe and respond to baby girls, and without intending to, mothers use more verbal and emotionally complex communication with daughters than with sons. It is perhaps no surprise that girls go on to be more verbally and emotionally articulate—and boys learn early not to be crybabies.

This is different in the Netherlands, where it is more acceptable for boys to cry and where I'm often struck by the demonstrative ways in which Dutch dads show tenderness and physical affection with boys right up through elementary ages. A few days standing outside school at pick-up time is all it takes to remind me how freely Dutch fathers kiss, cuddle, and comfort sons in public.

By contrast, back in the United States, it shocked me at first to see fathers kick, punch, or elbow their sons—only to realize the gestures were meant kindly. *Kick*—Here's your hot chocolate. *Elbow*—What a spectacular sunset! For Rob Lehman, a Seattle pediatrician who teaches father-son sex-ed classes, a "play-punch" is often his only sign that attendees have bonded over the information he presents. But are boys really poor at showing affection and caring for others, or do they just need examples and more practice?

A few months after repatriating to Seattle, we found a house to rent in a little cul-de-sac on a hill. On the dim winter day when our moving truck arrived, our neighbors came out into the cold to introduce themselves. Gwen, the mother of two adolescent boys, smiled to see three-year-old Caroline and encouraged me to hire her eighth-grade son, Colin, to babysit. "He'd be wonderful," she said. He was ready to begin learning the job.

We lived on that cozy street for eighteen months, during which time Libby was born. We socialized often with the neighbors and definitely needed babysitters, but I never called Colin. I was unsure about hiring a boy to babysit, and at the time I didn't take time to examine my reasons. I just hired girls.

"I want to interrogate that now," I told Gwen as I was writing this chapter. At the time as a mother of young children, I imagined my way of thinking about domestic life as alien to any adolescent boy's perspective. I wasn't confident we'd communicate well. I felt more certain that I could lay down my child care and household expectations with a female babysitter—wouldn't it be more intuitive for her, since she'd probably done a lot of similar work already in her life?—or maybe the truth was that I was most comfortable bossing a girl. I had no doubt that my kids would be safe with Colin, and yet, and yet—what was my fear, my resistance?

Although Colin didn't end up with many babysitting jobs, his younger brother, Beck, eventually spent many hours caring for kids as a babysitter and a summer "manny."

As a junior in a high school of more than a thousand students—and just before being elected school president—Beck told me he knew "tons" of girls who babysat, but not a single other boy. "It's just the stigma around it," he explained. "Honestly, [adults] are taken aback. Babysitting is a thing that girls do. Even when you're talking at school, people are like, 'Oh, okay, you babysit, that's a little weird....'"

"Here's what was going through my head when I advocated for my guys babysitting," Gwen, a community engagement director, told me in a bulleted email:

- Kids need "first" jobs where they can safely fail. Babysitting for a neighbor when your parents are 20 feet away is lower risk for all parties involved.
- It's hard to get jobs before you are 16; it's not fair if the girls only get the opportunity for this kind of work.
- My kids are responsible and make good decisions; you can trust your kids with them.
- My kids grew up in a house with a dad/mom who are 50/50 caregivers. Childcare was never just women's work in our house—they had a great nurturing role model in their father.

- My kids have something to learn from babysitting, and they both have things to teach younger kids.
- Babysitting in your neighborhood helps build community.

Knowing how the tide would shift, I could hardly begrudge girls an early hiring advantage, but I couldn't argue with Gwen's clear reasoning. So why is there so much social resistance to entrusting boys with child care roles? Back to the harmful stereotypes: First of all, adolescent boys are typecast as oversexed. They're too often assumed to have lewd impulses—for which they are both valorized and demonized—and they are also supposed to lack self-control. I suspect these unfair thoughts motivate parents to keep young kids apart from teen boys. In Beck's case, only one family who hired him had a daughter. She was the oldest of three kids, a sixth-grader who mostly kept to herself while Beck played with her younger brothers. There was never a time when Beck was hired to watch a single child alone. Only groups, only boys, and only, it turned out, the wild ones: "It was my niche market," he told me soon after quitting babysitting for regular hours and steady pay at a neighborhood grocery store. Parents with particularly rowdy kids would seek out a babysitter who they thought could keep up with their kids. While Beck could do it, matching the energy of rambunctious kids was his least favorite part of babysitting—it was exhausting.

It didn't escape his notice that he was never invited to babysit a boy who was quiet and liked to read books. And although parents of girls interviewed him, often thanks to a connection his mom had made, "they just never called me back. I would have taken the [opportunity], but it never came up." Still, in a way his niche was better: comparing notes with female babysitters he knew, he discovered he was being paid considerably more per hour.

Ultimately, the fact that I never attempted to hire Colin to babysit meant that we all missed out. My kids didn't get the opportunity to be nurtured by a boy, and perhaps Colin didn't get to practice life and relationship skills that could have served him and others. Beck seemed to know it: "I'm a big believer in that you should always have as many people skills as possible," he said. "Even if those kids are eight years old, that's valuable." He said he sees himself as having a skill too many high school boys lack—something at once simple and revolutionary: "I can take care of kids."

Ribbons and Sighs, Laces and Leers: Blending Roles, Leveling the Field

Early in my first pregnancy, Dan and I found out that our fetus happened to have two X chromosomes. That is, we were expecting a girl. But despite the intelligence about her sex, I had the quaint idea that I wouldn't be able to say much about my daughter until I started getting to know her. Dan and I filled her drawers with tiny clothes in a mix of colors, picked out an orange stroller, and left the walls of her nursery yellow just as they'd been when the room held my writing desk. We avoided speculating much, but we did quietly dream. Dan hoped for a kid who liked to play ball, go camping, and take airplane trips. I hoped she would be a singer. I looked so forward to hearing her voice. And I wanted her to be confident and resilient and to laugh at my jokes at least sometimes. But for the most part, all we did with our curiosity about this never-before-seen individual was to wait. She would arrive as her own unique self, beyond the capacity of our imaginations. Or so we thought.

It turned out that plenty of people—particularly strangers—knew all kinds of things about our gestating child. One of the first things we learned was that we should be relieved: our little girl would give us far less trouble than a boy would. People told us she would be simply adorable in all the little dresses, and that I was so lucky I'd get to do her hair, and that she would probably wind up tall and pretty, at which point—sorry to say—she would start giving us far more trouble than a boy would.

Having been a girl who rejected dresses, who hated the way long hair interfered with sports, and who adroitly provoked her parents from birth onward, I bristled at people's certainties about my child so long before she had the chance to speak or cry or even breathe for herself.

So by the time a lady at the neighborhood bus stop asked, "Do you know what you're having?"—friendly small talk, nothing more—I'd gotten a bit cheeky.

"Hoping for a human," I said cheerily.

"What?"

"Fingers crossed," I smiled. "No hippos!"

She did not find me funny, and I couldn't blame her. We had been standing on the sidewalk side by side staring into space, and this was Minnesota; we needed *something* to talk about. The weather wasn't really noteworthy, whereas my belly looked like it needed its own bus ticket. But by that point in my pregnancy, I was feeling increasingly certain that gender should not be the subject of small talk any more than ballots, bills, or birth plans. Small talk loves generalization, and gender is just too individual.

Later when we lived in the Netherlands, I saw that parents there had reached an unspoken social contract that now in the United States we are just beginning to explore: the idea that deemphasizing gender by going neutral creates a safer, freer, and more egalitarian social climate for children. We moved to Amsterdam when Caroline's wardrobe was pretty much comprised of clothing purchased in the girls' section at Target. I didn't think she wore much pink, but I quickly observed that my daughter's wardrobe gave her a more stereotypically feminine style compared to other girls in her peer group. It didn't take long to notice that pink was an uncommon color for girls or boys in Amsterdam. Most kids wore dark neutral colors and even the tiniest ones looked bad-ass in their moto jeans and bomber jackets. It was rare to see a child gussied up to look especially frilly, and certainly children's fashions never came across as sexy or risqué as they sometimes do in US stores. As time passed, whether we were rambling around the city or visiting the countryside, I noticed how often I struggled to tell boys from girls.

Michele Hutchison, a British expat raising kids in the Netherlands and co-author with Rina Mae Acosta of *The Happiest Kids in the World: How Dutch Parents Help Their Kids (and Themselves) by Doing Less*, noted the same phenomenon. When she showed her mother

her son's middle-school class photo, the grandmother tried to count the number of boys and girls. But with so many gender-neutral outfits and hairstyles, she simply couldn't tell.

Time and again over the years as our family went to and fro between continents, we would see that the gender lines for kids in the Netherlands—and to an extent elsewhere in Europe—were simply less rigid than at home in the United States. In Amsterdam, a big pink heart on the ballcap didn't necessarily say "girl"—we knew, because when Caroline wore one around the city at age eight, she was (mystifyingly) presumed to be a boy twice in one day. Long hair certainly wasn't gender exclusive. Nor did florals, stripes, or dots count boys out. Most children's shoes were for any gender, all styles and colors lined up together in the shops. The message was clear: before they were boys and girls, kids were kids.

Such fluid and flexible rules made dressing myself and my kid way more fun than before, but I became aware that looser gender expectations also provided important public health functions. Generally, there was the implicit message to the next generation that gender roles are individually rather than collectively defined. Specifically, the trend toward neutrality offered cover for kids who might not quite fit in their assigned gender. For Penny, the younger of two girls in a Dutch-Australian family we befriended in Amsterdam, this meant that when she was five and insisted on playing pirates, choosing male playmates, and wearing cropped hair, soccer shorts, and sport sneakers, she could do all of these things without attracting curious looks or needing to explain herself. Her parents explained that because it was socially acceptable for her to express herself in the way she preferred—as unambiguously masculine—it hadn't become necessary for her to change her name or pronouns. But if they saw her begin to suffer from being called a girl, then they would seek help in supporting her social transition to life as a boy. They just weren't in that position yet—and still weren't by the time Penny was eight—because a particularly flexible aspect of their culture allowed them to take their time with that decision.

This does not mean that transgender and gender-nonconforming kids don't exist in Dutch society—they are numerous in the Netherlands, as around the world. Dutch researchers working in the 1990s pioneered much of our current understanding of gender dysphoria—a distressing mismatch between a person's assigned sex and experienced gender. The "Dutch Protocol" remains at the forefront of evolving standards of care for young people who want to change gender socially, medically, or both. One of the most important reasons for children with gender dysphoria to seek clinical support is the high association of their condition with mental illness, particularly anxiety and depression, which can increase the risk of suicide. But remarkably, Dutch transgender kids suffer fewer behavioral and emotional problems than North American kids do, which researchers attribute to greater social acceptance among their peers. Similarly, because they experience less homophobia, Dutch kids raised in planned lesbian families are more socially open about having same-sex parents and suffer fewer emotional and behavioral problems compared to their American peers. This means that Dutch and American parents are probably making significantly different calculations of risk when determining if it's socially safe to allow a gender-nonconforming child to freely and publicly explore a range of gender expressions—or if it's better to commit promptly to a "typical" gender in order for a child to pass without raising questions or the specter of bullying and intolerance.

Living in Holland, I learned that Dutch people typically reject "antisocial" behavior, reminding each other just to blend in and *doe normaal*—act normal…*because normal is weird enough*, the rest of the saying goes, allowing sly room for plenty of diversity. Despite a high gender equality ranking for the Netherlands, different norms do persist for boys and girls. Buttered biscuits with anise-seed sprinkles coated in pink or blue are served to celebrate the birth of a new baby. And in terms of gender roles, many observers see the Netherlands as a relatively traditional place, given that men work more hours and make more money overall than their female partners, and many women choose to work part-time or not at all. But it happens that research shows these women, particularly the mothers, are some of the happiest in the world compared to their counterparts in other countries.

(Still, Dutch feminists disagree over whether this means women in the Netherlands are truly liberated.)

A 2017 article in *de Volkskrant* exposed the ways in which a sexual double standard still exists to the detriment of girls in the Netherlands. Importantly, though, Holland's world-class school sex-ed program is well positioned to address social problems of gender and sexuality. In 2017, a nationwide campaign aimed to teach elementary-age children why it is unfair to hold girls and boys to different sexual standards.

I may not have been living in a perfectly gender-neutral society in the Netherlands, but as a woman who had quite contentedly settled into the Dutch way of things, I distinctly noticed the calming effect of life in a place largely unobsessed with sex and gender. Interacting as adults with neighbors and shopkeepers and strangers, it did seem that before we were men and women, we were people. There was no winky, teasing manner in which men spoke with women, no deferential or distrustful tone women generally took with men. With less attention on my gender, I simply felt happier in it.

Cognizant of the way that loosening gender roles levels the playing field and even puts everybody more or less on the same team, some parents have rejected the social gender script in the extreme by choosing to hide their child's biological sex from their community in hopes of eliciting a gender-neutral experience for the child. The most public examples have been families in Canada and Sweden who provide their children gender-nonspecific clothing and pronouns, and don't tell anyone outside the immediate family what genitals the child was born with. This lasts until the child is old enough—somewhere around three to five years of age—to name their own preferred gender and pronouns. But even in Sweden, which currently ranks even higher than the Netherlands for gender equality, there are limits—limits that Lotta Rajalin and the teachers in the gender neutral preschools she directs in Stockholm have pushed against since their founding in 1998. She describes their work as a matter of democracy, and says that children deserve to be well-prepared for the world in which they're living: a place where traditional gender norms have diminishing relevancy.

In a 2016 TEDx talk, Rajalin said that even in famously egalitarian Sweden, if a person walks into a baby boutique or a bicycle shop to buy a gift, the salesperson's first question is always the same: Is it for a boy or a girl? Swedish boys and girls face different thresholds for the same gender-stereotypical behaviors Americans would recognize. For example, Rajalin said, a boy might be free to wear a pink shirt, but head-to-toe pink, which is acceptable for girls, would draw stares for a boy.

As an antidote, teachers at her preschools, Nicolaigården and Egalia, work to create an environment that avoids categorizing children. They aim to make all activities, expressions, and feelings available to children of any gender. The children can express themselves and their genders however they like, but because psycholinguistic studies show that careful language choices powerfully influence young children's ideas about the world, the teachers use conscious terminology and grammar—"friends," not "boys and girls," as well as *hen*, a gender-neutral pronoun newly adopted into the Swedish language—to avoid implying that certain ideas or activities are reserved for particular genders. The teachers arrange play settings for the children that mix objects, jumbling any preconceived notions about which children a toy is "for": A dump truck is presented full of colorful beaded necklaces. A poster on the wall depicts a beefy robot wearing a pink tutu at the ballet barre. A wooden train set is accessorized with dinosaurs, doll families, dragons, puppies, motorcycles, and ponies. By turning theories of gender equality into practice, the schools have attracted media attention from around the world, including plenty of criticism calling the approach draconian, confusing, or just plain silly.

Gabriella Martinsson, a teacher at one of the preschools, explained in a mini documentary how the schools' critics miss the point:

> I think that there might be a fear with some people that when we work with gender-equal teachings we will rob their child of something. That we will take away something from a little boy, for example, which could be associated with boyishness. That...he wouldn't

be allowed to play with a football or play with cars. Or in the same way rob a girl of something that could be associated with girlishness. This is not how it is. We do not take anything away from anybody. We only add. That is how we see it. We think that the traditional teaching methods divest children of things because it steers the children into two different directions where there's one way to be a girl and one way to be a boy.... *This* is to rob the children of something.

Every culture has its adherents to traditional gender roles. Many people find peace of mind by embracing traditional stereotypes and trusting that differences in status, opportunity, influence, and sovereignty simply reflect the natural order of things. That's the spirit behind snarky newspaper articles and dismissive reader comments about efforts at gender inclusivity—whether in Swedish preschools or American restrooms. But social scientist Fine would seem to back up Rajalin's efforts: "No single factor is overwhelmingly important in creating sex inequalities. Every influence is modest, made up of countless small instances of its kind. That's why everything—a doll packaged in pink, a sexist joke, a male-only expert panel—can seem trivial, of intangible effect. But that's exactly why calling out even seemingly minor points of sexism matters. It all adds up, and if no one sweats the small stuff, the big stuff will never change."

The wait lists for Rajalin's schools are long, and although I haven't heard of any similar projects in American schools, I have to say that scenes from Nicolaigården and Egalia classrooms actually don't seem markedly different from the many innovative American classrooms and community places where people are making an effort to be conscious of gender bias. My Los Angeles friend Jenny told me that although her younger son's best friend is a boy whose favorite colors are pink and purple, "It's really big at our school that kids don't say 'those are girl colors.' Those are anybody's colors. I love that. I wish that more people did that around the world. I wish there was less judgment about what belongs to who."

The US gender gap is currently worse than in almost every other rich country and many poor ones. While Switzerland, Denmark, and the Netherlands took the top three spots for gender equality in the 2016 United Nations Human Development Report, the United States sat way down at number 43, a slight improvement from the previous report but still only a few places ahead of Russia and Saudi Arabia—and behind countries such as China, Libya, and Kazakhstan. Unfortunately, a 5 percent improvement in our American gender gap score would only nudge us up a single spot in the rankings. We would need to improve our score by 300 percent to hit the top ten. But a nice thing about Americans is that we already know the value of hard work and serious practice. Once we see the sense in something, we sally forth and own it.

To conclude her TEDx talk, Rajalin offered her audience something to practice. For the next twenty-four hours, she suggested, "avoid words like 'men,' 'women,' 'boy,' and 'girl.' Say instead—and *think* instead—'person,' 'human being,' 'child,' 'adult.' Try that," she said, "and see what's happening in your head."

Speaking for myself, I found some wiggle room there. Five percent, at least.

8

Consent

*C*ome on. *I'm not gonna hurt you. Just real quick. But I need you to! It'll be easy. What's the matter? You did it last time! It's no big deal. You're making me sad. If you do it, I'll…*

Want to guess the scenario?

These comments—all of them—are ones I jotted in my notebook over the course of a few weeks the spring Libby turned five. They are things men said to her after she refused something they wanted: usually a high five or a fist bump, occasionally a hug. One day at the neighborhood pocket park, I saw her chin quiver as she tried to stand up to a perfectly well-meaning father we knew who kept bugging her for a high five. She retreated with small backward steps until she pressed into my legs.

Later, when I asked if we could talk about what had happened, her face flushed with humiliation.

"I don't want to talk about that!" she yelled, covering her ears. Clearly my raising the issue brought up bad feelings. But there was something I needed to tell her, and I waited until she calmed down enough to make eye contact.

"When somebody asks you to touch them and you say no, it's not okay for them to keep asking," I said. "It's hard to keep saying no, but you have the right to do that."

She burst into tears.

After that, it was as if a switch in my awareness had flipped. I began paying closer attention to the coercive scripts people practice with girls. These men—many of them dads of daughters themselves—certainly did not mean to do any harm. But how could such wheedling not leave its mark by wearing children down and teaching them to relent against their own instincts and comfort level? With time and practice, girls learn to think of acquiescence as simply a kindness—doing someone a favor. *All they want is a smile. All they want is a wave. All they want is one quick flash and then it's over.* Pressure also sows doubt by suggesting to a child that her gut reaction—*no, I don't want to*—is unreliable. Pestering is a kind of practice that raises a child's tolerance for being bothered, bullied, or harassed. Coercion of girls for the gratification of boys eventually becomes normalized, and resistance is just the middle act in a play that is expected to end with surrender.

Kelly, a Seattle mom I know, shared her concerns with me about her daughter experiencing unwanted chasing on the playground. It may sound like small potatoes, but I agree with her that chasing, like tickling and roughhousing, calls for consent.

In a 2017 *New York Times* Modern Love essay, twenty-four-year-old Heather Burtman wrote about the male gaze and how, after puberty, it seemed as if men could ogle, catcall, and touch her simply for being a woman in public. Among several examples, she described having her buttocks and then her hands grabbed by a man in a club. "You can say no 100 times, and he will still pull…. The harder you pull away, the harder he pulls closer. It is like a game to him."

This is the gender dynamic that puts the lie to victim blaming. When a girl or woman reports that she has been sexually harassed or assaulted, skeptics may ask why she didn't resist more, scream, or fight. The simplest answer is that in a lifetime of pressure and cajoling, a typical American girl learns that resistance only brings pushback, whereas the path to capitulation is well-worn and familiar.

By the time she was six, Libby loved to chase a particular older boy at school. One day as they looped through the school foyer, I stopped her—*5 percent*—and asked if she happened to know whether he *wanted* to be chased. She said yes, and I looked to him to confirm it. I wanted neither one of them to lose the distinction between something wanted and something tolerated. He nodded with a smile. "I like it," he said. *Fine.* And around and around they ran some more.

Like most women, I know how it feels when someone helps himself to contact with my body, from the adolescent boy who grabbed my crotch through my shorts when I bent to choose earrings at an outdoor market to the distant relative who recently paused behind my chair at a restaurant and, while casually chatting with someone else, conducted a suggestive massage I couldn't wriggle out of. The experiences may be mundane, but they always leave me with a certain skin-crawling muteness. But as a child, even if I never learned a good way out, I *did* learn that touching another person against their wishes for my own gratification is unacceptable. It didn't require a complicated lesson.

When I was in fourth grade, I spent a period of weeks convinced it was totally fine for me to spank my best friend whenever I felt like it. I don't quite know where I got it, but those were heady times for NBA basketball—my favorite TV characters were Magic Johnson, Larry Bird, and Punky Brewster in her Chuck Taylors—so my best theory is that I was inspired to adopt the infamous man-to-man butt slap of professional athletics. Except I missed the context piece. My brother, sister, and parents no doubt received plenty of the same attention, but I saved my best whaps for Casey. She was my favorite. I did it as a friendly greeting. It was code for my love. She never knew when it was coming. She always wore leggings. I couldn't resist. On a foggy spring morning, I walked up to the line outside our classroom door. Delighted to see my friend's rear end before me, I laid one on her. She usually said, "Ow!," but this time, disconcertingly, she said nothing as she turned around. I smiled good morning, and she put her knuckles up my nose.

At that time my idea of consent—for which I knew no word—was rudimentary at best. Before the day she set me right, I have no recollection of Casey ever telling me not to touch her butt. She certainly at least whimpered every time I hit her, but I ignored her reactions because I didn't think they mattered. I know we don't sound like much of a pair, but we really were buddies. We had grown up together. We spent most of our time at school together, our families hung out on the weekends, we liked a lot of the same things, and I can't remember any time we fought. We didn't even fight the time she punched me. I just nodded and then fast-walked into the classroom with my head tipped back. I crumpled up some brown paper towels, pressed them to my gushing nose, and went to sit quietly at my desk waiting for the bell. My teacher, no doubt suspecting something since I hadn't come tattling, drifted my way and casually asked what had happened.

"Casey punched me, and I deserved it," I said.

She nodded—said exactly zero words—and went to greet the line. With that I realized even my teacher had known all along that I'd been wrongly hailing my friend with unbidden spankings. Had everyone known this moment was coming except me?

I was a child then and learned my lesson soundly. As a mother in 2017, when women established the #MeToo movement by rising en masse to call out harassment, assault, and sexual misconduct, I thought about the media men sent packing from their power positions, including longtime Fox News pundit Bill O'Reilly and Hollywood executive Harvey Weinstein, not to mention those politicians still in their posts despite serious accusations of sexual misconduct and assault, most notably President Donald Trump. At first I imagined those guys thinking like dopey fourth-grade me: *Why didn't anybody* tell *me?* But the truth was probably insidiously closer to *I thought I could get away with it.* We'd all been told plenty of times—just not in language we chose to hear until it blew up in our faces—and in some cases, not even then.

Clearly, stereotypically "masculine" and "feminine" misbehavior do not always belong to boys and girls, respectively. Yes, boys and men are usually the ones doling out unwanted touching, but not always. So every child needs to learn about asking and giving consent, and even best friends need to ask permission. I could have learned that lesson bloodlessly if we'd had a great sex-ed curriculum like the ones Dutch four-, five-, and six-year-olds receive about body sovereignty, boundaries, and consent. My peers needed it too—especially the ones without a friend like Casey to set them straight young.

Years later, I was dancing at a wedding when a burly drunk college acquaintance dashed onto the dance floor, cranked his arm all the way back, and hit me so hard on the backside that I stumbled and nearly fell. (My dancing may have been subpar, but no one else got violent about it.) I had learned my lesson in fourth grade about spanking: ask first, *duh*. But clearly my peers and I had not all learned the same lessons about body sovereignty—aka keeping one's hands to oneself. I like to think that Casey would have known what to do at that wedding, but I just retreated to a table in tears. (It didn't occur to me then that I had been criminally assaulted—after all, we were no longer children.) Although the pain was intense, the worst part was the lack of consequences. The party simply went on.

When people have true body sovereignty, they live not in a land of submission and domination, but in a grown-up world of mutuality and consent. Yes, those ideas sound less cinematic than the old-fashioned chase-her-down-and-woo-her-senseless storylines, but that might be just because we haven't seen many great depictions of how sexy it can be for two people on equal footing to have a conversation about what they're going to do next. If you can get over the looming presence of a third-wheel narrator, Planned Parenthood's 2015 video series on consent offers some fairly provocative possibilities.

"I think there are tons of opportunities at home to talk about gender roles and gender stereotypes, but if you're not also talking about consent and boundaries, then you've missed it," Kari Kesler, a sexual and reproductive health educator and curriculum author, told me over coffee one morning alongside her colleague and co-author Andrea Gerber.

I thought to mention a recent *New York Times Magazine* tidbit in which philosophy professor Kwame Anthony Appiah, in his weekly "Ethicist" column, had fielded a question about tickling:

My husband often engages in horseplay with our daughter, who is 9. Sometimes when she's had enough, she will call out "Stop!" or "No!" even if she instigated the tickling or wrestling. My husband doesn't always stop, saying, "Oh, but you started it!" or "You're just trying to get away!" It's generally in good fun, although sometimes it all ends in tears. If I call him on it, saying, "No means no" or "She said stop," he'll usually tell me not to butt in, that he is her parent, too.... Am I overreacting?...Or is a line being crossed? —Name Withheld

I was floored by Appiah's opinion: he saw nothing necessarily wrong with a father overriding his daughter's no. He defined it more as a problem of parents failing to see eye-to-eye and suggested that the letter writer go find out from a psychologist whether physical play to which a child doesn't consent is really anything to worry about.

The letters to the editor came in hot: "When a child's pleas of 'stop' or 'no' are ignored, the kid will come to expect that from others and will be vulnerable to aggressive behavior. The lesson she is learning is that standing up for herself is useless," came one response.

Another said: "I believe Appiah missed the main ethical issue in his response to the mother writing about her husband tickling their daughter: control over our own bodies. Does the father have any right to do what he is doing to his daughter over her objections?"

"I wonder if @nytimes should maybe think about having a woman ethicist," another reader tweeted.

Kesler laughed wearily and shook her head. When it comes to consent, "tickling is the *best* example," she said. "I use that all the time, because everyone thinks that it's okay to keep tickling someone even if they don't want that." It's such good practice for sexual consent, she said, because "tickling is a fun activity. You're doing it because it makes them laugh, it feels good. And there's all this coming and going from it: someone may want to take a break and then reengage. People can say no to this, but not to that. There could not be a better example. Roughhousing can be similar but isn't as good as tickling."

She added that parents can seize the moment to teach about consent—particularly how to know if it has been granted or revoked even if the cues are nonverbal.

"It's not just 'I hear your brother saying no,' but also 'here are other ways you can tell he doesn't want it even if he *isn't* saying no.'"

Gerber nodded and gave examples: "'I can see he's telling you with his body that he doesn't want this anymore. Here are all the ways you can tell that he is not consenting. He is saying no, he is turning away—'"

"'He is asking for help,'" Kesler added. "'He's not laughing anymore.'"

Despite increasingly familiar definitions of consent in which all parties are clear, comfortable, and enthusiastic about what's happening, recent surveys have shown that American adults are confused about consent. We haven't had lessons, and we haven't had practice. So it should be no surprise that even ethicists are confused. In a 2016 survey commissioned by Planned Parenthood, two in ten adult respondents strongly agreed that if a partner is "not saying 'no,'" then it's okay to go further, while the same number of people (not to mention just about any Dutch kindergartener) strongly disagree. Most important is an enthusiastic *yes*.

Erasing that confusion is the first step in shifting a coercive culture toward a consent culture. According to Rivers and Barnett, having unambiguous rules levels the playing field. "When kids play such games as Red Rover or King of the Hill that have clear rules, even though they involve some rough-and-tumble play, girls and boys behave similarly. Rules become another 'situation' that shapes behavior, perhaps more than gender." Thinking back to the Dutch rules for *doktertje spelen* [playing doctor], this rang true.

Kesler said parents can ask themselves, "What can I do right now with [my child]? What are the skills they need, what are the attitudes they need, what are the norms they need to change to prevent them from one day, when they are all alone with another person and I'm not there, being like, *I'm just going to keep going here*?"

Visits to doctors and dentists offer other teachable moments. Must we follow a nurse's request to hold down a child who is panicked about receiving shots, or can we ask for some prep time to ensure the child is ready, even if that means returning a different day? Do we force a crying toddler to have every tooth polished on the first dental visit, or agree to begin with just one tooth, and clean more the next time? And will we consider driving across town if it means we can see a pediatrician who asks for a child's consent and listens for the answer before a physical exam?

Dr. Elizabeth Schroeder, a US independent sexuality educator, told me she thinks today's American parents and preschools are already doing more than in previous generations to teach toddlers about relationships, which is key to healthy sexual development. "Parents say, 'Hands are not for hitting,' or 'Hands on your own body.' That's about boundaries," Schroeder explains. "If it's not okay to hit a friend, it's not okay to hit anybody. And it's not 'Don't hit girls,' it's 'Don't hit *anybody*.'" Those directions, Schroeder says, are foundational to ideas of gender equality as well as good relationships, platonic and romantic alike. And now that consent has become a critical area of concern in young Americans' sex lives, plenty of parents consciously teach very young children to ask permission before touching another person's body and to listen when their friends say no. Teaching this lesson, she says—and meaning and modeling it—is nothing less than the making of a less violent society.

9

No Cooties Allowed

Caroline was still only two when she started begging for play-dates with Renzo, an older boy in her preschool class in Amsterdam. One night she tossed and fussed at bedtime, unable to sleep out of pain from a knee scrape she'd received in a stumble while chasing him at recess.

"I love Renzo," she told me as I rebandaged her at the bedside. "He's funny. And strange. And a little bit sweet. He's such a great guy." *A great guy?* Did two-year-olds actually talk this way?

But she wasn't alone. There was something magnetic about the tall-for-his-age, curly-haired, twinkle-eyed, fun-loving Renzo. When he arrived at school in the mornings, children from all corners of the little school screamed his name like Beatles fans.

"*Please* can Renzo come to my house?" she asked for the zillionth time as I tucked her back in.

"We'll see," I answered yet again, still unwilling to admit the truth about my hesitation. I was intimidated by this almost-four-year-old boy whose family I hadn't met. Would his parents be taken aback by an invitation to a girl's house? Particularly one only two-thirds his age? I had seen Renzo at school in his padded Spiderman suit. Would he be disappointed with a playdate at our house, where peace-loving Caroline liked to sing and dance and have imaginary birthday parties with stuffed animals? And what about Caroline—would she have the interaction she envisioned?

So I put off inviting Renzo over, and put it off some more, hoping the infatuation, or whatever it was, would pass. I asked often about the other girls at school, not so subtly steering her toward same-gender friendships. I thought it was important to encourage female alliances for my daughter, to emphasize the power of sisterhood. If I was going to manipulate her social life, which was somewhat against my nature anyway, I wanted to send a message about how great girls are.

Living in the Netherlands, I saw and took for granted that boys and girls sat together at school, played together in the park, walked together in middle school, and held mixed-gender birthday parties at any age. But I didn't really think about how these childhood gender relations came about. It hadn't clicked for me that each time I declined to invite a boy to play with Caroline, I was depriving her—and her prospective playmate—of chances to form the kinds of friendships that really *do* foster equality.

Renzo graduated at age four, when preschoolers in the Netherlands go on to kindergarten. Caroline was dejected at first, but soon her eye roved to Alfredo. And after that to Sammy, and then to Pedro. But I didn't invite any of those boys to our house either, and eventually her constant babble about them gave way to stories about the girls in her class. At least, those were the stories she chose to share with me. For better or worse, I had already signaled which friendships I wanted to hear about and which kids made more likely after-school playmates.

Like most American parents and teachers, I had always assumed that it's natural and inevitable for girls and boys to grow apart and play separately, especially after preschool. The data is clear: American kids observed by researchers in school settings spend their middle childhood years highly gender-segregated. It's considered perfectly normal—I've even seen it chalked up to "hormones" at that early age. Since it's so commonly expected to see a widening gulf between boys and girls, I assumed it was harmless—or inevitable—and never thought to say anything to counteract the pattern. Accordingly, by the time we moved back to the United States and Caroline joined a new preschool, I supposed that her interest in cross-gender friendships was fading and would not reignite until middle or high school. Back among American families, we slipped into a familiar pattern: girl- or boy-only birthday parties commenced around age four. Parents responded to their kids' requests for other-gender playdates the way I had responded about Renzo in Amsterdam: *Wouldn't that be nice? Maybe some other time.*

This was the new normal until Caroline reached first grade. In a parent meeting, her teacher explained that she would be encouraging mixed-gender work and play groups. As parents, she said, we should be seeking and supporting boy-girl friendships for our kids. "It's very good for them," she said, explaining that anthropologists consider middle-childhood gender separation to be a modern phenomenon and not, in fact, a particularly natural one. Was Caroline's teacher saying that modern American culture actually *causes* cooties? In no uncertain terms, yes. Cooties are human-made, and as conscious parents and educators, we can choose whether to let them march in.

That meeting was my first hint that what I'd seen in the Netherlands—boys and girls starting friendships in toddlerhood and maintaining them right through childhood and adolescence into adulthood—wasn't just happenstance. Parents and teachers must have been actively encouraging boy-girl bonds. And they must have had reasons for doing so.

Early and astutely, children sense which types of social relationships are off-limits. Going against convention to form those bonds comes with social risks. For example, elementary-age children in American classrooms who are known to have cross-gender friendships endure disapproval, teasing, and hostility from their peers (and sometimes from adults). This may be one reason children are more likely to cultivate and keep cross-gender friendships outside of school. And it is precisely why the Dutch approach is to actively push back, coaching and expecting children to form and keep gender-diverse friendships.

Deborah Roffman, a Baltimore-based sexuality educator who has taught, lectured, and published on the subject for decades, agrees that childhood gender segregation is "self-imposed" and not inevitable: "Parents and teachers can do their very best to actively encourage girls and boys to sustain good friendships and positive, relaxed interactions with one another throughout the elementary school years," she writes in *Talk to Me First: Everything You Need to Know to Become Your Kids' "Go-To" Person about Sex.* "It truly does not serve them to think of each other as 'opposites,' or an entirely different species ('Ooooh, cooties!')."

When Dutch child psychologist and *J/M voor Ouders* parenting website contributor Tischa Neve received a question from a parent whose five-year-old daughter had started ignoring her best friend, a boy, after a bout of teasing from classmates, she offered this advice: "It may only be temporary. If the other children lose interest, the friendship may resume." Still, adults can help, Neve said, suggesting that the teacher should intervene, perhaps by initiating a class discussion about friendship and love. She also suggested reaching out to the boy's parents to heal the friendship and seeking out television shows and movies that center on boy-girl dyads (something American parents have told me they can't find enough of).

Psychologists studying four-year-olds have found that teachers who make positive remarks about instances of cooperative cross-gender play caused a significant increase in that behavior, noting that the rate of cross-gender play *doubles* when children hear multiple instances of teacher praise mentioning boy-girl cooperation. But making no comment is the same as making a negative comment: children revert to previously learned patterns—boys with boys, girls with girls.

"Encouraging boys and girls to play together more often could have a number of beneficial effects," the researchers wrote. "They might affect the children's tendency to view opposite-sex as well as same-sex children as playmates, friends, and co-workers. Such attitudes, if maintained, might have far-reaching effects on men's and women's ability to perceive each other as equals." Furthermore, the authors wrote, more cross-gender play allows boys and girls to learn behavioral and cognitive styles as well as play activities "typical" of other genders, expanding everyone's horizons. A mix of styles, researchers say, serves best for psychological well-being and healthy relationships. In addition, a proliferation of mixed-gender pairs and groups "might make it more difficult for boys and girls to be treated differently or exposed to different learning experiences by their teachers."

As the preschool study makes clear, caregivers and teachers of children whose friend groups are becoming gender-homogenous can give clear reasons, advice, and logistical support for branching out. Teachers can say to kids, "Hey, did you know it's actually healthy and important for you to play with boys *and* girls?" A parent might ask, "Who could we invite over to mix it up a little?"

As a foundation, five- and six-year-old children in many Dutch public schools receive a simple classroom talk asserting that boys and girls can be friends. The lesson concludes with a group brainstorming session about the kinds of activities they can do together: just about anything. Eventually they become so used to working together that cross-gender partnering is a nonissue. Many Dutch parents and teachers have long since put these lessons into practice, and their effects have rippled outward into broader social norms.

Every other year, Dan and I take Caroline and Libby back to their neighborhood elementary school in Amsterdam to spend a month re-immersed in Dutch classrooms. One day after school at the beginning of fifth grade, Caroline came home from her Amsterdam classroom wide-eyed. "Mom, there's something I have to tell you"—she knew I'd be interested—"You know how at home when a teacher tells us we have to pick a partner from the opposite gender, and everybody goes *uuugh*?"

"I can imagine," I said.

"Well, here, when Tom tells us to do that, everybody just does it. Nobody says *anything*."

"Nobody says anything?"

"Well actually," she smiled, "I heard a couple kids go *yesss*."

Similarly, when expat Margaret's son was nine, her family moved to the Netherlands from her home country of Ireland, a place where, as in the United States, boy-girl friendships in middle childhood can be scorned by peers and not always actively encouraged by adults. "My son sometimes makes comparisons between how young boys/ girls relate here" in the Netherlands, she commented in a Facebook group focused on Dutch education. "He far prefers the relaxed interactions here, how boys and girls are much more comfortable with each other, how they can be friends without any teasing from other kids, how school classrooms are mixed as a rule rather than the exception, how girls play football and are really good at it and so on." These behaviors don't simply happen by accident; they are cultivated and encouraged.

Ailsa, who had moved with her parents from Scotland to Holland when she was in high school and was now the mother of a sixteen-year-old daughter and a thirteen-year-old son, joined me on a fall afternoon in 2017 for tea in a museum café in Haarlem, the city outside of Amsterdam where she had settled with her Dutch husband. She laughingly described the extreme gender separation she'd grown up with in her traditional Scottish primary school. Until age six, she said, boys and girls played together in the schoolyard. After that, they were assigned separate playgrounds. There was a small gap in the fence, she said, where children could peer through and try to observe how the other side played. When it was time to enter the school building, the children used separate doorways marked BOYS and GIRLS. But when she transitioned to school in the Netherlands, "suddenly it was okay to hang out with boys at the interval and actually talk to them without it being a big deal." As she fell into friendships with boys and with girls, her surprises were no longer about differences, but "wow, boys are just like us in a lot of ways." Ailsa said she values the fact that her own children have grown up in a society where boys and girls spend more time together: "You sort of realize what you have that's the same and what's different *together*," she said. I was struck by that: the idea that boys and girls who learn about one another *with* one another gain an inherent sense of fairness and equality through their linked experience of going through life side by side. "Us" and "them" become "we."

As in many Dutch schools and preschools, the Amsterdam elementary where Caroline and Libby have dropped in over the years has one bathroom per floor—and the unwritten rule is that particular stalls are for particular classrooms, not certain genders. One UK-born mother raising two sons in Amsterdam marveled to me that while gender separation is so important to Americans that we get up in arms about which bathroom transgender students will use, her fourteen-year-old son was allowed to tent up with two girls while on a school campout.

Shea, an American mother, moved from New York City to Amsterdam when her son Quincy was three years old. As a self-described "tomboy" who grew up with mostly male friends, she said she'd always planned to raise her kids to have playmates of different genders.

"I would play football in the street with the boys," while other girls watched from the sidelines. "The girls would be whispering 'How did you get to talk to him?' and I would say, 'I don't see what the big deal is. It's just Justin.' I think it really helped a lot when the dating years started," she said. Since boys weren't mysterious, she felt confident about conversing with them and well-grounded when love interests started to blossom. And, she added, "it was less of a rush to have sex." The reason for this, she explained, was that by the time adolescence rolled around, she regarded boys as full-fledged, multifaceted individuals rather than reductively as potential objects of desire. To her, "boy" meant "person" before it meant "possible love interest." She didn't reflexively bring sexual assumptions or expectations to her adolescent interactions with boys—some of which were still plenty awkward, she assured me with a laugh. She felt secure in that it was possible to have adolescent relationships with boys that weren't dating relationships. Perhaps those friendships also had a greater possibility of enduring.

"What if the boys you wanted to date had healthy cross-gender friendships as kids too, and knew how to talk to *you*?" I asked her.

"How different that would have been," she laughed again. "Maybe I would have gotten married younger! I might have found my friend, that person I can talk to, where it just seems natural to be together."

Shea was right to think that boys and girls learn by experience how to relate successfully and meaningfully with one another in both platonic and romantic relationships—there's plenty of research to support her intuition on this. But how to go about encouraging those childhood bonds?

"I picked up on it from other Europeans," Shea said. As a newcomer to Amsterdam, she had tested the social waters among fellow parents just as any American might. "I probably initially said something like, 'Oh my god, Quincy wants to have a playdate with another girl,' and they looked at me like 'What's the big deal?'" She got the message from her parenting peers—the message that I missed when Caroline still had the chance to play with Renzo—that adults are the ones responsible for children's gender segregation and its consequences.

"Living here made it so natural," she said. "Most of his playdates when he was young were with girls. There was always a girl that was his best friend. And now as a teenager, the boys and girls hang out together. It's not a big deal. And I didn't have to do anything to make that happen." But I suspect Shea wasn't quite taking credit for everything she had done, including stretching her initial willingness to reach out to Quincy's girl playmates for get-togethers and bringing a normalizing sense of approval to his friendships with kids of any gender.

Quincy, at fourteen having spent most of his life in the Netherlands, easily attested to his friendships with girls. I asked him if he'd been able to hold onto his preschool friendships with girls, or whether teasing from friends in elementary and middle school prevented those from lasting. "I think it was fine to hold onto them," he said. "They still lasted. But I mean, I wouldn't have as many sleepovers or playdates or stuff like that with them toward the later years, but we would still talk and hang out in class. It wouldn't be like, 'Oh, I'm not going to hang out with them.' In my class, all the girls and guys are pretty much friends." He told me about a girl from England with whom he'd maintained a regular friendship since they met at school at age six. "Back then, we'd just play around on the playground," Quincy said, "and now sometimes we might go to the movies or do something like that."

American parents who want to support their children's gender-diverse friendships might be on the right track, but they still run into friction, Shea said. She told me about her friend, a mother whose three-year-old son had bonded with a same-age girl in his Connecticut preschool classroom. Noticing that the two played together constantly at school, she approached the little girl's mother and proposed a playdate. But the girl's mother said she felt uncomfortable with the idea. Citing their gender difference, she asked, "What would they do together?"

"Just...play?" the boy's mom answered.

It was an answer I could have used a few years earlier. But as with Caroline and Renzo, the get-together never happened. Without support for their friendship, the boy and girl grew apart.

While gender-segregated institutions including schools have long since been abolished in the Netherlands and much of Europe, single-sex schooling is on the upswing in the United States, Canada, Australia, and the United Kingdom. The shift is in large part a result of public speculation from Michael Gurian and Leonard Sax beginning in the early 2000s that boys and girls learn so differently that they should be educated separately. In 2001, the No Child Left Behind Act provided funding for new single-sex public schools. In the United States we now have hundreds of public classrooms and schools offering single-gender classrooms, up from only twelve in 2002. It's a paradigm under challenge by the ACLU and seen by many to reinforce antiquated, harmful ideas about fundamental cognitive differences between genders—not to mention leaving no place for students with nonbinary identities. Since sex-segregated schooling has resurged in the United States, an exhaustive review of the literature showed no educational advantage to separating gender. But there are disadvantages: "Today, much of the so-called 'science' of sex difference has been debunked, but that hasn't kept public schools from modeling programs on bogus theories," wrote UCLA gender studies professor Juliet A. Williams in a 2016 *Los Angeles Times* op-ed. "As a result, boys are being deprived of the opportunity to develop crucial social skills, such as working collaboratively and thinking creatively, while girls are being denied the opportunity to build test-taking skills and learn how to succeed under pressure." To make matters worse, boys who attend all-male high schools (Donald Trump, for one) graduate with less egalitarian views toward women. There is value in learning to live, learn, and work together.

Furthermore, sorting kids by gender—whether to quickly divide them into work groups or to dismiss them in an orderly fashion for recess—is increasingly understood to damage their ability to see one another as equals. "Too often the classroom is a place where gender becomes an issue even though it actually has no relevance to the main job of teachers and kids: learning," write Caryl Rivers and Rosalind Barnett in *The Truth About Girls and Boys*. "It can start with the ordinary greeting of teachers to their class. 'Good morning, boys and girls.' Teachers would never say, 'Good morning, blacks and whites.' Or 'Good morning, Latinos and Asians.'"

Hoping it was not too late, as Caroline was already moving through early elementary school, Dan and I took pains to change our message. I made sure to show interest when Caroline talked about boys she enjoyed working and playing with at school. I encouraged her to seek them out at recess, and I suggested playdates—although she hesitated. By the time Libby turned four and Caroline was finishing third grade, both kids knew we favored mixed-gender birthday parties even if they still required some coaxing.

During dinner one bright evening that spring, Libby, veteran preschooler, had an announcement to make: "I don't like *any* boys. Except Dad."

He looked at her. I looked at her. Caroline, who had taken a keen interest in gender identity ever since her Calico Critters first swapped boy and girl clothes years ago, put down her spoon. A giddy gleam came over her seven-year-old face as she too turned to look at her sister. It was chili again, but this meal was about to get interesting.

In the sudden silence, Libby blinked and thought some more and then added: "Except Dad *and* the boys in my class."

"What about Papa?" Caroline asked, meaning their grandfather.

"Yes," Libby said.

"Both papas?" Caroline asked.

"Yes."

"What about Uncle Luke?"—my brother, a kind and caring uncle who had just crocheted a baby penguin for Libby.

"Yes."

"What about Uncle Rob?" My sister's husband, father of baby cousin, Rosie.

"I like Uncle Rob. And I like Rosie!" Then panic swept Libby's face. "Is Rosie a boy or a girl?"

"Girl," we chorused.

"PHEW!"

"Libby," Caroline paused to explain between bites, "It's good to have friends who are boys *and* girls. Then you get to do more things."

Her reasoning caught me. It was a painfully sharp observation. Without having read the studies piled on my desk, she'd named exactly what researchers have painstakingly recorded: boys and girls who spend time together in friendship actually *educate* one another in important ways, including communication and negotiation styles and technical knowledge. In this way, they equip one another with relationship and practical skills that persist through the teen years and into adulthood, coloring not only romantic relationships but also professional ones. Especially striking to me was a study revealing that college men in intimate encounters with women routinely guess wrong about their partner's state of mind, seeing implied consent where in fact there is none. I wondered if this combination of his tone-deafness and her difficulty getting through to him might go all the way back to missed opportunities to swap communication styles in childhood.

"Libby, how would you like a playdate with Dexter?" I asked, already texting to his mom.

She threw her head back: "YEEEES!"

If he couldn't come over soon, then we'd try Alexander or Sebastian.

The conversation felt like a small triumph, but I still hadn't fully grasped all of the important reasons why boys and girls should spend more time together. And I still wasn't doing much to encourage specific, meaningful, *deeper* cross-gender friendships for my kids.

By fourth grade, Caroline had become even more articulate—and sadder—about the limits of friendship. At school, boys in her class were doing and saying and playing different things from the girls. She wanted some of everything, but she saw the lines separating boys from girls and knew teasing came for kids who crossed them.

In the United States, "the boys and the girls are more separated," said Karen, a Dutch mother raising three daughters, a seventeen-year-old and twin thirteen-year-olds, in a Seattle suburb. "Because as soon as you have a friendship between a boy and a girl you have 'Oooh, boyfriend-girlfriend!' I think in the Netherlands, even in our generation, it was really normal" to have a mixed-gender group of close friends throughout childhood. Karen shared that one of her thirteen-year-olds had been best friends with a boy since kindergarten. "They used to have sleepovers all the time, and they still want to have sleepovers. Fortunately, his mom is open-minded and says it's fine as long as they don't share a bed."

This gave me pause. The last sleepover either of my daughters had with a boy was…never, unless I counted trips to visit with family friends.

As Karen noted, the teasing endured by mixed-gender friend pairs inevitably accuses children of being in love. We all know the old singsong taunt that puts two friends sitting in a tree and *k-i-s-s-i-n-g*, which of course leads right to marriage and babies.

One day I heard Caroline grumbling over a writing prompt in a journal for girls she'd received for Christmas.

"What's up?" I asked.

"Listen to this question: 'What's the best thing about being a girl?'" she read, looking unhappy. "*That*'ll be interesting."

She was attuned to the fact that the question pitted boys against girls. Frustrated by that, she put off writing in that section. But I was curious, so I posed the question to her again a few days later.

"So, what *is* the best thing about being a girl?"

She flopped sideways on my bed, annoyed. She sighed, and then she said, "I was just picturing someone saying, 'Having long hair,'" she said, all too aware of the stereotypes. "So I don't know. Just being myself. I don't have an answer to that."

I thought it was a pretty darn good answer, and now I had another question.

"What's the worst thing about being a girl?"

Here she didn't hesitate. "Having people say that I can't play certain games, or that I'm not good at something because I'm a girl and it's more of a boyish thing. Like football, telling me I'm not strong enough to do it." She added that she saw many rich friendship possibilities among her classmates, but some of them seemed out of reach only because of "one tiny thing: their gender."

"So then how might your life be different if you were a boy instead of a girl?"

"I just feel my mind would be different and I'd learn different things because of the friends I'd have. My [girl] friends teach me certain things, and lots of the boys in my class get taught things by other boys that are not the same as what girl friends are like."

"Have you thought about talking to the boys in your class about it?" I asked. "Maybe they really just don't know that boys and girls can be friends." I saw her eyebrows flick up as an idea took root, but she said nothing more. That is, not until three weeks later on our way home from school one afternoon. As I pedaled up the hill toward home—even in Seattle we did our best to keep our Dutch bike life rolling—Caroline, perched behind me on the long tail of our cargo bike, suddenly slapped her knee. "Mom!" she said. "I almost forgot! I'm so proud! I did it!"

"Did what?"

"I talked to Lee," a courteous, bright-smiling boy with whom she'd been classmates for more than three years. The two of them had gone on a classroom errand to the school kitchen, and Caroline saw her moment.

"I told him I think he's funny, and I like him a lot, and that boys and girls actually can be friends. He was so happy to hear that! I told him I wanted him to come to my birthday party, and he said he's going to invite me over to play."

With their friendship agreed on, the playdates commenced. What did they do together? On her first afternoon at his house, a boat docked on a ship canal in Seattle, he took her out in his little sailboat and brought her safely back to shore. They played with his rabbit for a while, then had a hide-and-seek session around the marina with his German shepherd. After that they played a long game of Monopoly that kept tipping over as fishing-boat wake jostled the board, and finally they ate a fish he'd caught for dinner. When Lee came to our house, the two rode skateboards down the kiddie slide in the basement. They bounced balls off the roof and fought for the catch. They went to the park to dig for hibernating ladybugs at my request (my indoor citrus trees had a winter aphid infestation). The two of them walked to the corner store for hot chocolate and pushed the living room furniture aside to make room for charades.

And when Dexter came to play with Libby, the two of them hit Wiffle balls. They kicked the soccer ball. They bounced for ages on two side-by-side tiny trampolines in the basement, starting off maniacally but quickly becoming eerily robotic about it, as if bouncing was a job that just had to be done. Later on a warm spring day they pulled out the hose and made a water park out of the backyard. They played a little with stuffed animals, but soon switched to Legos. There's research suggesting that in cross-gender play sessions, girls adopt more boy-typed behaviors, perhaps because they're more experienced at predicting what a friend would like to do and altering their own behavior accordingly. (As a teenager I drove my poor parents nuts by adopting not only my guy friends' hobbies but also their laughs, of all things.) The more Caroline and Libby expanded their friendships with boys and broadened their ways of playing, I thought perhaps there was another reason activities in cross-gender friendships tend toward behaviors considered boy-like: that stuff is just *fun*.

But Dexter's mom, Jen, pointed out to me later that her sons showed the same kind of consideration to their friends. "Both Miles and Dexter anticipate what their friends might like to do," she wrote to me in an email when the boys were thirteen and seven:

When Miles would host female friends in early elementary, I remember that he changed his room around. He went up to the attic and pulled out his dolls and stuffed toys. (Curious George at one point had his own set of homemade bunk beds and clothing).

Miles truly wanted to host his friends and provide things that they wanted to do. It wasn't necessarily that they were girls (or that he made any assumptions about what "girls" like) but he did know what they liked, so he tried to prepare ahead of time. Now when he hosts friends in middle school, he prepares similarly by fixing up his work bench or organizing his tools. The last playdate, he pulled out the Christmas lights so they could decorate the outside of the house.

Further to Jen's point, it had been five-year-old Dexter who'd once sent a note, painstakingly composed on his big brother's typewriter, inviting Libby to his house for a tea party. (She eagerly accepted.) Dexter had concocted the vision for the tea service, complete with a plate of French macarons, with Libby in mind because he was certain she, in particular, would enjoy it—and he was quite right. He also had art supplies—more of Libby's favorite things—ready for the moment the teapot ran dry. As Jen's family made clear, learning to consider others and to form thoughtful, flexible friendships builds relationship skills for children of any gender.

Still, without seeing plenty of examples, maybe it's not so surprising that we're easily thrown by the question of what boys and girls might do when they're invited to play together. And when they're older, the question shifts: What will they *talk* about? An article about boy-girl friendships on the website of Focus on the Family, Dr. James Dobson's influential evangelical organization opposing LGBTQ+ and women's rights, advises parents to set boundaries for their children's cross-gender interactions: "Teach them that there are certain discussion topics that should be saved for same-sex friends. For example, it would be inappropriate for a young girl to talk with a male friend about shopping for a bra or getting her period. Those subjects should be saved for 'girl time.' The same goes for boys, who should limit conversations about their own body development to 'guy time.'"

Compare that to what happens on *De Dokter Corrie Show*, a popular Dutch public television program for children nine and older designed to teach—or reinforce—healthy, accurate lessons about bodies, puberty, sexuality, and love. In a 2015 episode on menstruation, the exuberantly rubber-faced host starts by smacking down the idea that periods are gross or only a girl thing. Periods are a part of life, and everybody should be comfortable with that—boys and girls alike. Later in the episode, we see a mixed-gender group of sixteen- and seventeen-year-olds sitting together in a room in Dokter Corrie's studio (with subtle flying-penis wallpaper in the background). The boys are there to ask questions about periods, and the girls are there to explain things. It's mostly unscripted, and it seems no question is off-limits. The boys want to know a lot: *What's it like to use pads and tampons—does it feel unnatural? How do you know when to change them? Does a tampon string ever break? Do any of you have your period right now? In dealing with women, should I take into account whether she has her period?* There's plenty of laughter as the kids educate one another, but none at any individual's expense. Even when one of the boys asks if you can reuse a tampon and one girl covers her mouth as she laughs—*That's disgusting!*—sixteen-year-old Donna keeps a neutral expression and answers straightforwardly, using her hands in an expanding gesture: "It spreads out. There's always something in it, so you won't get it back in."

It's a respectful group in which everyone is served: the boys are educated, and the girls are validated. It's hard to imagine an outcome like this if the subject of their conversation were taboo except for "girl time." I thought about this more when I listened to a 2017 episode of *Mom and Dad Are Fighting*, a Slate podcast, in which hosts Allison Benedikt and Gabriel Roth discussed whether boy-girl friendships matter much.

"Having girls who I had a long relationship with and...could talk to about stuff, I think that was a helpful thing for me in my life," said Roth, as the father of a kindergarten daughter and a younger son. "It makes me a little sad to think that kids might go through long stretches of childhood without having a friend of the opposite sex," he said. "Because then what, that whole gender is like, a mystery to you?"

"I definitely never had boy friends," said Benedikt, the mother of three sons, ages eight, six, and three. "I guess it doesn't bother me," she said about the fact that her sons didn't tend to play with girls. As an example of how boys gain from not having girls around, she said, "I drove a carpool home the other day of three boys from basketball, and one of them said, 'What does it mean when a girl says you have a cute butt? Don't all butts look the same?' It was great for the three of those guys to be like, back there sort of wondering....I mean maybe *What's up with those weird girls?* isn't great, but I don't know, it feels, it just feels regular to me. Maybe it's insidious and it snowballs into territory that I wouldn't be comfortable with, but it feels okay now."

I couldn't help thinking that sounded like a perfect example of a time when boys and girls need one another's perspectives—which can be a by-product of simply spending more time hanging around together.

For her part, podcast guest Diane Levin, an education professor at Wheelock College and author of the book *So Sexy So Soon*, brought an unequivocal view: "It's important to encourage friendships with kids of the opposite sex. This is something to be nurtured." She told Benedikt and Roth: "What's happening now is boys and girls get so alienated from each other [that] when their relationships come back [in adolescence], it often is around sexual behavior." With "so little opportunity to relate to each other when they're younger," she said, kids develop "fewer skills for having positive, caring, connected relationships."

It's a disconnect that persists into American adulthood, in which the default concept of male-female relationships is romantic and heterosexual. Adult Americans are reluctant to form—or even acknowledge the possibility of—platonic friendships between straight men and women.

When Janine, the American mom I'd met through our kids' Dutch-language Saturday school in Seattle, began dating her future husband, Bastiaan, a Dutch man, friends teased about the fact that she kept up her friendships with other men while her husband continued to socialize with his female friends. But the couple felt, and continue to feel, that cross-gender friendships are important for adults, too. That jived with my experience living in the Netherlands, where many of my heterosexual Dutch parenting peers had easygoing male-female

friendships. I had to face my own warped ideas about healthy companionship when one sunny Amsterdam afternoon I found it almost
unbearably awkward to share a picnic blanket with a Dutch work-
from-home dad I knew while our kids played in the park's wading
pool after school. Simply lounging together on a blanket in the grass
felt suggestive of romance.

That was just the way I'd been socialized, and I was not alone. I had
to think my Dutch friends would fall off their chairs laughing if they
could see the most popular searches that popped up when I Googled
"man woman friends" in 2017:

platonic friendship between man and woman
do men ever just want to be friends with a woman
can a man and a woman be best friends
can a married man and a woman be just friends
pure friendship between man and woman

Not to mention a parade of articles stoking more of the same in-
security about whether such relationships can even exist, let alone be
okay: "Can Men and Women Be 'Just Friends'?" (*Psychology Today*),
"Can Men and Women Really Be Just Friends?" (*Shape*), "Can Men
and Women REALLY Just Be Friends?" (*Huffington Post*), and on
and on.

Such questions and their regrettable answers (some of the articles
conclude that no, it is not possible for adult men and women who are
straight to form platonic friendships) are an unsurprising outcome of
childhoods in which boys and girls are tacitly permitted—or entirely
pressured—to go their separate ways. The idea that nonromantic
friendships between straight men and women are somehow dangerous is reinforced by the fact that cross-gender friendships between
straight and gay or lesbian adults, such as a straight woman and a gay
man, are often deemed "safe." (Bisexual people are generally disre-
garded in these scenarios.) There's perhaps no better way to test the
question of which friendships can be socially permitted than to ask
about the experience of transgender adults, who may change gender

but remain the same individual. And sure enough, some transgender people who transition in adulthood say the hardest thing about no longer identifying with their former gender is the loss of deep, previously same-gender friendships, which somehow don't seem permitted to remain so close.

Just as I was thinking about obstacles to cross-gender rapport, the New York Times published an article about a poll they'd commissioned asking men's and women's opinions on the appropriateness of going alone with someone of the "opposite" gender (who is not their spouse) for lunch, dinner, a drink, a car ride, or a work meeting. A majority of the women and half of the men polled said it would be "unacceptable" to do dinner or drinks. In workplaces, a quarter of respondents felt it was inappropriate to meet alone with a different-gender coworker, making it even clearer how cooties in childhood persist. After youths spent apart, American men and women just aren't comfortable with one another.

In other words, Caroline had been right: in American friendships, gender is just "one tiny thing" that makes too much difference. That point sat vaguely on my mind one late-fall Saturday when I started texting parents of Caroline's fourth-grade friends in search of a sleepover for her. Dan and I had tickets to a comedy show, and we'd forgotten to hire a babysitter. But it wasn't a good night at Olivia's house, or Zoe's house, or Mia's house, and it was time to cast a wider net. Feeling a bit reckless, I texted Wanda, Lee's mom, and invited my kid over to their place for a sleepover. "I realize it might seem radical since they're classmates," I typed out, "but I didn't want to rule it out." In fact, I regretted not thinking of Lee sooner.

"We would love to host Caroline overnight," Wanda answered immediately.

When Caroline got home from Dutch class, I told her the plan. Her eyes widened for a moment, but she nodded and went to get her sleeping bag. She was excited. And she was putting on a brave face.

"I'm nervous," she told me in the car on the way down to the bay, where Lee was coming off the water from a sailboat race.

"Are you up for it?" I asked.

"Yes," she said. "I just can't picture how it will be." When she said that, I thought the boy-girl aspect was the problem. But once again, that was my own bias. It turned out she just wasn't sure how they'd configure their sleeping bags in the boat.

Here's how it was: A family outing with his parents for burgers followed by a walk to the ice cream parlor with a few games of pinball, then board games at home on the boat, then nestling down side by side on the floor with reading lights and chapter books in hand. Wedging her way in, Shep the dog made three.

The next morning, we collected a very happy Caroline. (And this was before the next sleepover, when she'd awaken to the smell of pancakes and Lee's rabbit sitting on her head.) "We loved having her over," Wanda told me. "They're so precious together. The age of innocence. You should experience it too."

Since then, we have. Wanda had been right: it's a heartwarming friendship to observe. We hope against hope it will last—if not the childlikeness, at least the close companionship. But it was easy for me as an adult to look on and idealize. Come Monday, Caroline and Lee would have a dilemma.

"Did you and Lee talk about your sleepover at school?" I asked super-smoothly when that afternoon arrived.

Looking me right in the face, she enunciated every word of her reply: "We did not talk about it at all."

All right, so I could help my daughter interact with boys, but I couldn't make the other kids like it. Naturally, both Caroline and Lee dreaded the burden of needing to prove they were not in love or planning a wedding.

For the record, their friendship didn't smack of the same infatuation Caroline had shown for Renzo and other boys at other ages. Their connection came across as entirely platonic, each child grounded as their usual selves. The thing was, they just clicked. They played like windup toys, laughing their heads off, charging through every possibility they could find in a day, then sleeping like angels in striped pajamas at night.

But what if they *had* been in love? Even though nearly all of us have felt it as something important, childhood love is easily dismissed in American culture. If it's not "the real thing" with wedding bells, it can only be "puppy love"—meaningless infatuation. Children face the paradoxical message that love, felt by people of all ages for all genders, prefigures marriage, which is only for adults. This forces them to decide if their childhood affections are illegitimate—not meaningful and not worth learning from—or inappropriate, which may lead to shame, confusion, and an inner rejection of their own tender affections. But what if we could change this story? What if we admitted that kids *can* be in love, and kids and adults all knew it, and everybody treated falling in and out of love as a normal and important part of growing up?

Ask a Dutch parent or teacher, and they're likely to assure you that yes, of course young children can be in love. It's almost a silly question. At home, Dutch parents are far more likely to validate their children's emotions as they fall in and out of love. And at school, at least in one popular curriculum, romantic love is a lesson that begins in third grade.

Despite the social risks, over time Caroline enlisted other girls in her class and pulled aside more of the boys to spread the good news: forming friendships was okay! Before long, others in her cohort were sending invitations for mixed-gender birthday parties and inviting friends of different genders to play after school. One spring morning, as her fourth-grade year was coming to an end, I reminded her that it was class photo day. She paused. "I think this is going to be the most meaningful class picture I've ever had."

"Why?" I asked.

"Because," she said. "We've all gotten so much closer."

10

Spring Fever

When American parents hear that Dutch schools start sex ed in kindergarten, first comes surprise, then skepticism: "Okay, but they don't *really* talk about sex at that age—do they?"

Then intrigue: "So how does *that* work?"

I was on my way to find out. From the window of a commuter train, I glanced out to see massive barges on the huge, tree-lined Amsterdam-Rhine Canal as it cut through the flat green countryside. Along the towpaths, morning cyclists in flapping jackets propelled heavy black bikes against a brisk spring wind. Across from me, a man in a trim suit pulled out his breakfast: a pair of cheese sandwiches. I turned back to my flashcards. *Aanraking*: touch. *Houden van*: to love.

It was March 2016 and I was back in the Netherlands getting to know a world-famous sex-ed curriculum for students ages four to twelve—and building my Dutch vocabulary at the same time. *Geslachtsdelen*: genitals. *Wrijven*: to rub. *Twijfel*: a doubt.

That day I was headed to an elementary school in Utrecht, one of the largest cities in the Netherlands and home of the country's biggest university as well as Rutgers, the global sexual and reproductive health foundation. Since 1994, Rutgers has produced a widely used curriculum recently renamed *Kriebels in je buik* (*Butterflies in Your Stomach*) based on internationally agreed sexuality-education standards from a collaboration of UNESCO and other United Nations agencies including the World Health Organization.

The Rutgers curriculum is a model of what is known globally as "comprehensive sexuality education," or CSE. This type of sex ed is based on the principle that sexual, emotional, and interpersonal development begin at birth, from which time children have the right to age-appropriate, culturally relevant, medically accurate, and nonjudgmental information that they can use to make well-informed decisions to protect their physical and emotional well-being. A key feature is the social-emotional element: teaching children to form secure, respectful, safe relationships safeguards human rights and advances gender equality. *Gelijkwaardig*: equal. *Belangrijk*: important.

Comprehensive sexuality education is also a major line of defense worldwide against the spread of HIV and other infections. It can allow girls to stay in school longer by protecting them from unwanted pregnancies, and particularly in the parts of the world where childbirth is most risky, CSE saves girls' and women's lives by protecting them from deadly complications and reducing demand for unsafe abortions. In places such as the Netherlands, where STIs and unwanted pregnancies are very few and unsafe abortions are all but unheard of, CSE can still have meaningful social effects by keeping girls' economic opportunities open, affirming sexual diversity, reducing sexual violence, and nudging attitudes toward the acknowledgment that all people have the right to feel desire and pleasure. Schools in the Netherlands are required to give lessons about personal health, boundaries, and respect for sexual diversity, and the Rutgers curriculum is the most popular, having been used in 2,500 schools since 1994. With the first digital version offered in 2017 reaching an estimated minimum of 150,000 students in more than five hundred schools, the curriculum offers the country's leading sexuality lessons for primary-school students.

Comprehensive sexuality education never was a Dutch-only concept; it has simply found a fit in the Netherlands, a by and large open and tolerant society where many of today's children experience a legacy of frank guidance about sex from parents and grandparents thanks to the Dutch women's movement and sexual revolution of the 1960s and 1970s. Their movement was more successful in changing minds than the simultaneous American movement, largely because

Dutch men were more motivated to adopt a feminist stance on gender equality. For women and men, fear and negativity no longer informed people's everyday ideas about human sexuality. Birth control became easy for anyone to get, traditional notions of chastity until marriage faded, and at-home birth became standard maternity care. All of these developments underscored the idea that sexuality and reproduction are normal and healthy parts of life and that, with education and preparation, they are likely to go well. Accordingly, the famous Rutgers curriculum aims for children ages four to twelve to gain respect for themselves and others. They're taught to increase their awareness of their own and other people's feelings, needs, boundaries, ideas, and potential, and they learn to make healthy decisions in relationships and sexual life. "As a teacher, you don't have to be afraid children will get too much information about sexuality," the teacher's guide explains, echoing similar advice given to parents by the national health service. "Children will pick up the information they're ready for."

Speaking of which, I could see I was way behind on my Dutch scatological terms—*krabben*: to scratch; *boeren*: to burp—which came up in a lesson about the body functions we perform privately when we wish to be polite. When I got to the last word in my deck—*gewoon*: normal—I drew a box around it. It was the perfect description and the perfect irony for this mind-blowing yet entirely practical set of lesson plans.

Scheetjes laten: to fart. Time to get off the train.

At the center of a tidy, quiet, working-class neighborhood on the southwestern edge of the city, I approached a modern, cheerful building of red brick, pastel paneling, huge windows with bright yellow awnings, and a bike rack spanning half the building. The school Het Schateiland—Treasure Island—sits in a network of streets named after famous explorers. The Dutch government funds all kinds of schools—public, independent, and religious—so that families may choose where to send children without worrying about tuition. Het Schateiland is a Catholic school, but I wouldn't have known if I hadn't been told. I saw no prominent religious symbols, and let's face it: I was here for the stellar sex ed.

The Week van de Lentekriebels, or Spring Fever Week, is a Rutgers special project week that takes place in hundreds of elementary schools around the Netherlands. That day in the atrium at Het Schateiland, heart-shaped red balloons with the Spring Fever Week Logo—a butterfly (for that fluttery feeling) and some little circles and squiggles like confetti strings (or gametes, depending how you looked)—floated from the handrails along a broad, rainbow-striped staircase. Given the spring sunshine pouring through the skylights and the twitterpating theme of the week, I expected a buzz, some charge of off-kilter kid energy in the atmosphere. But I found calm all around, and the gently floating balloons were the only sign that anything special was going on.

School assistant Lucienne Berndson greeted me with a smile and introduced me to Henk ten Hoeve, the lead teacher for groups five to eight (equivalent to US grades three to six). As we walked together to Henk's office, I glanced around the open-plan school and noticed many students wearing colorful headscarves. Before the customary tiny cups of coffee got around to everyone, I had to ask: "You said this is a Catholic school?"

"Our school is 99 percent Muslim," Lucienne nodded, which did not clear up my confusion. "Mostly Turkish and Moroccan," although recently, she said, more students from Syrian, Iraqi, and Afghan families had joined the school. "We are becoming more diverse," she smiled.

"We ask the parents if they can understand our Catholic identity and do our Christian *feesten*," such as Christmas and Easter, Henk explained, "and we also celebrate Muslim *feesten*."

Okay, but how again was Spring Fever Week jibing with a 99-percent-Muslim Catholic school?

Henk acknowledged that Spring Fever Week is a reach for the school's parent population. "We want to bring the students something about sexuality every year, but we have to be very prudent how we teach it. Children are like their parents. When they see someone kissing, they can—" and he quickly shielded his face with both hands. In the nearby village where he lived, Henk said, "you can talk about anything. But at school, we have to do it in a way they don't get wrong ideas."

Lucienne reminded me that parents must actively choose Het Schateiland for their students. In many cases they're intentionally seeking a more "typical" Dutch influence for their cross-cultural children. Other Muslim parents in the neighborhood, she said, prefer a different nearby school with a more conservative reputation. On top of that, even though Rutgers wants parents to get to know their curriculum, Lucienne sugar-coats the pill: "In the newsletter, I say the week is about relationships and boundaries. I say it in a general way."

So when I walked into teacher Hasan Hotamis's room full of four-, five-, and six-year-olds, I expected the lesson to be somewhat reined in.

Against a backdrop of self-portraits drawn by the children, Hasan, in an oatmeal-gray sweater that matched his hair, beckoned the room's twenty-two children into a ring of tiny wooden chairs around a red rug in the middle of the room. Teaching assistant Malika Dardouh, wearing a floral headscarf and fresh eyeliner, closed the picture book she'd been reading and shushed the children, steering them to the circle. Hasan had something made of blocks on the floor to show them: a life-size outline of a waving child.

"Is it a boy or a girl?" he asked, feigning puzzlement. "Hmm… how do you know? Today we'll learn about boys and girls: what is the same and what is different."

He asked for volunteers to stand on a small stool arranged like a pedestal at the front of the room. A boy in a hoodie hopped up, and his teacher turned him around.

"This is a boy," Hasan said. Then girls' hands flew up, straining. He reached for one nearby, a kid in purple sneakers and a wheat-gold sweater. She hopped onto the stool, and he guided her in a gentle spin.

"A girl. But," he said, putting his knuckles to his chin, "what is the difference? Look at each other," he said. "How do you know the difference between a boy and a girl?"

Still without beginning to answer the question, he took up a stylus and used a fat black line to make a pair of drawings on the digital whiteboard: two circles for torsos, plus a head and limbs for each. Soon he had simple outlines of two kids running toward each other with three dots apiece for nipples and navels. Then he sat on the floor, his height matching the children's in their tiny wooden chairs. "Look carefully," he said, peering up at the screen though black-rimmed glasses. "I have two figures. They each have two nipples and a belly button, two legs, two arms and two hands, two feet. And I *still* don't know who is the girl and who is the boy."

A girl in pink gasped, while others began pointing and raising their hands.

"Ohhhh," Hasan murmured, as if he'd just thought of something. He returned to the board. "Who will help me?"

Arms flew up. "I want to help!" one boy exclaimed despite himself. Hasan mock-counted and gasped: "*Everyone* wants to help! Shall we make one boy and one girl? Beginning with what? Can we see their backside?"

"No," the children chorused. Teaching assistant Malika, sitting with her hands resting on a little boy's shoulders, shook her head along with them.

"Can we see the front?"

"Yes!"

"What do boys have, then?"

"*Piemel*," came a handful of voices.

"How does it look? Like this?" he asked, making a stroke in the air with the stylus.

"Yes!"

"Downward?" he confirmed, then placed the pen at the base of one oval torso and drew a short line between the legs.

"Is that a boy?"

A handful of kids said "eww," and a few more chimed in. Hasan gave a half second's attention to their reaction, briefly covering his mouth and hunching his shoulders as if in a giggle, then got back to business.

"And what do girls have?"

"Vagina," came the single voice of a brown-haired girl in a white dress with tiny pink polka dots. "Vagina," the other children repeated after her. (As in the United States, "vagina," not "vulva," is commonly used in the Netherlands as the term for female genitals.)

"Vagina," Hasan nodded calmly. "And how do I draw that?"

"So small!" yelled the girl who'd stood on the pedestal earlier. She jumped up from her seat and stood in a straddle, pointing emphatically between her legs.

"Here?" he asked pointing to the chest on the second figure.

"No!" the children shouted.

"Here? Between the legs?"

"Yes!"

This time he drew a short upward line, a cleft at the base of the torso.

"Is that good?" Everyone seemed satisfied with the drawing except the girl who had said "so small," who shook her head. She seemed to have something more specific in mind.

Implicit in Hasan's lesson and intentional in the curriculum was the message that all genitals are created equal. Eventually the curriculum also teaches that not everyone with a *piemel* identifies as a boy, nor vice versa.

When it came time to give the figures underpants, Hasan opened the floor to all of the children's ideas about gender expression: at their request, the girl's underpants would be pink, and she would have a skirt, a necklace, and long wavy hair. ("Long enough?" Hasan asked when the curlicues reached her legs.) In contrast, the boy's hair would be short and spiky, his underpants blue.

Treading carefully just at the edge of the gender-role landscape that children hold firmly in mind at this age, he made no challenges but quietly began drawing nail polish on the boy.

"No!" the kids screamed. They were having fun with this game.

"But I want nail polish too! Can't I?" Hasan said, stamping his foot with a quick pout. But then he granted their wish, shifting the nail polish to the girl. It looked more as if he might be strengthening stereotypes rather than rooting them out, but this was simply the beginning: exposing beliefs comes before examining them. The lessons for this age group and slightly older children, I knew, went on to tackle gender stereotypes with toy- and clothes-sorting activities that teachers can then radically question: "What would happen if a boy wore a dress? Why can girls wear pants?" The manual reminds teachers to add a culturally sensitive caveat that not all children are free to choose their own clothing.

Just as I began to wonder how this was all going to play out at recess time, Hasan delivered his last message about bodies for the day. "Look," he said. "Just as with your nose, just as with your ear, just as with your mouth: you have them, yes, but we don't go around talking about them. Can we agree?"

"Also not about penises," a girl volunteered.

"Also not about penises," Hasan nodded. "And not about your ears, nor your tongue, nor your belly button," he said, pointing to his own. He stood up. "Also not about your buttocks," he said resting his hands on his backside, "or back, or shoulder. If you need the words, you can use them, but not otherwise."

It was a complex message handled simply and positively: *These are your body parts. They are ordinary. When necessary, we speak of them.*

Reined in or not, these children were receiving some of the highest-quality sexuality education on the planet—light years better than anything offered to their average American peers.

It was time for recess, but the lessons would continue. During Spring Fever Week, kindergarteners also begin learning about touch, consent, and communication. Testing on their own arms, they consider their preferences among tickling, stroking, scratching, and pinching. How do they know if they like something? How do they know if they don't? They practice saying no, and they're taught about secrets—the kinds to keep and the ones to tell. And yes, naturally: the lesson plans include a story about pregnancy, birth, and how babies get made in the first place:

> How do the sperm and egg come together? That happens if a man and a woman have sex, because they care for and love one another. The man's penis comes into the woman's vagina, and sperm cells come out of the penis. These swim toward the egg cell. When the sperm reaches the egg, a baby can be formed.

As students get older, the lessons give more detail and more nuance, striving toward inclusivity. For example, regarding reproduction, young elementary students learn that not all babies are made in the same way; sometimes doctors help by combining egg and sperm and placing them inside the mother to grow. Not all babies are born from the vagina; sometimes surgeons deliver babies from the abdomen. Not every couple can make a baby. Not all parents are a woman and a man. Adoption is another way to become a parent. Not everyone wants to have children. Fertile couples who want to have sex but not have a baby can use contraception, and so on.

Once I started to see how simple it could be to communicate clearly with four- and five-year-olds about bodies and reproduction, it became less difficult to imagine kids leaving elementary school with a well-developed understanding of relationships and human sexuality—just in time to start (or in actuality, delay) making the informed decisions that produce such exemplary Dutch sexual health statistics. This is why the Netherlands tallies fewer unintended pregnancies, abortions, and cases of sexually transmitted infection than almost any other country. Even though the US teen pregnancy rate has declined as a result of increasing contraceptive use, American teen girls are still giving birth at five times the rate of their Dutch peers. And when it comes to social-emotional health and relationship skills, it's telling that Dutch teenagers—male and female—are twice as likely as their American counterparts to characterize their first sexual encounter as fully wanted and enjoyed.

Across the atrium from Hasan's room, Liesbeth de Groot had a question for her classroom of eight-year-olds: "Do you know the difference between love and being *in* love?" Standing at the front of the room wearing a Valentine-crimson dress, silver sneakers, and a big smile, she taped up a large red poster she had filled with pictures of her loved ones.

"Love is big," she said. "Being *in* love is smaller, and special. Wherever you are, love is everywhere. It's something very important, and we are going to talk about it."

Here was a subversive approach to the problem of elementary-school teasing about love and *k-i-s-s-i-n-g*: validating, supporting, and normalizing kids' crushes.

Liesbeth went over her poster with the class, naming people she loves: her brother and sister, her children, her students. Then the children were given paper and colored pens and pencils to make similar posters of their own. They drew hearts and names extending from the hearts for everyone they loved.

The teacher emphasized that this was *jouw liefde* (*your* love) so the children should use whatever colors and materials they wanted to. An energetic boy by the window whose family had recently emigrated from Egypt bounced out of his chair and interrupted to say he knew someone in the class who was in love.

"Yes, and we already talked about that," his teacher said gently, carefully balancing the other student's emotional privacy with the curriculum's aim of normalizing talk of love at all ages.

"Who do *you* love?" Liesbeth asked the boy.

"Myself," he answered.

"That's very good," she replied, "because if you feel love for yourself, you can also feel love for others."

Then it occurred to him to add a name to his heart: "Teacher." He showed her, and with demonstrative flair, Liesbeth returned his gesture with a hug.

While the children worked on their love lists, I asked Liesbeth what other sex ed lessons she'd given that week.

"About crushes, the differences between girls and boys, and against stereotypes," she said. "That works well in my class because there are girls here, for example, who really love *voetbal*." (Even though "football" is the word for soccer in the Netherlands, it's like American football in one sense: it's seen as a boy's sport.)

Other key lessons for seven- and eight-year-olds encourage children to know how they feel about being naked and being touched. Aside from yes and no, feelings of confusion, ambivalence, and doubt are discussed. Teachers might also choose an optional activity in which students learn and share about their own birth stories.

Eight- and nine-year-olds go on to receive lessons fostering self-esteem, describing reproduction and childbirth, debunking gender stereotypes, encouraging diverse friendships, and reinforcing that every person has different preferences about whether and how to be touched as well as different desires about how they want to be treated.

In Liesbeth's class, the children were free to cover up the names on their big hearts or to hold them up for all to see. Most of the children didn't seem to mind if others looked at their love lists. Sitting near me, a tall, round-faced boy from a Hungarian family hunched over his work as names filled the space around his heart and began running off the edges of the page. He seemed shy but raised his hand anyway when Liesbeth asked if anyone would come to the front of the room to share about their love.

Then I saw something I couldn't quite imagine happening in an American third-grade classroom: a boy standing up in front of his classmates to speak directly about his love for others. With one nervous hand scratching the back of his head, he read out loud from his paper: "I love my teacher, family, boy friends, girl friends, my best friend, sister, brother, mama, papa, cousins, school, grandma, and grandpa."

He finished reading, dropped his hand from the back of his head, then looked up and smiled. Everyone clapped as he strode back to his seat.

Regardless of what messages the children received (or didn't) outside of school about love and friendship, every kid in class that day knew that they were *expected* and *understood* to love, and that their peers and their teacher, too, had lives full of people they loved in different ways. Liesbeth made it perfectly clear that the children were never to be ashamed of loving someone, and no one should try to make them ashamed.

As part of this lesson, some teachers show a love-themed episode of *Huisje Boompje Beestje*, a public television program for children ages five to eight. In the fifteen-minute episode "Verliefd!" ("In Love!"), nature clips of animals courting, mating, and giving birth are interspersed with the story of classmates Merethe and Juriaan, a girl and a boy of about eight. They make eyes at each other from their desks. He passes a love note: *I like you.* Daydreaming, heart doodling, playground chasing, and hand-holding ensue. The two are all smiles, appearing to equally seek and like the interaction. Other kids on the playground watch the affair in bemusement, but there's no teasing in the script.

"The Dutch concept of *verliefd zijn*, which means 'being in love,' blurs, rather than sharpens, the line between love and lust," writes Amy Schalet in her important book *Not Under My Roof* comparing Dutch and American attitudes toward teen sexuality. Dutch parents "describe their children, even young teens, as capable of experiencing being 'in love.'" She quotes one Dutch mother saying her teenage son was "interested in girlfriends at a very early age" and matter-of-factly stating that during his childhood he was often in love.

In another public television clip noted in the curriculum, Melle, a boy, and Hannah, a girl, are real-life schoolmates of about eleven or twelve who have been "going together" for two years. They tell an interviewer how it feels to be in love. (The curriculum and other suggested materials also reassure children that it's just as normal to fall in love with someone of their own gender.) For Melle and Hannah, it all started when they sat side by side in school and began liking each other more and more. Asked to describe Hannah, Melle says she has brown hair and brown eyes, and he thinks she's "nice" and "cool." With her long bangs reaching nearly to her freckled cheeks, she smiles to hear this. She describes the blond-haired Melle as good at math, not so good at spelling. Their courtship started when Hannah dropped off a letter at Melle's house asking him to be her boyfriend.

"Have you kissed?" the straight-faced interviewer asks.

Hannah smiles. "Yes."

"Yes?" the interviewer says. His tone is even—no teasing, no patronizing.

Melle looks at him and nods. "Yes."

"How did it happen?"

"We were playing at Hannah's, and she asked me if I wanted to kiss her—"

"And you didn't say no?"

"No, I didn't say no."

"And was it nice?"

Hannah smiles again.

"Yes," Melle nods sincerely, not showing off but not bashful either. "It was nice."

Even though teachers at Het Schateiland had been offering the Spring Fever Week lessons for a decade, I realized that their school, with its inflow of children from diverse cultural and religious backgrounds, made a surprisingly apt comparison to many American public schools. While some American students grow up receiving good-quality sex ed from outside sources, many others arrive at midstream still clueless about bodies and relationships. At Het Schateiland, the teachers seemed to agree that all students should end up on the same page. That is, each child should have the same accurate information as their peers, and just as importantly, students should hold expectations about respect, equality, and consent in common.

On her coffee break I caught Eva van Nijendaal, who teaches eleven- and twelve-year-olds, the school's oldest age group. She reapplied her bright red lipstick and pushed back her lively cloud of brown curls as she told me why, even though some teachers pick and choose a handful of lessons, she teaches the entire Rutgers lesson packet from front to back. In a few months her students would graduate to secondary school, where "there's more sexuality and more pressure," she said. "I want to make sure they learn in a safe environment. And I have to say I'm really open. I name everything there is to name. They have a lot of questions, and they're afraid to ask their parents—it's still taboo. I tell them they can ask me anything," although she reserves the right not to answer especially personal questions.

Her students receive lessons on knowing and caring for oneself, puberty, genitals, sexual orientation, reproduction, safe sex, masturbation, beauty distortions in the media, internet safety and social media, porn literacy, and the challenges of saying no and getting help in cases of sexual transgression, assault, or abuse. Optional extra lessons cover circumcision, love and dating, different ideas about virginity, and legal age requirements for sex. After twelve-year-olds have completed the lessons in *Kriebels in je buik*, they are likely to encounter another well-known CSE curriculum, *Lang leve de liefde* (*Long Live Love*) in secondary school.

But for now, Eva said, her students just needed more basics in an ongoing, nonjudgmental context. "The other day during a math lesson," she told me, "one of the kids said, 'What's a dildo?' I said, 'It's a plastic penis that you can use when you're older.'" And then, to hear Eva tell it, they got right back to numbers.

A softball like that doesn't shock her, but she was surprised by how little her students that particular spring knew about puberty. "They keep saying *it's gross, ew*, even after the third day. Falling in love is strange to them—*ew*." And even though they were all eleven or twelve years old, "they had no idea about girls getting periods."

"I keep in mind the things they learn at home, not just about sexuality but also relationships," Eva said, explaining that outside school, most of her students received little to no sexuality information from their Muslim parents and then had to balance that lack of knowledge with the distorted messages of pornography, ubiquitous in the age of screens and devices. "So school comes in the middle."

It was a sentiment I had been hearing a lot: the idea held by experts at Rutgers and enshrined in their lessons and publications that children have the right to accurate information about relationships and sexuality, as well as to a clear framework of social skills and self-knowledge from which to make decisions. This touches one of the most contentious ideas out there when it comes to sexuality education: Who should deliver it? Almost everyone I've asked, including Dutch sexuality experts, says that parents are primarily responsible. But many parents, of course, can't or don't do the job—or try, but fall short.

Take me, for example: I might have been researching high-quality sexuality education, but that didn't necessarily make me a sufficient teacher for my own kids. I certainly wasn't teaching full-fledged lessons bolstered by activities, picture books, films, and games. I knew my kids deserved to be well-schooled in sexuality, and I knew exactly what outcomes I wanted for them, but despite my efforts—and Dan's—we were under no illusions that we could deliver a comprehensive education. I often made mistakes a trained teacher never would, such as forgetting to revisit past lessons and failing to repeat critical information. Even with access to great curricula and a fair ability to read Dutch, I found myself perpetually behind on teaching key concepts. The gap between what I *envisioned* delivering and what I *actually* delivered reminded me of my wonderment watching primary teachers teaching children to read. I might have been a writer, but thank goodness my kids didn't have to learn to read from me. Knowing how to do it is not the same as knowing how to teach it.

Even if I had every resource to teach my children's comprehensive sex ed flawlessly, I wouldn't be able to do the crucial job of reaching their peer collective. When students gain their sexuality education together in the community of their peers, everyone—adults and students alike—examines the same information and becomes party to the same agreements about how to behave and get along. Furthermore, the best comprehensive sex-ed lessons send kids home with updates about what's being taught and homework assignments to complete together with caregivers, all designed to help families pick up the conversations at home, where individual values can be discussed in more depth. This design allows students to know what their peers know and keeps parents and teachers in clear communication about where young people's knowledge stands. When comprehensive sexuality education becomes a community fixture, its value increases even more. Doctors, policymakers, social workers, law enforcement officers, and other influential adults know what they can expect young people to have learned. And those who prey on children can no longer benefit from their ignorance.

Therefore, schools—and to an extent other community institutions, such as churches and community centers—are best positioned to step into the breach. And when it comes to school sex ed, "parents should not have the right to a veto," said Margaret, an Irish-born mother raising children in the Netherlands, in a Facebook discussion of Spring Fever Week. "I think children should be educated regarding their bodies and sex etc. in school, regardless of their parents' wishes, as I think it's the right of a child to be fully educated regarding their bodies/autonomy."

When it's put that way—that it's more important for children to be accurately informed about their own bodies than it is for parents to control the message—the entire question of whether sex ed belongs in schools begins to seem off the mark. Henk ten Hoeve's delicate task of delivering information about sexuality to his students without offending their parents seems more of a strategy problem than a moral one. Same with Lucienne Berndson's candy coating in the parent newsletter.

That day, I stopped thinking of school sex ed as a safety net or a backup plan. A school sits squarely on the front lines when it comes to equipping children for healthy, happy, secure futures with body autonomy and balanced relationships. I thought of what Henk had said—*children are like their parents*—and I wondered what American children, sweetly ignorant as they blunder through adolescence and deadly secretive as they discover physical intimacy, say about us.

Her coffee break over, Eva introduced me to her colleague Cherisch Deel, who also taught eleven- and twelve-year-olds. We chatted across a small desk in a narrow office. Where I had sensed playfulness and activism in Eva's approach, I saw an almost painful concern driving Cherisch to teach her students as much as possible about their bodies and the changes and encounters to come.

"I think they're too young to explore [sexually]," she said, characterizing her own background as much more conservative and religious than her colleague Eva's. "But you need to have knowledge: How does my body work? Boys are having their first *zaadlozing*"—ejaculation— "and girls are getting their periods. And they may be shocked." One girl in her class "didn't know the anus from the urethral opening." Another one of her students, she said, had the all too common idea that babies are born from the navel.

"It's about 'How do you see yourself? your self-worth? How does your body develop? What's the development of a baby?'" She said she sees it as her critical role to set all of these misconceptions straight.

"I'm not afraid to discuss it if a parent complains to me," Cherisch said. "One mother said 'No, I'm not talking about it with him.' Well, then one year later her son got a girl pregnant."

Cherisch invited me into the classroom to meet her students. "You can practice your English," she told them as she brought me to the front of the room.

Seven girls and seven boys listened carefully as I introduced myself and explained my visit. These were the oldest kids in school but seemed very much still children.

"What questions do you have for them?" Cherisch asked me.

I looked at the students, each one in jeans, every girl with long brown hair pulled back, every boy in rumpled play clothes. "I want to know what you all think of the Week van de Lentekriebels," I said. "What have you learned about?"

Some nodded and smiled while a few softly laughed. A boy with deep umber skin and braces raised his hand. "About what is miscarriage," he said.

"How…feels it to be in love," said a boy in a striped hoodie.

"How does it feel for the body to change," a girl added.

At the back of the room, four red heart balloons bobbed softly above a gold-papered box covered in hearts. It was the *vragenbox*: a place for anonymous questions about love, relationships, puberty, reproduction, and, yes, sex. It would be there all week, maybe longer.

"What about your parents?" I asked. "Are these lessons okay with them?"

A few of the students shifted in their seats, smiling a little. For some of them, to be sure, this was knowledge they would guard from their families. But a girl in a gray jumper sitting close to me raised her hand.

"I am a Muslim," she said, "but my father says I need to learn more. He says I need to be a little bit more free."

11

The Joy of Sex Ed

The jokes started right on schedule, 'round about fourth grade. All of a sudden Caroline's classmates couldn't keep straight faces when their teacher asked for a volunteer to grab the ball bag on the way out to the playground. Anybody who had peanut butter for lunch and dared to say so—*pee! nut! butt!*—was liable to set off a round of hysterics. Just as the first girls in upper elementary started getting their periods and developing breasts, some boys ramped up their teasing about female body parts and tossing around the word "boobs" in particular. Before long, Caroline's friend and sports teammate, who had just started wearing a bra, couldn't face her math assignments because the division symbols with their two dots looked like breast graffiti. She was too uncomfortable to look at the symbol, let alone write it.

But I hadn't heard about any of it until the day my daughter came home from school with a question: "Mom, when will we get sex ed in school?"

She knew I had been observing sex ed in classrooms in the Netherlands as well as in our own state. But what about *her* classroom?

"I actually don't know," I told her. "Probably not until sixth or seventh grade." Whereas Washington State public schools must deliver HIV education by fifth grade, and many public schools use *Family Life and Sexual Health (FLASH)*, a medically accurate curriculum for grades 4 and up, my kids' independent school didn't routinely cover anything about sex until middle school. "But why do you ask?"

She told me about the wave of teasing and discomfort between boys and girls in her class. "I can tell the boys and girls haven't learned things about each other's bodies. I was just thinking that if the kids weren't so confused, they wouldn't make as many jokes."

It was an awfully perceptive thought for a nine-year-old—one of those moments when a child seems generations wiser than her parent. I wasn't sure what to say.

"Have you thought about anything you could do?"

"Well, I brought one of our books on a field trip"—also news to me—"and I looked at it in the backseat with Caleb and Matteo. So that was good."

The father driving that day hadn't mentioned this to me. Had the music been turned way up, or had he perhaps seen the usefulness of the conversation?

"But we need lessons for the whole group," Caroline said.

"Why the whole group?"

"Then everybody knows, and nobody has to feel embarrassed."

"And everybody *knows* the others know," I added. "You all know you can expect each other to be mature and respectful."

She nodded. But her thoughts were off ahead of mine. "I made an appointment to talk to the school director," she said.

A chat with the head! I couldn't have come up with a better idea myself. The better part of me knew to keep out of it.

Still, the occasion stirred questions for me. I felt a little sheepish, first of all, to realize I had gotten to know the finer points of Dutch sex ed before I really knew much about formal sex education in my own country—let alone my own kids' school.

Starting in fourth grade (not bad!) the public elementary I attended taught accurate, if limited, scientific and medical details about puberty, reproduction, pregnancy, and disease prevention. At home, thanks in great part to conversations with my mother, I got a handle on the social-emotional side of sex ed. In addition to her approachability about basic body and puberty questions, she happened to excel at discussing the intricacies of emotions and relationships. She made being in love sound like the best thing in the world—something to look forward to. We didn't get much into specifics about female pleasure, and I didn't inform my parents before (or after) I had sex for the first time as a college student, but for the most part I had the knowledge I needed for physical health and the self-esteem to choose my own my time. (At eighteen, I was a little later than average for my generation.) But even with the advantage of earlier sex ed, I now knew there were times I'd put myself unwittingly at risk for STIs. I was lucky not to add to those statistics. Many people raising or educating children in the United States today received only late-stage school sex ed if any at all, and they had either no conversation with their guardians or an awkward, one-time attempt. That doesn't bode well for our collective sexual health or for our own ability as parents and educators to hand down the lessons kids need.

Still, I had been puttering along assuming that organized sex ed in the United States—whether through schools, churches, or other community hubs—was probably about the same as it was when I was a student: okay, but not awesome. I knew American sex ed had a reputation for being notoriously bad, as in frequently ineffective or simply nonexistent. But was our sex ed *truly* poor, or was that just an outdated myth? I soon discovered that the present situation was worse than I imagined. But it was also, in some ways, far more hopeful than I ever would have guessed.

Despite long-standing cultural and resurgent political obstacles, I found significant progress afoot in US school-based sex ed. A new generation of parents, educators, and policymakers are changing old views on the kind of sex ed that works—and students' right to receive it. In short, I saw movement. It was slow, but it was positive.

When I started looking at school-based sex ed in this country, I was surprised—and maybe slightly absolved of my ignorance—by how incredibly difficult it is to get a clear picture of what goes on in classrooms. The portrait is so hard to paint because separate states, school districts, and even individual principals and teachers make their own decisions about whether and what to teach about human sexuality.

Here's what I learned when I went to find out how we really *know* American sex ed is bad. For starters, it's patchy. Fewer than half of all US schools require that students receive information about human sexuality. As of 2018, only twenty-four states plus Washington, DC, required schools to offer sex ed of any kind. No state prohibits schools from teaching sex ed, although many specify what may (or may not) be taught if lessons are offered. Only thirteen US states require teachers to use medically accurate information.

Twenty-six states require that if sex ed is offered, the objective of abstinence must be stressed. Some states such as Georgia, Ohio, and Utah require all students to receive "sex education" limited to an abstinence-only-until-heterosexual-marriage (AOUHM) message. AOUHM education, by the way, which used to be known simply as "abstinence-only" education, is now frequently called "sexual risk avoidance" (SRA) education by its proponents. This most recent euphemism may sound uncontroversial, but it's the same old wolf in sheep's clothing: lessons condemning nonmarital sex and focusing on cisgender heterosexuality while excluding other identities and leaving out medically accurate information that can improve health outcomes and potentially save lives. As of 2014, programs in half of US middle schools and three-quarters of high schools centered on the AOUHM message, which means students are subjected to sex ed in which teachers are not allowed to discuss birth control or infection prevention. (This is why you can see, on YouTube, Mississippi First sex-ed advocate Sanford Johnson demonstrating how he teaches students to put on a "sock" in case they're going to "engage in a shoe-related activity.") AOUHM programs, which also don't nonjudgmentally cover consent or abortion, tend to proliferate in the states with the highest teenage pregnancy and STI rates.

And while at least eight states require sexuality instruction to be culturally sensitive, unbiased, and fully inclusive and safe for students of all genders and orientations, three—Alabama, South Carolina, and Texas—have laws requiring that when sex ed is offered, being gay must be discussed, but only in a negative light. In many states, volunteer groups—some secular, some religious—are allowed to provide lessons in public school classrooms. When those organizations don't operate transparently, school sex-ed content— and the motivations of their authors and classroom presenters—can be even harder to pinpoint.

Even when it's offered and even when it includes information about both abstinence and prevention, American sex ed is light. Most schools fail to meet the Centers for Disease Control and Prevention's sixteen benchmarks for HIV, STI, and pregnancy prevention as well as essential information about sexuality. Whereas many Dutch students receive at least a week's worth of lessons each year on relationships and sexuality beginning in kindergarten, the CDC reports that American students receive 13.5 hours *total* throughout their entire public school careers, with most of those precious minutes concentrated in high school. According to data from the CDC's National Survey of Family Growth, that's a marked drop from a decade ago.

Despite my initial guarded optimism, I could see that as a nation we've been getting worse at educating young people about sexuality since my own school film-strip days in the 1980s and early '90s, when medically accurate sex ed was at its zenith in American schools as a result of urgent concerns about the spread of HIV/AIDS.

Even at six years old, Dutch kids do twice as well as their American peers at demonstrating an accurate understanding of conception and birth. The knowledge gap between children in the two countries only widens from there with increasing ramifications. While comprehensive sex ed—the kind Holland is known for—integrates social and emotional skills, only a quarter of US public schools, and almost no elementary schools, report that students practice communication, decision-making, goal-setting, or refusal skills as part of human sexuality. Yet that's the stuff that makes a sexuality education truly relevant, holistic, and applicable.

American adolescents get pregnant, give birth, and catch sexually-transmitted infections many times more often than their peers in other developed countries. Eight in ten American teens compared to nine in ten Dutch teenagers use contraception the first time they have sex, but the fact that our unintended pregnancy rate is five times higher and falling slower than those in other developed countries suggests that US teens who report using contraceptives still may not be using them properly. This seemed even more likely when I learned that only about half of sexually experienced US teenagers have received any formal sex ed at all, and only about a fifth of American students ever learn in school how to correctly use a condom. Most of that education goes to white students, whose adolescent birth rate is lower than that of Black and Hispanic teens. Specifically, one analysis showed, the students who receive high-quality (comprehensive) sex ed tend to be older, white, higher-income, and more urban. Students who get AOUHM instruction are younger and low- to moderate-income. Students who get zero sex ed are most often low-income, Black, and rural. (When it comes to preventing pregnancy, AOUHM education has proven just as effective as no sex ed at all.)

It's not only the high inconvenience of unplanned pregnancy, childbirth, and parenthood that's problematic. Girls who give birth as teenagers are more likely to drop out of school, live in poverty, and experience lifelong negative health consequences for themselves and their children. And for something so preventable, it's an expensive problem. Nationwide, unintended pregnancy and teen childbirth cost taxpayers more than $20 billion annually.

Meanwhile, young people under twenty-four account for half of all new STI cases in the United States every year—another preventable outcome. Finally, although cross-national comparisons are difficult to make when it comes to sexual violence, Americans are known to be highly at risk of perpetrating or experiencing sexual assault, particularly in college—a phenomenon of lesser proportions in the Netherlands, where the overall rape rate, while certainly not ideal at 9.2 rapes (reported) per 100,000 citizens, is three times lower than in the United States.

It all adds up to a pretty remarkable decline for the United States, a country that a century ago offered the most accurate sex ed available anywhere and whose ardent health educators even, for a time, took the concept of formal sex ed to schools around the world.

When I happen to share with a Dutch person that I'm writing about the different approaches to sex ed between our two cultures—theirs more open, ours less so—sometimes they'll challenge me. How significant is the difference really? Aren't all parents a bit uncomfortable talking to kids about sex? And anyway, what does it matter? Even if grown-ups blow it, there's always school to back us up.

But when I tell them that most American kids don't learn about healthy sexuality in school, they just about choke.

"Not at all?"

"A few do, but most of them are already teenagers."

Then I'll get a nod. That *is* different.

But what's the big deal with schools—or churches or other community centers—offering formal sex ed? Why *can't* family-based sex ed be enough?

First of all, public school sex ed is available to everyone. Beyond that, a school with an up-to-date curriculum can offer accurate and detailed information about everything from STI testing to new birth control methods—things that many parents understandably aren't keeping tabs on. For some students, there's a confidentiality issue at play: it may be easier to ask a teacher about tampons than a mother who has never used them, or to find out at school about one's right to medical privacy. Certainly at school there's the herd benefit of teaching everyone the same information together, filling the information gaps that can lead to gender disparities and opening productive lines of communication among peers. Also, schools already doing so can continue to meet diverse pedagogical needs, providing tailored sexuality education for language-learning students, students who are parents, and those with disabilities. People with intellectual disabilities in particular face seven times the risk of sexual assault compared to people without disabilities. High-quality sexuality education for more vulnerable populations (and the people supporting them) is essential to their protection.

In the Netherlands, the approach to school sex ed is more top-down. What Dutch kids have is a federal government with central oversight of public schooling. Therefore it can specifically mandate—and has since 2012—that all students, beginning in primary school, receive some form of sexuality education that includes sexual diversity and self-protective "assertiveness training." The core objectives as stated by the Dutch education minister are to prevent sexual coercion, crossed boundaries, and homophobic behavior, as well as to promote respectful behavior and increase students' ability to resist sexual pressure.

No such overall directive is currently possible from the US federal government. American kids are educated under a decentralized local-control structure in which the federal government can only influence what's taught by strategically channeling funding.

Learning about the state of sex ed in the United States reinforced for me why—and how—we sorely need to outgrow old-fashioned ways of talking about sex with young people. Without ever having received good-quality sexuality education themselves, plenty of parents simply do not have the necessary expertise to help a child thoughtfully navigate the inundation of pornography and popular culture, let alone the latest in medical knowledge or even what's new on store shelves for menstrual and contraceptive needs.

"If we're not teaching students from year to year about sexuality, how do we expect them to grow up to be comfortable teachers of sexuality?" said Laurie Dils, who oversees sexual health education for Washington State public schools, when I asked her why we need formal sex ed. "The more opportunities students have to discuss sexuality in an open, nonjudgmental space, the more comfortable they will be delivering information as parents."

So what's a concerned parent (or youngster) to do when school sex ed isn't comprehensive, is only offered late, or simply isn't offered at all? One option is to advocate for it. The Future of Sex Ed Initiative, a partnership among Advocates for Youth, Answer, and the Sexuality Information and Education Council of the United States provides an online toolkit, "Why Sex Ed?," for families who want to make the case for comprehensive sex education (CSE) in their schools.

Meanwhile, in the absence of CSE for most American students and with the unpredictable pace of progress, plenty of innovators are mining the gap. Over the decades, and especially recently with the advent of websites and apps, countless creative approaches to helping young people access information about sexuality have cropped up, many of them downright brilliant.

That fateful fourth-grade year when Caroline was nine and peanut butter was no longer just peanut butter, I started asking around among my Seattle friends with older children for suggestions about how to acquaint her with better sex ed than we could offer at home. Over and over, friends offered the same enthusiastic advice: I should take my daughter to Great Conversations, a short course taught at our local children's hospital. Great Conversations is the brain child of Seattle nurse and educator Julie Metzger, whose straightforward approach to filling the information gap for preteens around the Puget Sound (and now the Bay Area) is so well loved and so hard to come by elsewhere in the country that after reading a profile of Metzger in the *New York Times Magazine* in 2015, a mom in Nebraska booked plane tickets to fly with her daughter to Seattle for the class.

My family and I attended Great Conversations for Girls and loved it. The course, which Metzger and her colleagues have been teaching to children for thirty years, is intended to be primarily about puberty. The basics of body changes are offered in a nonjudgmental, accepting light. It was fun and pleasantly funny and wholesomely feminist. For example, our instructor, Amy Johnson, reminded everyone in the room that body hair removal is something most of the world's women don't bother with. And "some people like to wear bras," she told the group, "but not everybody."

I noticed something partway through the class that Metzger herself didn't hesitate to point out when we spoke later: Great Conversations does not attempt to offer a complete sex education. It's a puberty workshop, with almost no time devoted to larger aspects of sexuality such as intimacy, reproduction, diversity, pleasure, or relationships. It was a tiny bit troubling to think of how many parents might be dusting off their hands and thinking the birds and the bees had been dispatched after attending the course.

And although scholarships are offered, the four-hour course isn't cheap: in 2018 it cost $80 in Seattle and $120 in Palo Alto. Looking around the auditorium on the winter night when Caroline and I attended, I saw mostly white parents and children among the eighty or so attendees. Because Great Conversations aims to strengthen family communication about human sexuality—a buffer, experts say, against early sexual risk taking—adults must accompany children. Except for a special Spanish-language workshop Metzger and her colleagues had offered in a Northern California school community, the classes are delivered in English. Boys and girls attend in separate groups.

"I can tell you right now, we don't remotely make ourselves accessible to everyone," Metzger acknowledged when we spoke. "We have scholarship funds, but still somebody needs an organized family unit to sign up and have transportation, and they have to call and have the guts to ask for scholarship funds." After attempting partnerships with groups such as the local YMCA, she'd found the extra work overwhelming for her small operation. And aside from a lack of access for socioeconomically disadvantaged kids and kids of color who, statistics say, receive less sex ed than any other group, Metzger also pointed out the larger problem of unmet sex-ed needs for gender-diverse kids and those with disabilities.

Exactly as the course instructors predict for their participants, Caroline and I shared a cheerful talk on the drive home stemming from the evening's class—but our chat disturbed me slightly, too, because she was so focused on the mystery she was left with: What are the boys taught about girls when girls are not in the room? She speculated. She yearned to know. She brainstormed ways to get into the boys' class. If she'd been allowed in, I later learned, one thing she might have noticed is that while ejaculation is covered for boys, female orgasm isn't necessarily discussed in either the girls' or the boys' setting.

But why should a class such as Great Conversations be held to the highest standards for *school*-based sex ed? At a time of life when many adolescents experience an information vacuum, Great Conversations does a great deal of specific good for thousands of participants each year. Metzger was an early innovator, seeing an educational gap—particularly for ten- to twelve-year-old girls—long before many other people recognized it. She's a pro at delivering a particular package of information to kids in early puberty. She wants people to use her classes as a stepping stone or jumping-off point, certainly not as the whole story or final word.

"I get super disturbed that there are people who come to our class and say that because they've done that, they're going to opt out of [sex ed] at the public school," she told me. "Why would you do that? If sex ed in the broadest sense is a pie, a class like ours is one piece of the pie. I hope that kids are still having sex ed at school, talking about it at the dining room table, having conversations about it at seven and eight and fourteen and fifteen and twenty-one and twenty-five and thirty-six and forty-eight." Sexuality, she said, "is an endless dialogue."

In communities large and small, independent sexuality educators like Metzger, often with nursing, public health, or social work backgrounds, offer workshops and lectures in living rooms, school gymnasiums, libraries, community centers, and medical buildings—and reach beyond their localities by making and posting educational podcasts and videos aimed at adolescents and young adults.

For families seeking more thorough sex education in a group setting, one of the oldest and best-known lesson packages in the United States is *Our Whole Lives (OWL)*, the fruit of a collaboration between the Unitarian Universalist Church and the United Church of Christ. Developed in the late 1990s and recently updated, *OWL* meets many of the best standards for accurate, inclusive, nonjudgmental, and age-appropriate sex ed for kids from first grade on. But the very affordable classes must be taken over the course of a semester in a participating church location, which, acknowledges UCC's *OWL* coordinator Amy Johnson, the same instructor my family had for our Great Conversations classes, is a huge commitment for most busy American families. The *OWL* lesson plans are available for anyone to purchase, but they are costly. Still, for those who can access it, *OWL* is considered some of the best sex ed on offer in the United States. The curriculum continues to grow, with its very newest courses designed for senior citizens.

As for other alternatives, some middle school and high school–age Americans are reached by peer educators through local chapters of Planned Parenthood's Teen Council. Some large high schools provide teen health care centers, whose services may include confidential STI testing and birth control. In the retail sector, even shops such as Minneapolis's self-described "progressive" sex toy store, Smitten Kitten, have moved toward offering smutless sex ed for young and old in public workshops and personal wellness consultations. And doulas, health professionals, sex educators, and other personal coaches are beginning to provide, for a price, "first moon" or period parties to usher girls into reproductive maturity with more positivity and less shame.

Meanwhile, a stream of sex-ed websites proliferates, including the tried-and-true Scarleteen, Sex, Etc., and Tabú as well as adult sex-ed sites such as O. School, introduced in late 2017, and Jessica Biel's Tryst Network, launched in 2018. There are sex-ed apps such as Real Talk, Juicebox, and Tia (for women's health), online experts, and an ever-expanding collection of educational animated short films for kids (and sex-talk resources for parents) available at Amaze.org. All of these efforts aim to meet kids where they're at—on screens—and to cut through ideological filters to fill them in on knowledge they're not getting elsewhere.

Such work-arounds can start even younger. When she was expecting her second child, my sister invited me to join her and her three-year-old daughter at a childbirth-for-siblings class taught by Seattle's legendary childbirth educator and doula trainer Penny Simkin. Never having heard of the class despite its being offered since the 1970s, I decided to go and bring along six-year-old Libby. As the class began, Simkin, short, sprightly, round-faced, and nearing eighty, showed large photos of newborn babies and described the differences between babies with penises and babies with vulvas, and pointed out their nice umbilical cord stumps—all normal, she explained. Then she took a seat near the children and said, "I want to introduce a pregnant mommy," and brought out a nearly life-size hand-sewn doll called Anna. The doll mostly covered Simkin, who sat like a ventriloquist in a low chair with the children circling her on the rug.

"Anna says, 'Children, my baby is about to come. I'm going into labor.'" Soon Simkin was intoning the moans and eventual pushy grunts of a birthing woman with unbelievable verisimilitude—something that gave my sister and me goose bumps while those six and under took it entirely in stride. Simkin taught them about the uterus (it's not the stomach), the umbilical cord ("food hose!"), and breast milk. "Who can say 'contraction'?" she asked as Anna labored on. "This is hard work!"

"She's probably used to it," a four-year-old boy reassured the room.

Soon the baby was born, and then a volunteer mother from a recent class settled into the circle with her newborn girl named Holly and Holly's three-year-old sister, Agatha. After Agatha told about being a big sister, the children learned safety rules for holding a baby and observed a diaper change. "Let's see," Simkin said. "I'd love it if she had some poop to show the children."

As I scribbled notes during the class, which was held in the basement of a community center in Seattle, I kept having a funny problem: tears. And snot. I looked at my sister. Same thing. Why was this so powerfully moving?

"We have to do this because we don't have a village," my sister whispered.

Afterward, when I asked Simkin if she knew the class could be so touching for grown-ups, she smiled and said she thought it had to do with the children's openness, wonder, and acceptance at that young age.

I told her I was writing about sex ed, and she nodded slyly. "That's my whole mission, you know," she said. "To show them childbirth before negative ideas have a chance to get in."

It was exciting for me to discover so many innovative stopgaps, few of which had to rely on unpredictable federal funding. I was tempted to see these ideas as solutions. But in the end, I had to wonder if any of these independent efforts—or even all of them together—could be enough. Education scholars such as Jonathan Zimmerman, author of *Too Hot to Handle: A Global History of Sex Education*, argue that independent, private approaches will always be higher quality than what schools can offer. He reasons that specialists are better suited for the job than general-, physical-, or health-education teachers. But I would soon be reassured that teachers, many of whom are not necessarily "expert" sexuality educators, are still capable of doing a fine job, especially with the support of a fine curriculum. Ultimately, if the goal is to educate the populace instead of a privileged few, then schools must shoulder the task. I had looked all over and simply saw no effective way around that.

Even in the Netherlands, where school sex ed is high quality and plentiful, television shows such as the long-running *Dokter Corrie Show* and 2017's *Hotel Sophie* contribute to the perennial task of normalizing talk about bodies, sex, and relationships. Dutch sex ed apps, nonprofits, and websites such as Sense for twelve- to twenty-five-year-olds and the adult-education (and art) project Wipsite are plentiful too. In other words, popular culture and independent organizations support, normalize, and reinforce sex ed, but they don't replace it. When I was a kid, I loved a nerdy after-school detective show called *Mathnet*, in which mathematicians used numbers to solve mysteries. But nobody questioned my need for comprehensive math education in school.

Moreover, while this might be a hard thing to accept, deciding whether children should receive education about sexuality might not even be a parent's prerogative. The United States lags behind many countries in recognizing that children have the right to education about sexuality more than adults have the right to restrict it. Over the past twenty years, international laws and standards have evolved to recognize sexuality education for everyone, including children, as a human right. National and local practices that impede access to information and resources—most often for adolescents and women—tread on additional human rights as well, such as the rights to nondiscrimination, privacy, confidentiality, education, information, health care access, and freedom from violence and coercion. From restroom discrimination against transgender people to blocked comprehensive sex ed in schools to obstructed contraceptive and abortion access, the United States is rife with such violations. But as I soon discovered around the country and in some of the most unlikely places, educators and parents have been booting out old lesson plans—many from curricula several decades old—in favor of accurate, inclusive lessons proven to help kids make healthy choices. I saw how innovative people can be when there's a clear need to be met, how much progress we can make in a short amount of time, and how real, deep cultural change—a shift in beliefs among parents and today's educators—is driving toward a future of American sex ed that will eventually look a lot more European than Puritan.

Inexplicable to me was the mismatch between the stats about the amount and type of sex ed American kids receive and the stats about the sex ed parents *want* them to have. Various polls and surveys have shown that the vast majority of US adults across the political and social spectrum support school-based sex ed covering both abstinence and contraception, which is considered standard for effective pregnancy and disease prevention. Three-quarters support federal funding for this type of sex ed in schools. Still, activist groups—particularly religious organizations—are able to mobilize levels of formidable pushback. For example, in 2015 a cluster of Omaha, Nebraska, school districts proposed retiring a thirty-year-old curriculum that contained discriminatory messages in favor of a new, comprehensive set of lessons. But the updated curriculum would be "full of pornographic content promoting homosexual lifestyles, masturbation, and sexually graphic images," said a website called Save Nebraska Children, mounted by a conservative group called Nebraskans for Founders' Values. That organization, along with the Catholic Archdiocese of Omaha, circulated fliers and petitions and brought a wave of outspoken community members—not necessarily with schoolchildren of their own—to board-meeting podiums to fight the updated curriculum despite public health officials and students themselves speaking in favor of a new, comprehensive approach.

One speaker, who described herself as a mother, grandmother, and retired public school employee, told the board of the Omaha Public Schools at a packed meeting in 2016 that "our most important responsibility is to get children to heaven." Speaking in opposition to updating the curriculum, she said "it rapes children of their innocence" and went on to read a Bible verse about sexual sin. Considerable applause broke out in the room.

Another parent said the updated lesson plans, which would be inclusive of all genders and sexual orientations, came "straight from the pits of hell." Shouting and shoving broke out among audience members in one such meeting; at least one student reported being struck by an adult.

Still, after a bruising year of hearings and public-relations struggles, and with some deletions from the proposed curriculum, the majority of Omaha-area school districts did ultimately manage to switch to more comprehensive, medically accurate, and affirming sex ed. And Omaha's battle, which brought national attention, didn't appear to dissuade other parents and districts from addressing their own outdated or inadequate sex ed programs.

Around the country, students, parents, and educators are bringing to light other "shame-based" and inaccurate lessons, including ones that compare unmarried sexually active people—especially women—to used toothbrushes, chewed up pieces of gum or food, a cup of spit, and dirty old sneakers. Just a year after the Omaha kerfuffle simmered down, parents in St. Louis—which for a decade had held the nation's top spot for STI rates—took swift initiative, managing to quickly persuade school officials in several area districts to oust an AOUHM middle and high school sex-ed curriculum called *Best Choice*, which, like many of its kind, was authored and presented in classrooms by members of a religious organization.

"What I would really like to see is a curriculum that is sex-positive instead of being all about shame," Caleb Friz, the father of two young elementary students, told a reporter. "It should be out in the open—this is normal, this is part of our bodies and let's talk about this. It's an important part of being a human being."

Even though sex ed curricula used in schools aren't allowed to overtly promote religion, Bridget Van Means, the leader of ThriVe St. Louis, the Christian-affiliated crisis pregnancy center that brings *Best Choice* into local public schools, didn't hesitate to characterize the curriculum as religiously motivated when speaking with a sympathetic audience: "We are, believe it or not, teaching God's standard of abstinence until marriage in the *public schools*. Is that *crazy*?" she said at one speaking engagement. By the end of 2017, although *Best Choice* was still in scattered use around the city, parents had convinced officials in the majority of St. Louis–area schools that the curriculum could not meet students' needs.

Elsewhere, change happens more gently. At a public K-8 school in southwest Minneapolis, parent Krista Margolis was surprised that her son's fifth grade had no sexuality-education curriculum. As a women's health nurse practitioner who, inspired by her daughter, had developed a puberty class for adolescent girls, she collaborated with her son's teacher "to create a week-long blast of info. It was a huge success." The following year, the district hired a health teacher to provide sexuality education to sixth, seventh, and eighth graders. Margolis said she was thrilled with the turnabout and the high quality of the lessons offered by the new teacher.

Despite the hard road, when I asked policymakers and educators to tell me what's going *right* in American sex ed, they'd brighten up and tell me about two important federal funding streams through the US Department of Health and Human Services: the Personal Responsibility Education Program (PREP), which brings "adulthood preparation" as well as abstinence and contraception education to at-risk young people, and the big success story, the Teen Pregnancy Prevention Program (TPP), a grant-making initiative in the federal Office of Adolescent Health that identifies and funds communities using evidence-based or innovative approaches to reduce teen pregnancy. Begun in the first term of the Obama administration, the TPP approach is essentially this: we'll fund what you're doing if it really prevents teen pregnancy. Since piles of studies have shown that AOUHM education is as bad at preventing pregnancy as no sex ed at all, the

TPP mostly funds comprehensive approaches. People who receive CSE are shown to have less sex with fewer partners, and when they do have sex, they are more likely to use protection and less likely to contract infections or become pregnant. Therefore, while abstinence organizations such as ThriVe still do receive millions of taxpayer dollars in a legacy that began in the Reagan years and peaked during the George W. Bush administration (and is once again on the upswing), the TPP simultaneously channels millions into starting and supporting programs that reach students early with accurate, age-appropriate information. The TPP has been a jaw-dropping success. Even though the United States still has the highest teen birth rate of any developed nation, the number of American teens having babies has been cut nearly in half since 2010—a drop unprecedented in American history. In 2017, the Trump administration moved to eliminate the TPP.

Meanwhile, the CDC's Division of Adolescent and School Health has its own stream of grant money that has slowly but surely been changing the approach to sex ed in many of the nation's largest school districts. From San Francisco and Oakland to Boston and Broward County, Florida, districts have received funding to implement "exemplary" sexual health education, which in many cases means K-12 and always means medically accurate, age-appropriate, and inclusive of diverse populations. Broward County, for example, made comprehensive sex ed for grades K-12 a formal requirement in 2014. In 2016, the nation's most progressive sexuality-education law yet took effect in California, making comprehensive sexuality education mandatory for seventh- through twelfth-grade students—and permitted for all grades. Students must learn that not having sex is a preventive choice, but teaching abstinence without explaining other forms of prevention is expressly forbidden in California public schools.

But this wave of progress isn't only happening in big districts.

"More and more I think there's some momentum," Washington's sexual health education program supervisor Dils told me. "We're seeing more of what I would consider conservative districts choosing to adopt [CSE], saying, 'We want to update our sex ed offerings. We're doing a disservice to our students because our sex ed is either really limited, or it's really old. We haven't looked at it in a long time, and we're ready to update it.'"

But there's been a slight problem: How to get it taught? In some cases, schools and districts struggle to find the most qualified teachers to tap and train, particularly given how overloaded many teachers already are. Another problem has been finding truly comprehensive lesson plans in an educational climate that has been incentivized since the early eighties to avoid covering sexuality in a forthright manner.

"We sort of shot ourselves in the foot by calling it 'sex ed' because it is so much more," said Dr. Elizabeth Schroeder, an independent sexuality educator based in New Jersey, as she explained to me the decades-old uphill battle to get comprehensive lesson plans into American schools. "You can't say 'child' and 'sex' in the same sentence."

We were in Boston having a late cup of coffee on a sunny afternoon the day before a blizzard was forecast to strike the Northeast. She had been telling me how difficult it is to make the pitch for sex ed in the first place, since that three-letter word alone tends to make people "clutch the pearls," she said with a theatrical gasp and a laugh. So, she said, "what you can probably get away with is saying 'we want young people to grow up and be happy and healthy.'" As sexuality educators, she said, "we know that means sexually healthy as well."

We can say "medically accurate" and "age-appropriate" and "inclusive" and "comprehensive" and "effective" all day long, but what do students really need to know? And how will teachers know what to stand up and say? To answer those questions, an alliance of sexual health and child development experts and organizations convened to define core standards for what American children from kindergarten through twelfth grade should learn in sex ed. In 2012, they published the National Sexuality Education Standards (NSES), and with that document as a guide, the first American-produced, K-12 comprehensive sex ed curriculum with lesson plans fully mapped to the new standards became available for download in 2016. Schroeder had co-authored the curriculum, America's first K-12 CSE lessons truly comparable to the Dutch *Kriebels in je buik*. Philanthropic foundations with youth, health, and education missions such as WestWind Foundation, Open Road Alliance, and Turner Foundation ensured that the curriculum could be made available for free, positioning it to compete with the free AOUHM lessons offered in many public school classrooms by outside organizations.

Almost as soon as the online lesson plans went live, the authors of *Rights, Respect, Responsibility (3Rs)*, developed by the nearly forty-year-old youth sexuality-education organization Advocates for Youth, found themselves flooded with requests for training and information. Schroeder and her co-authors hit the road, traveling coast to coast busily training teachers and school administrators.

In the years since Schroeder and the other *3Rs* authors had visited France, Germany, and the Netherlands to get a better grasp on what they call "European" models for sex ed, Schroeder told me she'd noticed that "many folks who are not academics are by and large horrified by the Dutch approach." It doesn't seem right to be so straightforward so early—until you compare the sexual welfare of Dutch versus American teenagers.

Indeed, the *3Rs* curriculum *is* much more than the best material most American schools have had to offer since the 1980s, which, when medically accurate, focused almost exclusively on the potential negative consequences of sex: the threat of HIV and other diseases, with pregnancy as the wing menace. The *3Rs* curriculum, which is also available in Spanish, aligns better with the Dutch model, with lessons on different kinds of families, personal space, and bodies for kindergarteners; friendships, gender roles, and reproduction for first graders; bullying, harassment, and puberty for third graders; love, communication, and reproductive anatomy for fifth graders, and so on with the balanced mix of biological information, social-emotional learning, positive encouragement, and life skills that's proven to benefit kids.

On the whiteout March morning in Boston the day after I'd met Schroeder for coffee, I settled into a hotel conference room at a national conference of physical education teachers to observe a *3Rs* training. I watched various health and PE instructors plus school administrators and district-level curriculum advisors trickling in and finding their places at tables arrayed with stress-ball toys in case anybody needed to get their sex-ed anxiety out. The forecast was terrible: the nor'easter Stella was well underway, and many of the morning's airline arrivals had been preemptively canceled. Some of the chairs in the room would remain empty that Tuesday. But just before Schroeder began the morning's introductions, five additional attendees— who did not fit my expectations at all—filed in and sat in a row. I guessed they were barely out of their teens. Who were these kids?

In the daylong seminar, Schroeder and her colleague Brittany Mc-Bride brought the country's first comprehensive, evidence-informed K-12 sex-ed curriculum to a small, intent audience of two dozen participants. The instructors demonstrated how to teach first-graders that all living things reproduce and modeled inclusive ways to divide students into groups (definitely no more boys over here, girls over there). Outside, the blizzard blew so hard it looked like puffs of white smoke were rising past our eighth-floor windows. The streets below became impassable. By day's end, I had learned that the five young people who had walked in, three men and two women, were health and education students from Central Michigan University. Maddie, a twenty-one-year-old health major, had taken her first-ever airplane flight to attend the conference. Given the snowbound streets, even after a long day's workshop the group of students agreed to join me for a conversation around a food-court table in the mall below the conference hotel. With the smell of pizza thick in the air and snow buffeting the windows around us, they told me how comprehensive sexuality education landed on their radar—and stuck.

"I had girls in my class that were seventh-graders getting abortions," Maddie said of her own middle school years. "That's what motivated me to teach sex ed. Because I wasn't exposed to it through high school, and my parents refused to talk about it. I had no clue when I came to college what it all meant. I realized I was so blind to everything."

"You're not going to get it all from your parents anyway," added her classmate Nick, who at twenty-four and wearing a black tracksuit with a school-gold polo collar poking out in neat triangles nailed the image of a freshly minted PE teacher. "You need an expert that's going to stay up to date and figure out what students need to know and give them the resources."

Wendy, twenty-one, nodded. "Yep. I want to be a PE teacher and wear the sweat suit and all that, but I've gotten to the point where I see how in both majors, PE and health, it's about improving the life of the student. Especially in sex ed, you want them to be equipped with the proper tools to make their decisions."

Roundly, they credited Su Nottingham, a faculty member in their university's school of health sciences, with opening their eyes to the importance of CSE.

"At least once a day I'm sitting there in class listening to her and I'm like, 'Oh, I wish I had known that when I was seventeen. I wish my high school teacher or my parents would have taught me,'" said Kyle, twenty-two, a hockey player.

Garrett, also twenty-two, agreed. "As a college male, learning about comprehensive sex education has made me more sensitive toward understanding what's going on with women. I have two little sisters, and I used to be like, *I don't care*, when they got their period. I had no idea what the hell was going on. I never really cared about birth control; I never knew how that affected women. I really was taught that old-school kind of abstinence sex ed. Now I'm more like-minded toward women and more sensitive toward LGBTQ people. Men my age who are in these classes with me, we all agree we're learning so much. We're starting to become more tolerable, better men."

All but one of the CMU students had been raised in Christian households, and not all of them said they'd feel particularly comfortable letting their parents know about the workshop they'd attended that day. Just the previous weekend, Garrett had played during services in his church rock band. Nick and Wendy, both practicing Catholics, had also attended church. But, they each emphasized, their religious beliefs shouldn't play into decisions about what kind of sex ed to teach.

"Sometimes I have conflicting beliefs," Wendy acknowledged. "But it's more about giving students the knowledge, not just what I believe."

Nick nodded. "As sex educators and health educators in general, we have to take our beliefs and bundle them up and throw them out the window."

"It's not about me," Wendy said. "It's not about what I believe. It's about giving them the fullest knowledge to make their own choices. I made my choice, I've decided who I am, but I can't deny knowledge to students because of what I believe."

"You want to encourage your students to be independent," Nick added. "To think for themselves."

"My question as a future teacher," Wendy said, "is what are parents so afraid of? What's so scary about being informed?"

Later, as I sloshed through melting snowdrifts back to my hotel, I thought appreciatively about how these young teachers-to-be fell so cleanly outside the sex-ed-debate cliché. As faith-minded individuals with religious backgrounds who saw every reason to bring comprehensive sexuality education to the conservative American communities where they would most likely go on to teach, they were like ideological bridges between the past and the future.

"Nobody thinks you exist," I had told them.

But they didn't seem particularly surprised at themselves.

And when I went looking, I started seeing other young teachers bringing change to the places that need it most. In spring 2017, I drove through peach and apricot orchards deep into Eastern Washington's rural agricultural territory. At the edge of Okanogan county, where teen pregnancy and STI rates soar higher than the national average, I made my way to Pateros K-12, a majority-Hispanic school with a 7 percent migrant population. Yellow goat hoofprints painted onto the road led me from the highway to the school, home of the Nannies and the Billy Goats. There, first-year teacher Jayden Hawkins, the health and PE instructor for every grade in the single-school district, was preparing to teach one of a spring series of sex-ed lessons to her seventh-graders.

Hawkins had grown up even deeper in agricultural country, an hour north of Pateros near the Canadian border in Tonasket. There, while in school, a teenager close to her family became a mother.

"Her last three months of senior year, she actually did most of her work in the counselor's office," Hawkins told me. "Eventually people found out. They were accepting, but it was really, really hard for her to be that face." Hawkins remembered "just watching the things she had to go through as a single mom who got pregnant at a young age— how she had to really be cautious about sharing that information with people," knowing she was likely to be judged or shamed.

In past years, sex ed had been offered to Pateros students by Care Net Pregnancy Center of Okanogan County, self-described as "a Christ-centered ministry whose mission is to lovingly promote sexual purity." Care Net trainees, like numerous volunteers nationwide in similar partnerships, brought free AOUHM lessons into Pateros classrooms.

"As a kid, you talk to your friends. They say they're having sex, and you don't know what they're saying," Hawkins said. "I wanted to be the voice of truth about those things in this community." After looking over several options with TPP grant support and mentorship through a local social services agency called Room One, Hawkins selected a comprehensive middle school curriculum called *Get Real* produced by Planned Parenthood League of Massachusetts.

"Being here in Pateros, I was really, really worried about how accepting the parents and the community were going to be about the curriculum I was going to teach. It's not the abstinence-only education that's been seen throughout the county in the past. But this stuff that I have, it's so great." Although two students opted out of the lessons, she said, "I have not had one parent complaint. Overall I've had the best support from the community."

Get Real and the other lesson plans Hawkins used for younger students all featured a critical family-involvement component; she sent home follow-up lessons in English or Spanish depending on each family's preference.

That day's lesson covered STIs. While I observed from the back of the classroom, students learned about transmission, barrier methods, and the one sure thing: abstinence. As woodsy smoke from a burn pile in a nearby orchard drifted through the portable classroom's open window, the students scanned their workbooks while Hawkins quizzed them on everything from how certain infections are spread to which online information sources are reliable to the reasons why people might choose to have sex. "And what other ways could they show those same feelings?" Hawkins asked.

Totally relaxed and matter-of-fact as she led the group, she walked among the classroom's circular conference tables with a gray headband holding back her wavy brown hair, a matching sweatshirt with "Billy Goats" on the sleeve, and a radio device to support a hearing-impaired student clipped to her pocket.

"Sick!" one girl said when the subject turned to genital warts—easily the most skin-crawling STI Hawkins could seem to mention.

"Wait, wait, wait, I have a question!" another girl said. "You can get genital warts from skin-to-skin contact?" She touched her neighbor. "Like this?"

"No," Hawkins said. "*Genital* skin-to-skin."

"So you can't prevent it?" the girl asked, looking horrified.

"You can if you use a barrier method. So remind me, what's a barrier method?"

"Lotion?" the girl said.

"No."

"A condom," a boy volunteered.

"A condom," Hawkins nodded. "A condom goes between the skin, so that will prevent HPV."

"I'm helping them unlearn the wrong information," she told me as she erased the whiteboard after the bell. "How do I tell a bad relationship from a good one? How do I help a friend if they identify as gay or lesbian? How are Hispanics portrayed in the media? And girls, how are they portrayed? It breaks down all those biases, and that's the part I love teaching."

I hadn't yet learned from conversations with sex educators that white, privileged communities are the most resistant to adopting comprehensive sex ed curricula, so I was still marveling that this teacher and her administrators at a low-income rural school with a high percentage of Catholic parents and a ruby-red voting tendency could be so downright progressive. But, like the teachers-to-be from Central Michigan, Hawkins was composed in the face of my amazement. As if it were a simple no-brainer, she said this was just the way schools needed to go for their students' well-being. Hawkins held the door for me and another student as she headed toward the gym to teach PE. She planned for all of her elementary students too—from kindergarten up—to receive comprehensive sex ed in her classes in the coming fall. That was the way things had to be if the county's health statistics were going to improve.

And what if, in addition to learning how to keep safe, kids learn along the way that gender diversity and even pleasure are normal, healthy parts of human sexuality? I asked.

Hawkins shrugged—*why not?*—and headed into the gym.

By the time I got home from Pateros, Caroline had sat down with her school director for a chat about sex ed.

"How did it go?" I casually asked, trying not to seem as curious as I really was.

"It went really great!" she said cheerfully. "You know what was the coolest thing? She treated me like an adult."

"Like an adult? What does that mean?"

"She asked me really good questions and listened like I had something to say that she really wanted to know. She didn't just pretend to listen and say *uh-huh, uh-huh* like grown-ups do all the time. She even gave me tea."

That was about all I learned, and for a brief moment it was all I needed: a reminder of the way meaningful change begins so reassuringly and irrepressibly in the minds and hearts of the next generation.

12

Safe Haven

I was perhaps not the French innkeeper's best-loved guest. It was an otherwise pretty morning in the sunny hilltop village of Vézelay, but I was mad I'd booked a crappy room for the previous night: threadbare blankets, grimy floors, questionable sludge in the bathroom, and midnight billows of noise and cigarette smoke from outdoor dining just below our windows. It was midmorning, and I still hadn't had breakfast—the inn's wilted buffet was as overpriced as the room—and after a sleepless night I was a little bent out of shape.

"*Merci*," said the innkeeper, hardly glancing up from the newspaper as he unfurled a gigantic hand to accept the room key I held out. Dan and the girls, who were six and two at the time, had gone down the hill in search of baguettes.

"We were not happy with the room," I told him, scrounging up my years-latent French. Then I clarified. "Not happy with the *price* for the room. Everything was dirty and smoky and worn out."

The innkeeper, enormously tall and thickset with a white beard and a white ponytail and a coffee-stained T-shirt, looked surprised. "You don't understand," he said, thudding a knuckle against the faded patterned paper on the wall beside him. "This is an *old* house, not a *dirty* house. It is charming!"

"I like the house," I said. "I like the walls. But the room was not clean, and the blankets had holes." He shook his head at my ignorance and agreed to tally up my bill using the "regular" rate instead of the "luxury" rate.

"*Merci*," I said, laying cash on the counter as he wrote my receipt.

But as he scribbled, his pale cheeks flushed pink. "You Americans don't understand old things," he said, handing me the slip. "You want everything new."

"My house is a hundred years old," I said, but he wasn't finished.

"And now," he said, leaning forward to peer at me, "I will tell you two other things wrong with Americans." Holding up two big fingers in a V, he stood up from his stool, gazed down at me, and proceeded. "Thing one. Americans feel entitled to not be bothered by other people's cigarette smoke."

Quite true, I nodded.

"And two: Americans are hung up about sex."

That caught my attention. "Absolutely," I laughed.

He hadn't expected me to agree, and now he almost smiled. He leaned toward me again. "When my daughter was fifteen and she told me she had a boyfriend, I was so *happy* for her. Now she could really begin exploring! But when we see American movies, the parents of teenagers are going"—he put all ten fingertips onto his head—"*aghhh!*"

I nodded. "It's because," I told him, "parents are worried about pregnancy and diseases and bad experiences. And we're uncomfortable thinking about kids and sex."

"Yes, *yes*! The parents are too shy!" Wide-eyed, he shook his head. "Too shy even to *talk* about it!" It was a mindset he seemed unable to inhabit for even a second.

Eager not to fit *all* of his pigeonholes, I ignored the fact that his data came from Hollywood and told the innkeeper I was already well aware of this issue and that yes, the stock American approach to teens and sex is negative and unhelpful, and that a great many of us hope to do better. He was so relieved to hear it that he reached to shake my hand, and we thereby made amends.

But later that day as we drove south, I wondered if I should have been so smug. Buckled into car seats and eons from teen romance, Caroline and Libby had so far passed the day's drive shouting about cows and sheep. What were the chances I'd really want to take any-thing other than the typical, disapproving approach when my kids became interested in sex? Was I really so evolved and relaxed and lib-erated that the innkeeper's stereotypes didn't all apply to me? Or had he in fact described me perfectly? And wasn't there another parent who should expect to have a say?

I told Dan about the innkeeper and his daughter, and he laughed.

"But wait," I said, "I want to ask you a question. Is there any way you can imagine us being totally *happy* for our daughter if she gets in-volved with someone at fifteen? Like for us to be genuinely *thrilled* for her to start exploring her sexuality with a partner?"

He groaned a little. Then sighed. But he didn't say *no way.*

"So what would it take for you and me to get to that place?" I asked. "Would we even *want* to?"

He let out a hesitant yes but was quick to qualify it. "But in a way, that would take a whole social shift. Not just one family. It also de-pends on the parents of the boyfriend—"

"Or girlfriend," I said.

"Whatever. It also depends on the other parents and kids in the community. Even if *we* could get there, we'd still be living in the American paradigm where for the typical guy, sex is a conquest. And if that's the situation, if the guy's a shitbag"—he glanced into the back-seat and lowered his voice—"then no. I can't get excited about my daughter being a part of that. I'd want her to recognize the problem. But if it's an actual caring relationship, I don't know—then maybe that's different."

"Maybe," I said, still trying to picture it.

Some years after our visit to Burgundy, when Caroline was almost in middle school, I brought up the story of the French innkeeper with an American friend. She listened and then paused thoughtfully. "What nobody's talking about," she finally said, "is how do we *prepare* our daughters and sons for sex?"

It struck me as such a forward-thinking question, a modern, al-most radical evolution of the old "How do we keep them from do-ing it?" dilemma that has foiled parents and powers-that-be since the swampy dawn of time. But then I had to wonder: What would be the point of this preparation? Dan and I had talked about whether we could imagine jumping for joy *à la française* about a sexually active teen, and even whether we could bring ourselves to want that. But we'd left the bigger question unanswered: *Why* would we want that for our kids? That's what I wanted to learn about.

A young Dutch friend who had grown up in southern France had explained to me the cultural nuances of my lecture from the inn-keeper: while it is more typically French to swoon for sensuousness and romance, it is more typically Dutch to pragmatically accept that most people begin having sex in their teens. But in either culture, the basic reaction is the same: *Love it or not, we have to embrace this.*

That couldn't be more different from the conventional American stance, which runs a bit more along the lines of "over my dead body, darling." In fact, in *Not Under My Roof*, social scientist Amy Schalet observes that while nine out of ten Dutch parents say they would allow their teenager to have their boyfriend or girlfriend sleep over, an equal proportion of American parents say they would never consider it.

Both Dutch and American adolescents have a similar average age for first intercourse—about seventeen and rising. But the extent to which they describe their first sexual intercourse as wanted, well-timed, and enjoyed differs dramatically. Six in ten young American men and four in ten of their female peers say they "really wanted" their first sexual intercourse at the time it happened, with the rest saying they were ambivalent or unhappy with the timing. By contrast, nine out of ten Dutch boys *and* girls say their first intercourse was desired, within their control, and enjoyable.

It's worth noting here that I don't use "virginity" as a technical term because ideas about how to define that word are so varied that I find it has no specific meaning. As Scarleteen founder Heather Corinna puts it in *S.E.X.*, a thoroughgoing sexuality guide for teens and young adults, "what it means to be a virgin—if virginity is a construct you want to work with—really can be defined only by you, and it has to do with how you define sex." Of course, "sex" is another word with many meanings, yet this one I do feel comfortable using despite its occasional ambiguity. Here's the difference I see: unlike "sex," the word "virginity" is harder to separate from timeworn notions of judgment. I also don't want to put particular importance on virginity, or "losing" it, as a rite of passage. "As out there as it may seem," Corinna writes, "you might give some thought to abandoning the concept of virginity altogether. However nicely or in different contexts some present it now, it is an idea that throughout history has been sexist, heterosexist, classist, and oppressive." And besides, pinpointing a particular sexual moment as the most important one causes everyone to miss the point: sexuality unfolds over a lifetime—from babyhood, as we've seen— and it deserves ongoing care and attention. Becoming sexually active, when this choice is truly within an individual's control, is better understood as a progression of behaviors and activities that may or may not eventually include intercourse, which may or may not be heterosexual intercourse. Sexual activity can also be a stop-and-start venture over time with a particular partner or different people. So when I talk about sexual behavior, I want that term to encompass the many varied definitions of sex that individuals use for themselves.

Still, since data can help us shape better policies and approaches, experts do try to plot and understand what adolescents are doing when. Unfortunately, most of the "first sex" data we have to work with still focus on penis-in-vagina intercourse as the key indicator of sexual experience. This renders some of our most relied-on statistics entirely noninclusive and therefore not necessarily generalizable, so I use them cautiously with that caveat.

Although the number of Americans who describe their first sexual experience as wanted is thankfully trending higher—a sign of improved assertiveness, less coercion, or both (at least for first intercourse), more than half still say they wish they had waited longer. So either adults aren't doing enough to keep young lovers apart, or we aren't doing enough to teach them how to decide if they are actually ready for sex. Either way, we leave them infantilized and sorely unprepared.

Acceptance has slowly increased over the years, but the majority of Americans still consider sex between teenagers to be immoral. In a 2017 Gallup poll, 64 percent of Americans called teen sex morally unacceptable, rating it equally as objectionable as the use of pornography. The only sex-related measures less acceptable were polygamy and extramarital affairs. Yet attitudes are shifting: a strong majority of Americans now consider unmarried sex between adults, having a baby outside marriage, and same-sex marriage to be morally acceptable.

Given all that, I had to wonder: What exactly *is* so terrible about teen sex? Why does the very thought of it make so many of us cringe, freeze, or reflexively put our foot down? What are we most worried about?

The first and most obvious answers are pregnancy and infections, despite the fact that teens in other countries have proven capable of using birth control and barriers effectively. And certainly in some devoutly religious contexts, premarital sex is considered sinful and therefore not negotiable. Beyond that, many adults aren't sure that adolescents are capable of mature, committed relationships and see teen sex as nothing more meaningful than pots of hormones carelessly allowed to boil over. Some parents worry their children don't fully understand the emotional bond—sometimes wonderful, sometimes all too overpowering—that can follow sexual involvement. And honestly, we American adults, with all of the sexual shame and judgment and prudery we inherit, may not exactly have the most healthy, satisfying, and pleasurable sex lives ourselves. What, we might wonder, do they really have to look forward to? Our own ho-hum or negative sexual experiences may set us up as parents to suspect that adolescents have overblown expectations of physical intimacy and that our kids will get involved in sex only to find themselves disappointed and regretful— or worse, mistreated or even exploited. Plus, sex is an adult responsibility, so kids who do it should be living on their own. Isn't that the definition of adulthood? And anyway, many parents figure, *we* had to sneak around; wasn't that just part of growing up?

These concerns are not small, and they are not unfounded. But when I took a hard look, I couldn't see how any of them, except perhaps the religion question, present impossible barriers to finding a middle ground when it comes to teenagers and sex.

In some cases, our objections rely on outdated information. For example, parents and health practitioners have operated for years under the impression that the younger kids start having sex, the more likely they are to engage in delinquent behaviors later. Federal policy continues to reflect this view in section 510 of the Social Security Act, which funds abstinence-only education as described in the previous chapter, specifying that "a mutually faithful monogamous relationship in context of marriage is the expected standard of human sexual activity" and that "sexual activity outside of the context of marriage is likely to have harmful psychological and physical effects."

But recent research debunks the contention that teen sex is inherently harmful, revealing instead that people who first have sex as teenagers—even as younger teenagers—show no increase in antisocial behavior and in fact may go on to have healthier and more satisfying relationships. Furthermore, some experts say it stands to reason that pleasurable sex in a positive relationship can be healthy for teenagers in many of the same ways that it's good for adults, increasing overall well-being, including physical and mental health. And American gender experts, Schalet points out, "argue that adolescent sexuality— conceived broadly, to include feelings, actions, and identities—is a premier arena for the expression, transmission, and challenging of gender inequality." That "challenging of" piece captures my hopes for the next generation.

Dutch parents, too, have their prickling fears about teens and sex. They're just different fears. So while "Americans say, 'Oh, I don't want you to get pregnant, so you'd better not do anything at all,'" said Karen, the Dutch mother of three teenage daughters who has lived in the United States for twenty years, "maybe Dutch parents say, 'Oh, I hope you don't get raped; that's really emotional and devastating.'" Which is not to say that American parents aren't just as worried about rape, only that Dutch parents see sexual violence as something less reliably preventable than pregnancy.

Whereas American parents who forbid teen sex relinquish the opportunity to contribute guidance and advice on their children's first forays into sexual intimacy, Dutch parents have figured out that embracing their children's sexuality buys them the opportunity to stay involved and give input. And to my surprise, Dutch teenagers say they *like* being able to consult their parents when they face big decisions about dating, love, and sex—not to mention drugs, alcohol, and other potentially risky firsts of young adulthood.

From what I've seen, Dutch teenagers are almost unbelievably open with their parents about sex. Most Dutch parents anticipate that they will be informed before their children have sex for the first time—or at least soon after—and that they will contribute to relevant decisions, whether that's where to keep the condoms or where the young lovers will sleep. Schalet quotes a girl describing how her parents reacted when they learned she'd begun having intercourse with her boyfriend: "'My father said, "Sixteen is a beautiful age."...My mother thought it was really great. She did not mind because she knows how serious we are.'"

But that doesn't mean those parents want or expect to get too deep in the details. In general, they see the intimate particulars of a person's sex life—even if that person is their teenager—as private. The idea is that anyone conducting a healthy and responsible sex life is entitled to their sweet secrets.

Certainly some Dutch teenagers do go behind their parents' backs and sneak around, whether for sex or to do other things of which they know their families disapprove. But for the most part, and far more so than their American counterparts, Dutch parents know what's going on. By trading in strict prohibitions for "soft" power, Schalet says, they keep themselves in a position to teach, advise, and protect their kids both physically and emotionally.

The Dutch example also suggests that learning to sneak around *à l'américaine* isn't a necessary stop on the route to maturity. In fact, some observers suggest that the furtive, antisocial sex one learns while fearful of getting caught could be a source of the American "hookup culture" that parents and sociologists have increasingly worried about. The more I learned, the more I had to wonder: Could we steer American young adult sexuality toward meaningfulness and equity simply by taking the taboo out of teen sex and getting more involved?

On an unusually dark, rainy autumn evening in 2015, I saw how this might look when I grabbed a dish cloth to wipe down my bike seat and pedaled off across Amsterdam to a cozy, brick-front bookshop near the Rijksmuseum. As I made my way there, I thought I was pretty clever. Dan and I had brought the kids to stay in the Netherlands for several weeks while I researched the Dutch approach to educating young people about sexuality. I happened to see an event listing for *Pubermania*, a book by Ingrid van Essen and Kiki Mol, both puberty experts and mothers. This was going to be perfect!

But soon after I settled in, I realized I had brought my own limited definition to the word "puberty." The talk was interactive, with the authors presenting a roadmap to parent-*puber* relationships while the parents interspersed their most pressing questions about raising teenagers. But nobody talked about puberty the way I'd always thought about it. No periods? No shaving? No acne or horn-doggery? Mood swings did come up, but nothing about body changes and only a few words about sex. I sneaked a glance at the book's table of contents just to reassure myself it didn't skip over sexual maturation entirely. Nope—there it was. Honestly, I was confused. If this was a talk about puberty, where were the usual gory subjects?

Out in the open already, that's where. It dawned on me as the evening went on that these parents didn't need help talking with their kids about changing bodies or the nuances of love and sex. They'd been doing that for years already. And that meant they could focus on something they considered even more important: strengthening bonds with kids who are becoming independent. What I learned that night as the mom of two younger students was that in puberty, body changes and sexual urges are not the most important things going on, parenting-wise. The most important thing going on is nothing less than the forging of a new parent-child relationship. The quality of that relationship can determine whether a child's first steps into adulthood—including sexuality—will entail silence, sneaking, and deceit or be guided by openness, communication, and mutual consideration with their parents.

The parents sitting around me in the bookshop that night—a mix of couples sitting shoulder-to-shoulder with raincoats draped over their chairs, plus quite a few individual mothers and fathers—had clearly begun their work years earlier. All along, they'd been banking on something I'd never considered until that moment: the counter-intuitive (to me) yet totally logical idea that parents who start talking early, honestly, and openly about sexuality with tiny tots can expect a powerful return on that investment in the form of *more* control over their children's sex lives later. With countless early, normalized conversations, they'd built trust with their kids, priming them to share more and listen better when they got older. According to Schalet, those open lines of communication allow Dutch parents to hold more sway over when, where, with whom, and under what conditions their teenagers do eventually begin experiencing sexual intimacy. That doesn't mean that parenting teenagers becomes a breeze—after all, these moms and dads were still attending a book talk for insight into the *tienerbrein*. But there was a very specific flavor to the wisdom they sought: they wanted to know how to stay *close* with their kids. Nothing else, it seemed, mattered so much.

I was seeing the heart of the difference, described so well by Schalet, between Dutch and American attitudes toward adolescent sexuality. Fueling the difference of opinion about whether parents can reasonably support their teenagers' sexual activity are the two cultures' contrasting ideas about what adulthood is. American parents tend to define adulthood as being "on your own"—financially independent or married. Therefore, in order to become adults, teenagers need to separate from their parents.

But Dutch parents see a harmonious family bond as something that should not be disrupted regardless of whether a teenager has progressed to making their own decisions about mature activities such as sex. That's why even though they generally accept their teenagers' sex lives, Dutch parents are not indifferent about who their kids partner with. They want to meet and talk to their children's boyfriends and girlfriends, and, a lot like what Dan had once said, they wanted the chance to see for themselves whether their teen has settled for anything less than a fair, kind, and evenhanded relationship. This is how Dutch parents confound clichés about what it means to be "open." Some of their biggest reasons for supporting teen sexuality are to preserve a close-knit family, to raise young adults who self-regulate, and to help their kids avoid promiscuity and practice respectful monogamy. (Even though they become sexually active at around the same age as their Dutch peers, American teenagers are more likely to have multiple partners.)

One aspect of establishing monogamy is figuring out how to integrate a new partner with one's family, which obviously can't take place behind parents' backs. Schalet has pointed out that in contrast to American messages about abstinence, purity, and marriage, the more positive Dutch outlook on teen love and sexuality leaves room for courtship—serious partnerships between teenagers in which they can practice the benefits of steady monogamy as long as they practice its values: mutual respect, affection, communication, trust, and honesty. In this paradigm, Dutch boys aren't ashamed to feel and express romantic emotions, while Dutch girls are raised to defend not so much their "purity" but their right to seek and experience pleasure. This plays out well for everyone: Dutch men and women become equally assertive at telling partners what they want (and don't) in bed. This comfortable assertiveness goes well beyond the boudoir; it's also expressed in the everyday interactions of work, family, and civic life.

But "simply telling kids sex is fine isn't necessarily any more helpful than telling them sex is bad," Ariel Levy points out in her book *Female Chauvinist Pigs*. "Both of these approaches can ultimately have the same result: a silence about the complexities of desire, feminine desire in particular." So if it isn't just a matter of giving a thumbs-up when kids announce they're becoming sexually active, then what, I wanted to know, would it actually *look* like for parents like Dan and me to prepare our children for their first experiences of sexual intimacy—and to strike a note of wise welcome when (ideally with a bit of notice) the time eventually arrived? Certainly some American parents are already trying to accomplish this: they're among the 10 percent or so Schalet found who *would* consider letting their kids have an intimate sleepover at home. And although that's a small fraction, I didn't have to look far to find them. Plenty of American friends—mostly parents of younger kids—offered to connect me with families they knew who had chosen an accepting, pragmatic stance toward their teenagers' sex lives.

And so, on a radiant Seattle afternoon in October 2017, I settled into a study room at the local library to chat with a mother and daughter who, we quickly discovered, happened to live opposite my house on the very same block. Fresh from a walk in the blazing fall sunshine, the cheerful pair introduced themselves: first Melissa, the pewter-ponytailed mother of three adolescents. Originally from Minnesota, she worked for an environmental conservation firm. Then her sixteen-year-old daughter Kendra, with cropped blond hair and a sprinkling of freckles, reached to shake my hand with a big smile and a tiny glint from her slender silver nose ring. Kendra, who along with her two younger brothers was homeschooled, loved thrift-store shopping, the great outdoors, her family, and her boyfriend of two years. The young couple shared a sexual relationship, which was something their parents knew and accepted.

I wanted to hear about that from Melissa and Kendra. Given that my oldest child stood at the threshold of adolescence, I also wanted their advice. Although I had met Dutch parents who went along with their teenagers' sex lives, it was different to imagine how a typical American family could pull off that kind of openness in a social context that's so disapproving of teen sex.

Melissa said that when she was a high schooler in the 1980s becoming interested in sex, she wasn't free to talk with her parents about that. From a great distance, she admired the example of her same-age Swedish pen pal. Both girls started having sex at around sixteen, but while Melissa said she relied on her boyfriend to have a condom, she learned in letters that her Swedish friend was on the pill—and didn't need to hide her sex life from her parents. Melissa also sensed that her friend had more agency in her own decisions about sex. "I was pressured in," she said, explaining that she would have chosen different timing but didn't know at the time that she should have had more say.

Still, "once I was in, I was like *Oh, this is fun! This is enjoyable. I like it*," she explained. "But I still didn't have any information." On a visit to Sweden, the teenage Melissa got to know her pen pal's friends and connected with a particular boy in the group. Her host parents gave Melissa and her flame the same courtesy they offered their own daughter: privacy for intimacy right within their home.

By the time she met her husband and became a mother, Melissa knew she wanted to emulate the Swedish example. "I wanted to be super open. I wanted my kids to know anything and everything. I wanted to *talk* to them about anything and everything. But," she said, a wave of emotion clouding her expression, "I don't think I ever really thought, *This is when I want my kids to have sex* and *this is what it will be like* and *this is what I will do*." So when Kendra, her oldest, hit age twelve and started having boyfriends, "I think I started to panic a little bit. I remember feeling kind of flummoxed, like *Okay, now this is more real*. My big fear was that she would be pushed into something she wouldn't want to be doing."

So when the moment came, what *did* Melissa do?

It was a spring evening after dinner. Kendra was almost fifteen, and for six months she had been dating Thad—a boy three years older whom Melissa and her husband, as well as their two sons, had enjoyed getting to know. They liked his parents, too.

As Kendra recalled the moment, she'd gone to Melissa's side at the kitchen table after dinner one night and said, "Mom? I think I'm ready to have sex."

"And?" I asked.

"She wasn't pleased," Kendra said.

"I cried," Melissa told me, glancing sheepishly at her daughter.

"I was nervous to tell her," Kendra said. "I wanted her to know, and she wanted me to tell her. We wanted that relationship." But when it came down to it, "she didn't tell me that she was thrilled."

Still, she seized the moment, deciding to take out pen and paper to make a list of things for Kendra to consider and talk with Thad about. Particularly given the potentially complicated age difference between the two, Melissa wanted to be sure her daughter understood the powerful emotional bond that sex can forge. She also suggested that the young couple discuss who would decide what to do if, despite plans to use two types of protection, a pregnancy were to happen.

"I also wanted her to know that she still needed to be involved with her family," Melissa said. "She still needed to do all her jobs and her homework, and she couldn't just go off into this other realm."

The two came up with a substantive list, and Kendra used it.

"I probably still have the sticky note somewhere," she said with a soft smile. (Around that time I found a similar list of such discussion topics in the Scarleteen book *S.E.X.*)

"It mattered to me," Melissa said, "that it wasn't a whim. That they were willing to listen to my list, and willing to think and talk more before they jumped in."

A few weeks later, still feeling ambivalent, Melissa took Kendra to see an adolescent medicine doctor for birth control. Melissa cried again at the appointment.

"I have to say I went in dragging my feet," Melissa said. "At this point, I felt *she's supposed to wait at least a couple more years.* I think there's this big idea in this country that there's a certain age that it's okay, and she was not at that age yet. And all of my peers around me"—parents Melissa described as liberal and who'd had sex themselves in their mid-teens—"were all telling me they thought it was much too young. I felt crazy for considering it."

"And I think I felt guilty for not wanting to wait," Kendra said, turning to her mom. "I wanted you to be on board with it. I felt like I was hurting you by not waiting. However, I didn't want to wait. So I didn't."

It struck me that Kendra was clear on something at the very center of sexual health: whose decisions are whose.

A few weeks after her doctor's appointment, Kendra and Thad were unusually late to a family birthday party at the neighborhood beach.

"We were all at the beach going, 'Where's Kendra?'" Melissa said. "And Grammy's like, 'They're at your house having sex!'"

"She was right!" Kendra laughed.

Since then, Melissa said, "I've thought a lot about it, and I think so much of it for me was feeling like I was a bad parent" for not raising a child who would choose to wait longer.

I knew what she meant. Having spent several years of my young daughters' lives openly researching, writing, and talking about a book on the normalization of sex with a rather colorful avalanche of books and articles taking over our small house, I'd had plenty of similar concerns. Even though I knew that sensibly educating kids about sex doesn't harm them, I still had occasional niggling worries that my daughters might come to the kitchen table and declare themselves ready sooner than they might have if I had only…what? Kept my mouth shut and my fingers crossed? Spent more quality time talking about *other* things? Forbidden sex until they owed taxes? There was no logical or scientific answer, but I identified with Melissa's worry.

Melissa mentioned the doubt that creeps in when she sees articles suggesting that kids with high-quality parent relationships—ones full of warmth, closeness, and support—wait longer to have sex for the first time. Yet here was a mother who clearly had a warm and trusting relationship with her daughter. She took a close and loving interest in Kendra's schooling, friendships, and feelings. Their family of five loved to hike through Pacific Northwest forests and regularly shared family dinners at home, where a well-loved piano graced the dining area and two labradors kept company. Even though the research Melissa had read about only offers an association and doesn't suggest that detached parenting *causes* kids to have sex younger than they otherwise would, I could see the insult of the suggestion. Clearly, the pair sitting across from me simply enjoyed being together. After our visit, they planned to stop by the local thrift shop. And later that afternoon, I would see the two of them bicycling side by side through our neighborhood.

Sitting across from this mother and daughter, it struck me that we need to change the big question about teens and sex. What if our most cherished benchmark for a teenager's first sexual experience wasn't *when* it happens, but *how positively*? What if we could shift our focus to ensuring that kids have sex safely in caring relationships when they truly want to? What if we did everything possible to prepare young people for the potentially formative and deeply meaningful life experience that sex can be? What if it isn't anyone's fault if a teenager has sex for the first time at a particular age, but it's to a guardian's *credit* if that first encounter is safe, consensual, wanted, and nice? When we're dealing with what really matters about sex, I realized, agonizing about age (as long as laws are followed) almost seems arbitrary.

Looking back, Melissa said, "I wish I would have been less concerned about what other people thought. I wish I'd been less scared and more focused on Kendra and what she was experiencing. I wish I would have been more happy for her, and celebratory about the big step she felt ready to take."

Kendra said her closest friends have enjoyed fairly open lines of communication with their parents about sex. But she wasn't sure if their parents would go so far as to allow boyfriends or girlfriends to sleep over in their kids' bedrooms. There's something about that final logistical question—*where* adolescent sex will be permitted—that remains a hitch even for the most open-minded parents. And that may be where the biggest concrete difference between Dutch and American approaches to teen sexuality still rests.

"Not under my roof" is such a well-worn directive that even American parents who know and accept that their teens are having sex might never think to ask where it's happening. But Melissa thought about it and even raised the question with Thad's mom. "In the end, we were all in agreement: We wanted it to be in a good place." So, while it was a little difficult to welcome at first, Thad began sleeping over in Kendra's room, and vice versa.

Allowing the couple to sleep together at home "just seemed logical to me," Melissa said. "I'm okay with weird places if it's a good, safe place, but I didn't want them to have icky places just because there wasn't a better option."

Her reasons—safety and comfort—mirrored those of Dutch parents and experts. But the Dutch reasoning extends even further to safeguarding the intimate cocoon.

Bram Bakker, a Dutch father, psychiatrist and co-author with Marina van der Wal of the 2017 parenting guide *Vrij(be)wijs* on preparing children for love and sex, wrote about returning home from an evening out to hear his son and the boy's partner "groaning" downstairs. His reaction: "Better at home than in places not intended for that. And better relaxed than full of stress, because someone might pop up in a public place."

Reading that gave me goose bumps. It struck me that a parent who can think in that way—who would hate to see teen lovers startled—has gotten beyond simply tolerating a teen's forays into the territory of sex. A dad who wants to shield his teenager's early intimate encounters from disturbance and embarrassment extends the same tender regard as when he tiptoed past his crib to leave him dreaming in peace. He feels a *stake* in his child's development and truly wants things to go well. He still believes his role is to provide safe haven. Only now, he must also grant trust and let go.

"Ultimately it's about this: allowing them to experiment in peace and security. Their own room is the only place where they can have that kind of privacy," the authors write, finding little patience for hesitant parents. "Screwing is what happens in the bushes under the portico. But if someone wants to discover lovemaking, then you give them space in a secure place—one they choose themselves. And if that is your daughter's bedroom, then, as parents, sorry, you might see things. Or you'll hear noises. So be it."

Their advice is for parents to fully finance and help procure birth control and barriers, including condoms, which should be kept in a communal household space such as the bathroom that doesn't require getting past a parent. (They consider the old saw "If they're old enough to have sex, they're old enough to pay for their own protection" to be utterly reckless and irresponsible on any grown-up's part.) But don't count how many condoms are missing after the weekend. Teenagers should have confidential lines of communication with a trusted health care provider. And any adolescent with female reproductive parts whose partner has a penis should have an open door (or strong encouragement) to obtain birth control such as the pill or a long-acting reversible method such as an IUD or implant without judgment from parents or physicians. If an adolescent has a doctor or nurse who dabbles in the slightest bit of sex shaming, they should move on to someone more professional.

When it comes to offering our American kids their independence, we parents can go very different ways. Dan told me about a basketball teammate with a smartphone app set to sound a noisy alarm any time his high school daughter strayed too close to her boyfriend's house. "I'm determined to get her through her sophomore year without getting pregnant," the dad explained. (Dan didn't ask why only sophomore year.) Meanwhile, a friend recently decided not to buy a house he loved because his only child, who would soon be a teenager, would need to sleep in a bedroom with its own exterior door. "I don't *think* so," he laughed.

But then there are theorists such as architect Christopher Alexander, who describe that very sort of freedom as a solution to the painful schism that too often wrecks American parent-teen relationships. In his iconic design system *A Pattern Language*, he encourages families to accommodate adolescence by creatively modifying the home to include a "teenager's cottage":

> To really help a young person go through this time, home life must strike a subtle balance. It must offer tremendous opportunities for initiative and independence, as well as a constant sense of support, no matter what happens. A teenager needs a place in the house that has more autonomy and character and is more a base for independent action than a child's bedroom or bed alcove. He needs a place from which he can come and go as he pleases, a place within which his privacy is respected. At the same time he needs to establish a closeness with his family that is more mutual and less strictly dependent than ever before.

This, too, makes a compelling kind of sense. French parents, Dutch parents, and other parents who embrace, support, and even find ways to pleasantly anticipate their children's sexual emergence can't be explained away as careless hedonists. They choose to be supportive for entirely clear reasons: health, happiness, and social equality. At base, they think it's more important to protect their young from illness, pregnancy, and educational interruptions than it is to prevent them from having sex. Beyond that, they know that sex can be an overall positive aspect of human experience and should be nurtured as such.

As I thought ahead about my own children's first forays into sex, I saw the need to shift away from trying to manipulate *when* that milestone will happen and instead to start focusing on ensuring that it will go *well*. The future is built on the lessons we learn in relationships, and parents who find ways to be involved with their teenagers' decisions about intimacy have a hand, at least, in shaping those lessons. So for me the question became how to be more like my one-time adversary, the French innkeeper. First, don't clean; grime is so charming! But also: find the part of young love that warms your heart as a parent. Could I get beyond simply preparing my kids to be safe and all the way to the enthusiasm Melissa wished she'd felt when Kendra told her she was ready?

I'm probably more like a Dutch parent than a French one; I'm not daydreaming about super-zingy orgasms for my kids, although I do wish them pleasure. But it was in daydreaming about the future that I recently felt the first inklings of joy and anticipation. What I visualized was nothing graphic, only my small living room with four people gathered: me and Dan in the armchairs, our daughter and her sweetheart arm-in-arm on the couch. The conversation is about sex, something the two teenagers are thinking about and want to be prepared for. Each of us blushes now and then, but the tone is cheerful, and there's laughter as we talk things over. And here's the precise moment, the one that makes my heart thrill: I see my child's partner turn and look at her, make eye contact, think about her, squeeze her thoughtfully. She cuddles in return and smiles across the room at us. I see her in love, and loved beautifully back.

Ah, here it is, I imagine thinking. *I've been waiting for this for you!*

Conclusion: Bringing It Home

Cultures can change. They're actually pretty fragile.
All you need is critical mass on a new idea.

—Lisa Wade, social scientist and
author of *American Hookup*

Something funny happened the summer my girls were six and ten. We were on vacation, and I sat in the middle of the backseat of an Uber with an arm around each kid as we caromed through the heart of Rome on a sweltering August afternoon. Dan sat in the front seat co-navigating with the nervous driver, who told us he'd just moved from Florence and didn't know his way around yet. He kept apologizing, certain he'd chosen a poor route to get us from the Colosseum (too big, too hot, too exhausting) to the children's attractions in the Pincio Gardens (Pedal rickshaws? *Antiquities anschmiquities!*). But we didn't care which way we got there; we were riding around Rome, and there was so much to see.

As we zoomed down a wide, busy avenue, something caught my eye. It was a smallish vending machine not unlike the ones that dispense pads and tampons in public restrooms. But this one hung above the sidewalk just outside a pharmacy. In a flash I realized what it was.

"Oh my gosh, you guys!" I shrieked, startling everyone. "That's the coolest thing! Look!" I pointed.

"What? What?" the kids cried, craning their necks.

"It's a *condom* machine! Outside on the *street*! So people can get condoms even when the pharmacy is *closed*!"

"Geez Mom," Libby said, shaking her head. She took a breath and settled back down in her seat. Dan's only reaction was a tiny hint of a smile.

"What's a condom again?" Caroline asked.

The nervous driver, appearing a bit pale in the rearview mirror, blinked rapidly.

"That's that stretchy barrier that a person can put over their penis—or actually they have them for vaginas too—when they want to have sex without sharing germs. It's kind of like a rubber glove for those body parts."

"Oh yeah," she nodded. "But I still don't get why they need it all of a sudden. Didn't they know they were going to have sex?"

"A lot of the time people do, but sometimes people decide they want to have sex even if they weren't planning on it. So with those vending machines, no matter what time it is, they can be safe and protected! All they have to do is walk down the sidewalk and pop in a little money. That is just so cool to see!"

The driver turned on the radio—rather loudly, I thought.

Caroline turned back to watch the city whizzing past her window.

"Look there," Dan said. "You can see the Colosseum!" We were definitely going in circles. But in that moment I knew we had made other, more important kinds of progress. As random as it may have been, my outburst about the condom dispenser had been truly spontaneous. I hadn't thought about it. I hadn't rehearsed what to say or agonized over the perfect moment. I never paused to muster up courage or even take a deep breath. I was just genuinely delighted the way I'd been earlier that day when we'd spotted an adorable mechanical wooden Pinocchio pedaling a tricycle in a shop window—and so, quite naturally, I said so. As the mom who had not so long before quietly hoped the whole sex thing would somehow magically explain itself, I had to marvel at the distance we'd covered.

Only a few years earlier, flummoxed and tongue-tied about the facts of life, I had noticed that not every society treats bodies as shameful and sex as offensive. I saw that many of my international friends were raising kids far more likely to have optimal sexual health and self-esteem, better sex lives, and more advantages of gender equality than their average American peers. I'd gone to see how they accomplished this, and most of all, while my kids were still little, to find out if I could reinvent my own philosophy about sex, clarify my guiding principles, and discover approaches more practical and more effective than the old-fashioned birds-and-bees checklist.

Without knowing how much help these suggestions will be to you, I want to share some of the specific things I've tried in the past, the approaches I'm using right now, and ideas I'm thinking about for the future. Take what you want, leave what doesn't fit, and most of all, please reach out to share your own best tips and tools.

Baby and Toddlerhood: Bodies Are Bodies and Our Bodies Are Ours

Soon after we first moved to Amsterdam, Dan and I enrolled two-year-old Caroline in a Montessori school where teaching kids how to be independent with their body functions was part of the pedagogy. Toilet learning is not the same as teaching about sexuality, but it is full of learning opportunities for children and parents alike. Explaining that toileting contributes to a child's self-esteem, Caroline's teachers encouraged us to follow their lead in choosing our words carefully. At school, no diaper or its wearer would be called "dirty," "stinky," or "icky." Instead a diaper was simply wet, full, or dry. The teachers had learned not to wrinkle their noses or make faces when helping a child with a change of clothes or a visit to the toilet, and they instructed us to teach ourselves the same skill for normalizing body functions. Given that children who started school here were at least twelve months old and able to walk, the teachers changed diapers with the child standing up. This was considered a more respectful and dignified way of showing the children that they were no longer infants. Later, as they learned to use the bathroom (a row of tiny toilets without dividers in a non-gender-segregated bathroom), the children became more familiar with seeing genitalia and how they function. They began taking responsibility for every part of themselves, even where they couldn't see. They formed their own boundaries for privacy and touch, and as they discovered the difference between cooperating and interfering, they learned a key principle about equality. "There are always limits for each freedom," explained Heidi Philippart, the pedagogical director at 2Voices, Caroline's first school in Amsterdam. "A lot of people misunderstand freedom," she told me. "True freedom comes from knowledge and responsibility. Your freedom ends where somebody else's rights begin."

One of our most important lessons from 2Voices came the day one of the teachers stopped Dan and me at the door. She had something to say about our two-year-old, who was by then the oldest to wear diapers in her class. As her parents, we felt it was too soon to teach her to use the toilet. "She is ready," the teacher told us firmly in Dutch-accented English. "It is you who are not." After I got over feeling ticked off, I started trying to pay attention to the difference between my own readiness and my daughter's—in all areas of life—which meant giving her good chances to grow even when I wished she'd stay little and life would stay simple. Instead of telling myself *she's probably not ready,* the teachers pushed me to change my questions: *How can I give her more autonomy? How will this independence empower her?*

Later, I received a Dutch pamphlet about raising children ages zero to six that coached parents to begin normalizing body parts and encouraging their children's sexual self-esteem right from the beginning. Citing research that frequently snuggled babies ultimately think more highly of themselves and their bodies, it suggested that parents pause after removing a full diaper to "sweetly rub your baby with some oil. This way you make it clear that a soiled diaper change can also have a nice side." Yes, it might seem a little excessive to coo over a baby's diaper area, but think of how often we do just the opposite. These were our first small lessons about why and how to teach a child that her body—and all bodies—are normal and right.

"All those little aversions we have as adults, the child absorbs them," Heidi told me. "It gives them a warped image of the self and the reality of the body and life." Telltale of this, she said, would be a child who laughs or feels embarrassed to see nude sculptures in a museum—or the pediatrician's office in Seattle where, pressed by parent complaints, staffers pasted small bundles of fake leaves over the genitals of two fine-art nudes framed on its waiting-room walls.

By the time Libby was born, I was confident enough to tell the babysitter not to bother "redirecting" when the baby's curious hands flew down to explore during diaper changes. A child's hands, I was learning, should be free to wander over their own body. By then I also had begun turning over the idea, widely held among human rights organizations, that people of all ages and abilities are entitled to comprehensive information about sexuality. That meant honoring and answering my baby's curiosity about her body parts—and ours. We bade fond farewell to my "daddy" and Dan's "dangly bottom."

Teaching freedom from shame also meant using accurate, nondramatic body terminology in a pleasant tone of voice, just as we did around feeding and dressing. Even when Libby was too young to talk, it was good practice for me and Dan to normalize body talk around our baby and her always-listening big sister. Attending to a baby's natural right to learn about healthy sexuality also meant modeling very early lessons about consent. Even someone who hasn't learned to talk can express refusal. We practiced by paying attention to her cues about whether she liked our tickles, kisses, and cuddles, or whether she wanted her big sister to carry her in a bear hug around the house (almost always an open-mouth-laughing *yes!*)

As language emerges—or better yet, even earlier—we get to choose the terminology we'll use with the children in our care. There are purists for whom medical texts hold the only answers, but here's what I've come to: As often as possible, we should teach medically correct terms *first*, just as we teach "nose" before "schnoz." Language is flexible and naturally allows for wiggle room, so I've always liked this advice: in addition to being correct, everyday anatomical terms should be uncomplicated and should fit with what's commonly understood by doctors, teachers, and others in the culture. As a child's physiological and sexual vocabulary grows, we need to repeat and reinforce *way* more often than feels necessary. It helps to remember how frequently any person needs to review a new word or concept for it to really stick. (Five steps to proper hand washing, anyone?)

Finally, as inconvenient as this may be, it's critical to avoid putting too much stock in gender roles for babies and toddlers (or anyone else). There are no "girl" clothes or "boy" toys except the ones we can't bring ourselves to offer impartially. There is no women's work or man's job. Interrupting gender-stereotypical thinking while kids are still young isn't blue-sky idealism that helps only women by bringing men down a peg. Research tells us that a teenager or young adult who has formed gender-stereotypical beliefs will be less sexually healthy than equality-minded peers. And as the world's most gender-equal societies show us, the economic and social benefits of equal opportunities in school, work, and family life accrue to all citizens, not only to women.

Gender equality stems from early lessons like Heidi's that no person has an inherent right to interfere with another's freedom—a principle many of us know better as the golden rule. But it also comes from the roles we model as grown-ups. I'm proud of the times I've hired female carpenters and electricians, and even though my kids are getting old enough to take care of themselves at home, I haven't given up on finding boys to babysit them. I'm also working on simple little things: taking the driver's seat more often on family road trips and finding the tools or glue to fix broken toys on the spot instead of setting them aside for Daddy to fix later. Even though I'm still the main household chef, Dan has long since taken over weekend breakfasts and school-lunch-packing. And even though they're plenty old enough to pick outfits themselves, the girls still love it when he lays out their clothes.

I don't know if small role-tweaks like those really make progress, but there's one thing that certainly does make a difference, and that's teaching kids to recognize stereotypes and discrimination—in matters of gender and well beyond—all on their own. I hope we take every chance to point out to kids young and old the assumptions that marketers and even well-meaning family, friends, and educators make about gender. Why not explain how putting people in categories and then offering products to make us fit the boxes better is the oldest money-making trick in the book? As they get older, maybe we can remember to ask our kids how they like labels and limits and listen to what they say. When they can spot inequality, critique it for themselves, and identify the need for change, then they'll be good to go, and all of us future-thinking mothers can finally go back to eating bonbons on the couch.

Kidding, of course. I take my bonbons while marching.

Preschool: Facts and Fairness for All

At this age, things start to get really fun. It's time for chitchat about how babies can be made—and, often relevant for preschoolers soon to have siblings, how they can be birthed and fed and bathed and cared for. We can mention that sex is something that older people might do not only to reproduce but also because it feels nice. This is a time to remind kids that love and affection and partnerships and family can form in all variety of combinations. I liked using *The Family Book* by Todd Parr as an easy way to frame that conversation. No matter what a preschooler's felt gender or eventual sexual orientation, these messages will allow them to feel valued and know that their body and heart deserve the same attentive, loving care as anyone else's.

As any caregiver knows, preschool play makes all kinds of room for learning. Although they make for expensive toys, it wouldn't be a bad idea to leave the tampons and pads down where kids can play with them and ask about them. It wouldn't be against the law to do the same with condoms. And heck, the lube, too. Conversation starters, every one. But what about more difficult, unexpected subjects, such as pregnancy loss? Having been assured by several experts that it's better to say too much than too little, Dan and I decided to always try to explain the hard things too, daunting as they can be.

Building on the trust and listening we establish with babies and toddlers, we can continue coaching preschoolers to ask one another for consent before they chase, catch, lift, tickle, tackle, hug, kiss, or otherwise handle another person. Even tickling a child's back as they fall asleep at night brings opportunities: *Am I tickling the way you wanted? It's so great when you say what feels good to you.* And we continue reminding them that they get to decide whether to have their body touched. The day I learned how right that felt was the day four-year-old Libby recoiled at a nurse's brusque approach to administering vaccines. Libby was crying hard and refusing to be touched by any hand with an exam glove on it. The nurse made no attempt to hide how absurd she found my efforts to calm my daughter down—and my idea *was* a bit far-fetched: I was trying to get Libby to consent to the shots by proffering her own thigh. Finally, with a great roll of her eyes, the nurse turned to me and said, "You need to pick her up and put her on this table and hold her down so I can give her these shots."

That snapped me right to clarity. "That's not going to happen," I said.

I asked Libby if she'd like to try again some other time. She collapsed with relief in my lap. Just half an hour later, accompanied by a much more cheerful nurse, Libby proudly climbed up onto the exam table, rolled up her pant leg, and smiled. "I'm ready," she said. And she was.

Other delicate and wonderful opportunities come up at this age: The chance to normalize nonsexual nudity in the household, with freedom of choice about going bare. The discovery for children that genitals can produce nice feelings, and the chance for caregivers to acknowledge this and even say, "Isn't it nice to have body parts that can feel good?" More and more, opportunities arise to shame or not to shame. Do we insist that a three-year-old with a hand in the pants retreat to the bathroom or bedroom? Do we tell them that their body is truly their own, or only that their body is private? Those two precepts, I learned, simply cannot combine without creating a mixed message. Instead of outlawing "bare-bottom games," I found it far more pragmatic—and instructive—to offer clear rules: each child must agree to the game, no one may do pain, nothing may be inserted anywhere, and my own addition: friends should ask their parents if the same rules apply.

Preschool is also the time to start asking kids about any differences they're internalizing about boys and girls—and to start gently, playfully complicating things. Why *can't* Daddy wear Mommy's dress? What if I *did* get my hair cut shorter than his? And anyway, who gets to decide if a person is a boy or a girl? While so many young people are tenderly stepping into the freedom to be whoever they want within or beyond the old gender binary, we can practice gender-neutral language in simple everyday ways: "children" instead of boys and girls, "person" instead of man or woman. Even if we're only nudging our own minds out of gender-stereotypical thought patterns, that's worthwhile.

By the time Caroline was three and a half, I had lived in Amsterdam for a blissful eighteen months without feeling watched, ogled, judged, criticized, or shamed. From my first days in Holland, for reasons I couldn't put a finger on at first, I had felt simply acceptable, no matter whether I gussied up or went *au naturel*—without makeup, that is. Eventually, I realized one reason why I felt so very okay dwelling in this much more gender-equal society than my own: no one stared, pointed, remarked, or snickered at each other's bodies. Without that "male gaze" phenomenon first described in the 1970s by American film critic Laura Mulvey, it felt safer to slow down and walk with my head up, dwelling calmly in place. Over time, my senses reawakened, and I felt more comfortably curious about others, inhaling the passing scent of a neighbor's rained-out hair or a shopkeeper's woolen sweater. In a way I remembered from childhood, I felt attuned to the world and a renewed sense of belonging.

When we returned to the United States, I knew I'd experienced more than enough male gaze for a lifetime. "Something happens for girls between the ages of nine and ten and early adolescence, age twelve," I happened to read in a book called *Mother-Daughter Revolution* loaned to me by a friend. "A negotiation takes place where girls trade in parts of themselves in order to become women within this culture." It was a chilling point. I couldn't do anything to control how others looked at, talked to, and remarked about me and my daughters, but I *could* stop contributing to the problem, and I could model how it looks not to reinforce the game. I challenged myself to stop greeting my friends—women or men—with comments about their appearance. I decided to work on engaging with kids about something they're *doing* instead of what they're wearing. The ultimate task wasn't just to stop remarking on looks, but to actually stop *noticing* so much. All of which turned out to be super easy!

Ha.

But I must say, after a lot of practice, I did stop scanning people's outfits for points of entry to conversation. My opening lines improved, and conversations got more interesting. I discovered that even a young preschooler who would find an admiring comment on her shoes bafflingly irrelevant can offer an original response to the question "What were you busy doing before I got here?" I keep telling myself it's worth something to greet children—particularly girls, whose looks are talked about more than anyone else's—in ways that convey that they are valuable without regard to their appearance. In ways that teach them to expect to be heard and considered rather than eyeballed and appraised.

Elementary Ages: Formal Lessons, Lasting Friendships, and Feelings of Love

When my youngest hit the spring of her kindergarten year, I could hardly believe that by her age, the kids who get the best sex ed in the world—and who have the very best outcomes—begin receiving comprehensive sexuality education at school. Or that in a different context, her fourth-grade sister would have already received coed lessons with her classmates on the changes of puberty, how to maintain healthy friendships, and how to identify and react to bullying, harassment, and sexual abuse. In the United States we have our own recently updated, world-class, yet still only sparingly applied National Sexuality Education Standards (NSES) containing the core concepts about sexuality, identity, and relationships that kids need to grasp at every age from kindergarten through twelfth grade. When I want to remind myself of what health and education experts say my kids and their peers *should* be learning in their particular grades, I'll glance over the NSES, or the lesson plans in *Rights, Respect, Responsibility,* the only free, comprehensive K-12 curriculum as yet fully mapped to those standards. It's disheartening to think about what most American kids, including my own, are missing out on, but I'm prompted all over again not to give up pushing for progress. This is for no small reason: CSE promotes gender equality and reduces gender-based violence. It teaches the right to be treated with dignity and respect no matter your identity. Simply put, it elevates humanity.

Even in the rare American communities where CSE does begin in elementary school, it should be the same boogie at home: parents and caregivers repeating previous information, adding new information, posing thought-provoking questions, and grabbing ahold of whatever teaching opportunities come up. We keep talking about consent, and as kids approach adolescence, we talk about it in more nuanced detail. *Can someone who is drunk give consent? If someone consented once, does that also mean yes for next time? Do married couples need to bother with consent?* It's important, too, to remind preadolescents that feelings of attraction, desire, and pleasure can be strongly felt by anyone; they aren't reserved for a particular gender. They should know that masturbation is a normal, safe, and healthy way to feel good and to learn. And they should be taught how to end romantic relationships respectfully (for example, not via text). By sharing about our own ups and downs in love, we can help girls *and* boys learn to face rejection with integrity, emotional honesty, and grace.

In some areas of the country, independent sex educators offer talks and classes to kids and parents, but in most cases access is limited to those families with the resources to attend. More attainable offerings are available in libraries, bookshops, and online. By now I've realized that our once-hot household collection of books about bodies and babies grows tepid if it doesn't keep expanding. One of the newest additions to our shelf is Scarleteen founder Heather Corinna's *S.E.X.: The All-You-Need-To-Know Sexuality Guide to Get You Through Your Teens and Twenties.* Our oldest daughter now has a bookmark on her computer for the educational videos at Amaze.org, and she knows she can watch them whether or not her little sister is around. Parents can use the site, too, for video coaching and word-by-word scripts to help them have "the talks" with kids.

A big surprise for me was learning that the middle elementary years are a beneficial time for children to maintain substantive, authentic cross-gender friendships. Just as you wouldn't want your child to abandon cross-cultural friendships, cross-gender friendships shouldn't be left to wither without supportive adults querying the reasons and looking for ways to reinforce those connections. Many kids, it seems, *want* permission and support to maintain their cross-gender friendships. Little helps and nods of support from adults go a long way.

One of the most moving things I've learned along this journey is that it's perfectly possible and splendidly sweet for elementary-age children to fall in love now and then. Finding out that it's safe and instructive for parents to acknowledge and talk about their children's romantic feelings (rather than to pooh-pooh, negate, or minimize them) has allowed me to be excited about my daughters' occasional crushes. When my third-grader told me at bedtime all about the apple of her eye…and then another apple some months after…and then another…I could almost see her big heart fluttering against her nightgown. Sitting beside her as she radiated love and adoration, my own heart swelled. I loved knowing I didn't need to be afraid, that I shouldn't burst her bubble, and that I was free to savor those gigantic scrumptious feelings right along with her.

Adolescence: Welcoming Changes, Preserving Bonds

I used to be afraid of puberty—my own, and then my children's. What good could come of all *that*, I always wondered, despite myself. Ultimately I had very little to complain about. Body-wise, my maturation went pretty smoothly. My periods weren't crampy or unmanageable. My breasts didn't weird me out too much. The difficulty came with looking like a woman before I wanted to be one. Even though my parents were loving and supportive as my body morphed, each new physical development felt like a door closing. Eventually I came to feel at home in my body as a woman, but it's been hard to shake the worry that my own daughters might feel the same dread I did—or that despite my best intentions, they'll even catch that foreboding feeling from me. So one of my biggest stretches as I went back to reconsider how to get beyond boilerplate birds and bees as a parent was to search for ways of seeing puberty as joyful and positive. Could I learn to look forward to puberty for my kids?

Two things have helped. One is understanding far better than before that bodies are just bodies; *people* assign bodies certain values and taboos. Those are always changeable, and we can talk with kids about that. Second, nothing helps more than finding role models.

One friend told me that she had always talked up the positive about body changes but never realized how well it worked until her eighth-grade son screamed from the shower, "MOM! I need you NOW!" Hurrying that way, she thought perhaps he'd broken something. Her son charged out of the bathroom. "Look! *Look!*" he yelled with a huge smile, pointing down. She leaned in, squinting.

Yes.

There it was!

His very first pubic hair.

"Oh and it's even *curly*," she gushed without missing a beat.

To me, that story is pure triumph in a culture that so regularly makes growing-up bodies into sexualized bodies—something most young adolescents understandably wouldn't want to have. But here were a mother and son simply admiring the biological unfolding of the human form. Hearing about that moment made me think of the times my own kids had startled me with shrieks demanding that I come see: they were *finally* tall enough to turn on the bathroom faucet or reach the bedroom light switch. This was growing up: nothing less and nothing more. And yet I couldn't forget the story of another boy, nineteen years old, who had visited a therapist in my community. He had such intense shame about his pubic hairs that he'd been plucking them out with tweezers. It turned out that pornography—where the prevailing fashion was bare-shaven—had been his primary source of sexual "information." Until his therapist told him, he had no idea that pubic hair was a normal feature of mature human bodies.

And what about fashion? I can't yet know what choices my daughters will make as adolescents when retail offerings and ideas of beauty suddenly transform from childlike to steamy. For girls, clothing styles get sexier, body hair calls for attention, and fresh-washed faces might seem more conspicuous than those shining with glitter and gloss. For now, Dan and I have some basic messages for our kids. What to wear and how to look—even right down to whether or not you shave your body hair—is all about fashion (if it's not compelled by religion or other authority). I've tried to let my kids know that fashion choices aren't moves a person makes only because they identify as a certain gender, although fashion can be used to help a person express their gender. I also take pains to point out that fashions differ. Right now, I tell my daughters, kids in Moscow and Michigan and just across the city are striking different looks from the ones at our local school. Fashions come and go, they differ from place to place and culture to culture, and the most important thing to know is this: whether or not to follow a trend is always a choice. Maybe I'm hedging my bets (or making my bed), but we also talk a fair bit about the courage it takes to be an original.

As many caregivers do, I've paused often to ask myself what kind of example I'm setting for my daughters. One thing was obvious to me as soon as I had my first girl: I never wanted her to hear me complaining about my face or my body and its functions. Not the flab, not the zits, not the wrinkles, not the B.O. or the periods or the sore breasts or the bloat or anything else. And since kids can hear not only through walls but also, seemingly, across continents and between grown-ups' ears, accomplishing this meant I not only had to stop complaining but also to stop *wanting* to. I didn't have to worship my image in the mirror, but I did need to show myself some basic respect. Part of that meant getting rid of the bathroom scale before it chewed up my every good mood, and well before it became interesting to my daughters.

And I had to keep improvising. When I chose to wear makeup and my kids asked why, what reason would I give? When in midwinter I arrived home sporting fresh-lacquered toenails, how would I explain the vanity of a pedicure? What would I say about why I shave my armpits (but not often elsewhere)? Or if they saw me plucking my eyebrows or heard how much I'd spent on highlights for my hair?

The best I can do is to be clear with my kids that when I make those choices, it's not because I think something is *wrong* with my face or my hair or the other parts of me. Primping can be fun. But I want my daughters to understand that beauty treatments and routines do have high costs: not only in money but also, importantly, in time. And as my kids can see when a soccer teammate must sit out a game because she can't remove the earrings from her newly pierced ears or when a female presidential candidate is picked apart for her carefully crafted looks, fashion investments can have opportunity costs inverse to the social cachet they may bring. Kids should know that not every gender shares those costs equally. For every girl uncapping her first lipstick, there is probably a boy out exploring. And for every CEO or politician getting her hair done—something professionalism demands of her—there's a clutch of male colleagues swapping career strategies over drinks. This isn't helped by the "pink tax" in which similar products and services such as razor blades or dry cleaning, when marketed down gender lines, cost women more. And yes, many men do spend time shaving, and plenty have elaborate diets and self-care regimens. Everyone is subject to the suggestive power of fashion and advertising. Nevertheless, when it comes to looking just so, women dramatically outspend men in hours and in billions on beauty. In an accounting of her 2016 campaign, Hillary Clinton was chagrined to discover that she'd spent six hundred hours—twenty-five *days*—having her hair and makeup done. Overall, I aimed for a message about simplicity.

When my daughter wanted her first bras, a friend told me about a brand called Yellowberry. The founder's idea had been to make sporty, comfortable, colorful bras and underwear that girls would identify with—without any suggestion that pleasing onlookers has anything to do with choosing undergarments. *Gaze? Who's gazing?* After we'd put in our order online, the simple brown boxes arrived containing soft pieces wrapped in blue tissue paper and yellow ribbon. The hangtags bore empowering messages about being comfortable in one's own skin: "Girl, You. Are. Awesome," one read. "Seek and find a hug when you need one," said another. This was how I wanted to teach my daughter to shop.

Meanwhile, customized subscription period-supply delivery services and first-period kits from companies such as LOLA, Aunt Flow, and Bonjour Jolie, as well as high-design menstrual cups, environmentally friendly cloth pads, and various brands of "period panties," now aim to make menstruating visible and stylish—in some cases with rascally in-your-face advertising. (No female parts and scared of periods? Prepare to be razzed.) Normalizing periods and other changes of puberty reminded me of something Rutgers consultant Elsbeth Reitzema had told me she wanted her work to foster among Dutch adolescents: fellow-feeling across genders for the embarrassing moments of puberty—a stained skirt, a wayward erection. She said that one supportive thing schools can do is to keep bathrooms clean and well-supplied. Not all menstruating people identify as female, so emergency period supplies should be easily accessible to all genders. Every little effort adds up to combat the problem, especially for girls, of plummeting self-esteem with the onset of puberty.

But despite knowing better, when my friend informed me that her fourth-grader had gotten her first period, I blurted a pitying, "Oh, poor buddy!"

"No, you don't say that," she swiftly replied. "This is *great* news, and we are all excited about it." By "all," she meant not only herself and her daughter, Aubrey, but also the girl's father and brother. This friend of mine had always been on the ball with open, thorough sex talks, so nobody in her family was shocked by the idea of a period, and everyone around Aubrey knew it mattered to be welcoming and supportive. Her brother knew how to help if his sister (or any friend) ran into a period-related emergency (stained joggers, say, or a lack of supplies). And Aubrey was proud to tell her friends—one of whom, I am grateful to say, was my daughter—that her newly pierced ears were the laurel she'd chosen to celebrate menarche.

I kept watching and learning. While a "first moon" celebration may sound like a joke to some, others take celebrating the onset of menstruation seriously and throw period parties or host more ritualistic blessings to warmly shepherd a girl into a new phase of reproductive life. I wasn't sure at first about whether I'd want to make much fuss over a first period. Did celebrating menstruation truly normalize it, or was it a weird kind of overcompensation for what can certainly be an unpleasant part of a girl's life? I realized the decision about whether or how to celebrate should be up to my daughter. And I've come around to thinking it's best to make a plan for some—any—kind of reward. Better than leaving to chance a positive or negative association that could linger for decades.

When I think back to my first period, all I remember is the embarrassing suspicion that my neighbors could see my pad through my shorts as I pulled weeds in the front yard. So for me as a parent who has long looked askance at puberty, I must say that practice and planning do make a difference. And so does my biggest puberty role model of all: my middle school daughter, who cannot *wait* for her body to develop and whose enthusiasm is simply contagious.

Finally, about teens and sex: The Dutch approach makes it clear that adolescents should have unimpeded means to birth control, which means facilitating their access to health care providers and paying for their contraception and protection—or at least helping kids to locate free or low-cost birth-control providers in judgment-free settings. With parity in mind, I can also put my money where my mouth is by making sure my adolescent daughters aren't stuck spending their allowance on pads or tampons, which belong on the family grocery bill, and by explaining why paying their own way on dates helps rewrite unfavorable old views about who owes what to whom.

Furthermore, adolescents need to learn about the relationship gaps between sex and intoxicated sex, real sex and pornography, and sex for intimacy and sex for other reasons. When we talk to kids about reciprocity in their intimate partnerships, that's in part about satisfaction for everyone. It's also about getting beyond lessons about how to say no or yes. Everyone should know, too, how to say, "Shall we…?"

A big surprise for me, the more I've thought about teenagers and sex, has been a substantive shift in focus. I no longer fixate on the question of how long my children will wait before their first sexual experiences. Instead I think it's more important to consider how positive, healthy, and gainful those first experiences can be. That, I've decided, is where I want to put my emphasis. To achieve that, Dan and I will need to keep lines of communication wide open with our kids, even if that means parenting at the very edge of our comfort zones.

So when our daughters ask, quite possibly in high school, if a sweetheart can sleep over, we'll consider allowing it. We hope to know our children's partners well. We want to see that they are forming respectful, balanced, and caring relationships. We're preparing to talk openly with them about expectations and safe practices. And most of all, we aim to keep open lines of communication by giving trust and letting go as wisely as we can. Easier said than done, I know. But I've seen proof that it's possible.

When my children were quite young, I set out with personal urgency to relearn how to act, think, talk, and teach about bodies, sex, and love. Along the way, I'd blundered aplenty and surely had many more goofs to go. But on that scorching day in Rome, I decided not to worry about my mistakes. Instead, I thought about all of the eye-opening lessons I had learned and the unforeseen things I had dared to try. I'd even heard myself exclaim about a street-side condom dispenser as easily as if I'd seen a juggling clown. Yet I could clearly remember standing blushing and befuddled in the bathroom when my pointing toddler proposed a chat about pubic hair.

My journey beyond birds and bees was about changing what I wish for. It was about learning to push beyond the basic, reductive sex-ed goals of prevention and protection and raising my sights to a more expansive, holistic, and positive conception of sexuality. What began as doubts and fears really did evolve into hopes and dreams; knowing what I *didn't* want had been easy all along, but now I knew what I *did* want for my children in their sexual lives. In their bodies, I wanted them to have health, safety, and reproductive control, of course, but also sovereignty, confidence, desire, and pleasure. In their relationships, I wanted them to enjoy harmony, affection, trust, equality, and authentic love. In their wider lives as adults, I hoped they would know their full worth, meet their deepest potential, and contribute to society in ways that would fulfill them. All of those positive outcomes, I had come to see, take root in lessons as simple and fundamental as learning to name body parts matter-of-factly, understanding that everyone has a right to their own boundaries, and remaining unashamedly at home in one's own skin.

Thinking of the many unexpected ways in which I'd learned as a parent to face the facts of life, I remembered the growing-up cartoon I'd seen years earlier at the science museum in Amsterdam. *Great, isn't it?* the mad-scientist narrator had asked, making it sound like a joy and a privilege to behold children flourishing—body and being—in their sexuality.

Yes, I thought. *As a matter of fact, it is.*

Acknowledgments

Throughout the writing of this book, a whole village of bright and helpful souls has kept me informed, supported, protected, and loved. My agent, Caryn Karmatz Rudy, saw early on that I had buried the message of something worth saying. She cleared the air, empowering me to tell it straight, and her belief fueled the writing of this book. Stephanie Knapp, my editor at Seal Press, was the determined mind who connected with my mission and the thoughtful guide who saw sense in my approach. I am grateful to her and the entire Seal team for boldly bringing this book into the world.

In the Netherlands: I would like to thank Rutgers for support, information, and access, in particular Elsbeth Reitzema and Patti Krijgsman. I am grateful to the staff and students at Het Schateiland in Utrecht for allowing me to observe and ask questions; I must especially thank Lucienne Berndson for the immensely helpful photos, videos, and interpretive help. For teaching our entire family, thank you to 2Voices, especially Heidi and Victoria. The 14e Montessorischool de Jordaan has gone above and beyond in repeatedly opening the door to our family; special thanks to Ronald, Jacqueline, Tom, Jody, Michelle, and Sandrine three times over. Adinda, thank you for your uniquely brilliant cross-cultural interpretation and translation support—and for your friendship most of all.

Stateside: I owe thanks to the many families, friends, and experts who have helped me to understand the challenges and landscape of sexuality education in America and our diverse and exciting opportunities for progress. For their expert help in parsing the current state of things, I thank Laurie Dils, Nora Gelperin, Elizabeth Schroeder, Amy Lang, Julie Metzger, Amy Johnson, Andrea Gerber, and Kari Kesler. Thank you to the staff at Pateros K-12 for the opportunity to observe in the classroom.

The staff, students, and parents at the Oranjeschool on Saturdays have made this book better by keeping our Dutch connection thriving in Seattle, by sharing cross-cultural stories, and by paving the way for my children to continue experiencing school in the Netherlands. Special thanks to Illonka, Ilse, Carola, Astrid, Karen, and Carine, curator of the best Dutch-language children's book collection west of the Mississippi. Or west of the North Sea, for that matter. And I am thankful, always, to the staff and teachers at my children's Montessori school. If I've learned one thing, it's to get out of the way and to observe the magic of children's unfolding.

Carly, you arrived at the front door soon after I became the mother of two, and right when I was seeing the world of American girls with fresh eyes. With your gifts of curiosity, patience, compassion, brilliance, and humor, you helped me turn my fear into understanding, words, and action. Thank you for the light you shine.

For their willingness to be vulnerable and share—and to offer me advice and ideas—I'm grateful to the Oranjeschool focus group, Julie's book group, and the Bubbles & Brainstorms gang with Martha at the helm. Over coffees and texts and lunches and playground chats, friends at home and abroad have given me fresh perspectives and pushed me to think in new ways: Dani, Gijs, Madeline, Linda, Megan G., Anna A., Alex, Sarah, Jen R., Mary, Chrissy, Jenny G., Adam, Jessica P., Skye, Amy R., and many generous others.

Then there are those rare friends who are also partners in the vexing, exhilarating work of writing itself. Janna and Sarah, while I hope you will never tell how ghastly this project looked when I laid it at your feet some years ago, I would like the world to know what you did then: lift it up, smile upon it, circle the good parts, and tell me to keep going. Thank you. And Kate, even from five states away, I feel your steadfast support every day as I draw on your advice as a writer, teacher, and editor. To my colleagues and students in the Ashland University MFA program: thank you for inspiring me.

Certain organizations and individuals have supported me materially in the writing of this book. Foremost, I would like to express gratitude to the Seattle Public Library system and to public libraries everywhere. Some walk through the doors for the children's book section, others for the internet, some for tax help, and a few for a warm place with running water. For me, study rooms and physical materials at the Greenwood Branch, access to online resources, and the Eulalie and Carlo Scandiuzzi Writers' Room at the Central Library have made it possible to do well-informed, efficient work.

In addition, I would like to thank the Sustainable Arts Foundation, King County 4Culture, the Centrum Artist-in-Residence program, the Helen Riaboff Whiteley Center, and the Uncle Curt Writer's Retreat at Birch Bay. Anne Marie and Ruth, thank you for entrusting your space to my family over the years. In 2009, I finished writing a book in your house. In 2017, it happened again.

Jean and Jim, you have provided me so many crucial and restorative days and nights in your magical home, often simultaneously taking my spot in Seattle to partner with Dan in caring for the kids. I will always be grateful to have you for in-laws. My children are blessed to have you for grandparents.

Mom, you are the mother bear who, with your parenting and your book *Play It Safe*, started it all. You have always worked to make the world a better place for children. Dad, thank you for being a man who supports women. You inspire me with your curious questions and the speed with which you roll up your sleeves to try something new.

Thank you to my sister for being my steadfast first sounding board and unconditional confidante. I don't know why, but I can hear myself think when I talk with you. And gratitude to my brother for being the boy I grew up with and for becoming such an exemplary man. Not to mention a legendary uncle. And my Scrabble nemesis.

Dan, you know this process: she gets excited about an idea, she digs in, she goes on exploring, she hits speed bumps, she despairs, she keeps trying, things look up, the going gets harder, but finally: ta-da! A book! And the next thing you know, she gets excited about an idea....It's a familiar ride by now, but no less infernal. What I really want to say to you, of course, is thank you: for believing in me, for caring about things that matter to me, for helping me to make my voice heard, and for lending that same credence to our children. How lucky we are to love and be loved by you.

And finally, my daughters: When each of you came into my arms, a new world began. Thank you for leading me to seek and discover, to learn and rethink, and to meet life's changes with joy. I spent a lot of time writing this book that I could have spent with you. Instead of holding that against me, you put notes in my suitcase and happy posters on the windows and handmade presents by my bed to tell me *keep going! you can do it!* This book would not be here if it weren't for you. Thank you for a lifetime of lessons in love.

Notes

Unless otherwise indicated, translations in this book are the author's own. In some cases throughout this book, names and identifying details have been changed to protect privacy.

Introduction

xvii The Netherlands may have been the world's first: "Diversity in Amsterdam," I amsterdam, accessed November 24, 2017, https:// www.iamsterdam.com/en/living/about-living-in-amsterdam/ people-culture/diversity-in-the-city.

Chapter 1: Dreaming

7 Dutch children topped the charts: Peter Adamson: "Child Well-Being in Rich Countries: A Comparative Overview," *Innocenti Report Card 11* (Florence: UNICEF Office of Research, 2013). See also Rina Mae Acosta and Michele Hutchison, *The Happiest Kids in the World: How Dutch Parents Help Their Kids (and Themselves) by Doing Less* (New York: The Experiment, 2017), 1–2.

7 Their parents, too, ranked: Jennifer Glass, Robin W. Simon, and Matthew A. Andersson. "Parenthood and Happiness: Effects of Work-Family Reconciliation Policies in 22 OECD Countries." *American Journal of Sociology* 122, no. 3 (November 2016): 886–929. See also "12 Reasons Why Dutch Moms Are the Happiest," Stuff Dutch People Like, November 2016, https://stuffdutchpeoplelike.com/2016/11/29/12 -reasons-why-dutch-moms-are-the-happiest, and Rina Mae Acosta and Michele Hutchison, "They Raise the World's Happiest Children—So Is It Time You Went Dutch?" *Telegraph* (London), January 7, 2017: "The Dutch have reined in the anxiety, stress, and expectations of modern-day parenting, redefining the meaning of success and wellbeing."

7 And the Netherlands consistently stood: Selim Jahan, *Human Development Report 2016* (New York: United Nations Development Programme [UNDP], 2016), 214, Table 5. When the UNDP introduced its current Gender Inequality Index (GII) measurement in

2008 (published 2010), the Netherlands received the top ranking (meaning it exhibited the lowest gender inequality as measured by women's reproductive health, empowerment, and participation in the labor market) among 169 nations. This happened to be the period during which my family lived in the Netherlands. Since that time, the Netherlands has improved its GII index while remaining highly ranked, dropping as low as number 7 but recovering to 3 in the 2016 report, the most recent available at the time of writing. Over the same time period, the United States ranking varied between 37 in 2010 and 55 in 2015. Its 2016 position was 43. See also UNDP Human Development Data (1990–2015) to compare countries' GII progress over time: http://hdr.undp.org/en/data. By way of comparison, refer to *The Global Gender Gap Report 2017* (Geneva, Switzerland: World Economic Forum, 2017), which uses different indicators to measure gender inequality. In the most recent ranking available, the Netherlands backslid a dramatic sixteen places to number 32 "due to widening gender gaps in political empowerment and wage equality for similar work" (25). The United States ranked at 49, three spots lower than in the previous year's report.

11 judging by US data on poverty: "Nonelderly Adult Poverty Rate by Gender, 2016," State Health Facts, The Henry J. Kaiser Family Foundation, https://www.kff.org/state-category/demographics-and-the-economy/people-in-poverty.

14 A second featured video blogger: Hank Green, *Human Sexuality Is Complicated*, October 12, 2012, video, 3:48, https://www.youtube.com/watch?v=xXAoG8vAyzI.

15 a giant-size cartoon projected: Science Center NEMO, "Growing Pains," animated video. See *Teen Facts—Growing Pains / copyright Science Center NEMO*, September 14, 2010, animated video, 2:56, https://www.youtube.com/watch?v=aTY52flChKs.

16 Dutch teenagers had fewer problems: *Fact Sheet: Teenage Pregnancy*, Rutgers, 2017, https://www.rutgers.international/sites/rutgersorg/files/PDF/RHRN-HLPF_A4leaflet_NL.pdf. "Number of Teenage Mothers Unprecedentedly Low," CBS-Centraal Bureau voor de Statistiek, October 15, 2013, https://www.cbs.nl/en-gb/news/2013/42/number-of-teenage-mothers-unprecedentedly-low. Compare *Substance Use and Sexual Risk Behaviors Among Teens*, fact sheet, Centers for Disease

Control and Prevention (CDC), Division of Adolescent and School Health (DASH), April 14, 2017, https://www.cdc.gov/healthyyouth/substance-use/pdf/dash-substance-use-fact-sheet.pdf, and "Teen Pregnancy in the United States," About Teen Pregnancy, Centers for Disease Control and Prevention (CDC), last updated May 9, 2017, https://www.cdc.gov/teenpregnancy/about/index.htm. UNICEF's *Innocenti Report Card* has also compared children's engagement in risky behaviors by country.

Chapter 2: Dropping the Fig Leaf

24 eight kids sit in a row: Marianne Busser and Ron Schröder, *Hoera, ik krijg een potje!* (Vianen: The House of Books, 2001), 7. For other examples, see Busser and Schröder, *Liselotte op het potje* (Houten: Van Holkema & Warendorf, 1993), and Vivian den Hollander and Dagmar Stam, *Hoi, naar school!* (Houten: Van Holkema & Warendorf, 2002).

24 must appease American publishers by drawing clothes: Beate Bjørklund, "Beware—his Post Includes Banned Illustrations!" Intellectual Freedom Blog, The Office for Intellectual Freedom of the American Library Association, March 30, 2017, http://www.oif.ala.org/oif/?p=9008.

26 Discussions about the march of body shame: See special issue "Shame Shame Shame: Bangalijsten, slutshaming, wraakporno. Waarom pikken we dit" ("...Banglists, Slut Shaming, Revenge Porn: Why Are We Putting Up with This?") in *LINDA*, July 2017. With regard to parenting and differential treatment of sons and daughters, see Lisa Bouyeure, "De dubbele moraal bij seksuele opvoeding: Meisjes worden nog altijd met seksuele schaamte opgevoed" ("The Double Standard in Sex Education: Girls Are Still Brought Up with Sexual Shame), *De Volkskrant Magazine*, April 1, 2017.

29 the officer warned the family: "B.C. Father 'Shaken and Upset' After Naked 4-Year-Old Son Prompts Police Visit," *CBC News*, April 18, 2015, http://www.cbc.ca/news/canada/british-columbia/b-c-father-shaken-and-upset-after-naked-4-year-old-son-prompts-police-visit-1.3052126.

30 beachgoers in too-revealing suits: "Women Being Arrested for Wearing One Piece Bathing Suits, 1920s," Rare Historical Photos, October 28, 2016, https://rarehistoricalphotos.com/women-arrested-bathing-suits-1920s.

30 Today, activist groups in some states: Sarah Begley, "Here's Where It's Legal for Women to Go Topless in the U.S.," *Time*, April 24, 2015, http://time.com/3834365/map-topless-laws.

31 But a Fort Collins blogger wrote: Chloe Johnson, "Bringing Opposite Gender Kids into the Locker Room: What Are the Rules and How Old Is Too Old?," *Fresh Air Fort Collins*, February 28, 2013.

34 An old town crank: Rick Steves and Gene Openshaw, *Rick Steves' Amsterdam Bruges & Brussels* (Berkeley: Avalon Travel, 2009), 206.

35 In 2014, the judges of Texas's highest criminal court: Chuck Lindell, "Texas Court Tosses Out 'Improper Photography' Law," *Austin American-Statesman*, September 17, 2014, http://www.mystatesman .com/news/texas-appeals-court-tosses-out-improper-photography-law/isySsa7MHv2IoWeFX6D9CL.

37 "What exactly about that nudity": Stephanie Klein, "We Ask Police, Can I Be Naked in Seattle?" MyNorthwest.com, August 5, 2014, http:// mynorthwest.com/19795/we-ask-police-can-i-be-naked-in-seattle/?.

Chapter 3: Finding Words

40 Sandy K. Wurtele, a psychology professor: Sandy K. Wurtele, Anastasia M. Melzer, and Laura C. Kast, "Preschoolers' Knowledge of and Ability to Learn Genital Terminology," *Journal of Sex Education and Therapy* 18, no. 2 (Spring 1992): 115–122.

40 A third of American teenagers: Laura Duberstein et al., "Changes in Adolescents' Receipt of Sex Education, 2006–2013," *Journal of Adolescent Health* 58, no. 6 (2016): 621–627.

40 most sexually active American teenagers: *American Adolescents' Sources of Sexual Health Information*, fact sheet, Guttmacher Institute, December 2017, https://www.guttmacher.org/sites/default/files/ factsheet/facts-american-teens-sources-information-about-sex.pdf.

41 No wonder little kids tell: Wurtele, Melzer, and Kast, "Preschoolers' Knowledge," and Amanda D. Thackeray and Christine A. Readdick, "Preschoolers' Anatomical Knowledge of Salient and Non-Salient Sexual and Non-Sexual Body Parts," *Journal of Research in Childhood Education* 18, no. 2 (2003): 141–148.

41 That message comes from educators, doctors: In Good Company: Who Supports Comprehensive Sexuality Education? fact sheet, SIECUS, April 2010, http://www.siecus.org/index.cfm?fuseaction=Page.View Page&PageID=1198.

42 Republican and Democrat alike: *Sex Education in America General Public/Parents Survey*, National Public Radio/Kaiser Family Foundation/Kennedy School of Government, January 2004, https://www.npr.org/programs/morning/features/2004/jan/kaiserpoll/publicfinal.pdf. The finding that Americans across ideologies support school-based sexuality education is corroborated elsewhere; for an overview, see Leslie Kantor and Nicole Levitz, "Parents' Views on Sex Education in Schools: How Much Do Democrats and Republicans Agree?" *PLOS ONE*, July 3, 2017, https://doi.org/10.1371/journal.pone.0180250.

44 the smart, well-rounded female college students: Peggy Orenstein, *Girls & Sex: Navigating the Complicated New Landscape* (New York: HarperCollins, 2016), 60.

45 urging parents to teach: Perri Klass, "Teaching Children the Real Names for Body Parts," *New York Times*, November 1, 2016, https://www.nytimes.com/2016/10/31/well/family/teaching-children-the-real-names-for-body-parts.html.

46 A sexual development brochure: *Hoe komt die baby in je buik? Seksuele opvoeding van kinderen tussen 0 en 6 jaar* (Utrecht: Rutgers WPF, 2012).

Chapter 4: Innocence

53 According to a Rutgers guide: *Hoe komt die baby in je buik? Seksuele opvoeding van kinderen tussen 0 en 6 jaar* (Utrecht: Rutgers WPF, 2012).

54 Sex educator Lang knows it: Amy Lang, "Birds & Bees & Kids for Preschoolers: Bodies, Boundaries, and Baby-Making," PNW Parent Education Series Lecture, Ballard Church, Seattle, WA, October 23, 2017.

54 the year's most frequently challenged books: "Top Ten Most Challenged Books Lists," Banned and Challenged Books: A Website of the ALA Office for Intellectual Freedom, American Library Association, 2011, http://www.ala.org/advocacy/bbooks/frequentlychallengedbooks/top10#2011.

54 "How do Dad's sperm and your egg get together?": Dori Hillestad Butler, *My Mom's Having a Baby!: A Kid's Month-by-Month Guide to Pregnancy* (Morton Grove, IL: Albert Whitman, 2005), 11.

55 "the man and woman want to get even closer": Butler, *My Mom's Having a Baby!*, 12.

56 "Sometimes people don't want any more babies": Sanderijn van der Doef and Marian Latour, *Ik vind jou lief* (1997; reprint, Amsterdam: Uitgeverij Ploegsma, 2015), 18.

56 "Hi, I'm Elizabeth": Butler, *My Mom's Having a Baby!*, 1.

57 positive recommendations from children's librarians: Stephanie Zvirin, starred review of *My Mom's Having a Baby!*, by Dori Hillestad Butler, *Booklist*, April 1, 2005, and Martha Topol, review of *My Mom's Having a Baby!*, by Dori Hillestad Butler, *School Library Journal*, May 2005.

57 equal in number positive and negative: Customer Reviews: *My Mom's Having a Baby!: A Kid's Month-by-Month Guide to Pregnancy*, https://www.amazon.com/Moms-Having-Baby-Month-Month/ product-reviews/0807553484/ref=cm_cr_dp_d_show_all_btm?ie =UTF8&reviewerType=all_reviews. Product reviews and comments on reviews last accessed January 20, 2018.

58 "Giving a child facts about reproduction": "Talking About Sex and Puberty," Parenting, Focus on the Family, May 6, 2011. https:// www.focusonthefamily.com/parenting/sexuality/talking-about -sex/talking-about-sex-and-puberty, adapted from Paul C. Reisser, *Focus on the Family Complete Guide to Baby & Child Care* (Carol Stream, IL: Tyndale House, 2007).

59 it "disgustified" her: "Is Children's Book Too Graphic for Kids?" *Fox & Friends*, Fox News Channel, April 26, 2011, http://video.foxnews .com/v/4554700.

59 "These people don't see themselves": Dori Hillestad Butler, "Banned Books Month: Guest Post from Dori Hillestad Butler: How Censor- ship Has Changed Me," Write All the Words! (blog), September 2, 2013, http://www.ekristinanderson.com/?p=7651.

59 In 2007 when then Senator Barack Obama: Teddy Davis and Lind- sey Ellerson, "Sex Ed for Kindergarteners?" *ABC News*, July 20, 2007, http://abcnews.go.com/Politics/story?id=3395856.

60 In its Innocenti Report Card series: UNICEF Office of Research– Innocenti, Florence, Innocenti Report Card by Date, https://www .unicef-irc.org/publications/series/16/.

60 When researchers ask them directly: John Hudson and Stefan Kühner, "Fairness for Children: A League Table of Inequality in Child Well- Being in Rich Countries," *Innocenti Report Card 13*, (Florence: UNI- CEF Office of Research–Innocenti, 2016). "In part because of this broad

stability over time in its life satisfaction gap, the Netherlands recorded the lowest gap not only in 2014 but also in 2002, 2006 and 2010" (31).

63 In 2014, Jezebel blogger: Tracy Moore, "OMFG Teach Your Kids Accurate Names for Body Parts Already," Motherload (blog), *Jezebel*, September 24, 2014, https://jezebel.com/omfg-teach-your-kids -accurate-names-for-body-parts-alre-1637781018.

Chapter 5: Privileging Pleasure

69 a woman's genitals connect directly: Naomi Wolf, *Vagina: A New Biography*, revised and updated edition (New York: Ecco, 2013), 1.

70 According to a recent UK survey: "Straight-Talking on All Things Gynae…," The Eve Appeal, updated 2018, https://eveappeal.org.uk/ news-awareness/straight-talking-things-gynae.

72 Specifically in reference to very little kids: Deborah Roffman, *Talk to Me First: Everything You Need to Know to Become Your Kids' "Go-To" Person about Sex* (Boston: Da Capo, 2012), 232.

73 In some cases older children: Erika Frans, Thierry Franck, Kristin Janssens, and Oka Storms, *Normatieve Lijst 2017: Sensoa Vlaggensysteem Buiten de Lijnen*, Sensoa Vlaggensysteem, 2017, 18–19, https:// www.seksuelevorming.be/sites/default/files/digitaal_materiaal/ uitgebreide-normatieve-lijst.pdf.

73 British sex educator Justin Hancock: Daisy Wyatt, "'Stop Ignoring the Clitoris': Making Sex Education About Pleasure," *i News*, November 25, 2016, https://inews.co.uk/news/education/putting-clitoris-back-sex -education.

73 Over the centuries the clitoris: Suzannah Weiss, "'Fear of the Clit': A Brief History of Medical Books Erasing Women's Genitalia," Broadly, *VICE*, May 3, 2017, https://broadly.vice.com/en_us/article/ nejny8/fear-of-the-clit-a-brief-history-of-medical-books-erasing -womens-genitalia.

73 In his guide for parents: Luke Gilkerson, *The Talk: 7 Lessons to Introduce Your Child to Biblical Sexuality* (printed by the author, 2014).

74 an extraordinary collection: Douglas Harper, "clitoris (n.)," Online Etymology Dictionary, https://www.etymonline.com/word/clitoris.

75 two hundred million girls and women worldwide: "At least 200 million girls and women alive today living in 30 countries have undergone FGM/C," Female Genital Mutilation and Cutting, UNICEF

Data, updated December 2017, https://data.unicef.org/topic/child -protection/female-genital-mutilation-and-cutting/#.

75 "primarily for three objectives": Sarah B. Rodriguez, *Female Circumcision and Clitoridectomy in the United States: A History of a Medical Treatment* (Rochester, NY: University of Rochester Press, 2014), 10–11.

75 "Because of the relative ease": Rodriguez, *Female Circumcision,* 178–179.

76 Naomi Wolf has posited: Wolf, *Vagina,* 112.

76 In a French-inspired sex manual: Simon Schama, *The Embarrassment of Riches: An Interpretation of Dutch Culture in the Golden Age* (New York: Vintage, 1987), 424.

76 a digital lesson for fourth-graders: "De geslachtsdelen," lesson plan, *Kriebels in je buik,* Groep 6, Lichamelijk ontwikkeling en zelfbeeld, Rutgers Kenniscentrum Seksualiteit, 2017, slide 6, https://www .kriebelsinjebuik.nl.

76 The World Health Organization takes: "Gender and Human Rights," Sexual and Reproductive Health, World Health Organization, 2018, http://www.who.int/reproductivehealth/topics/gender_rights/ sexual_health/en/.

77 experts tell Dutch parents: *Hoe komt die baby in je buik? Seksuele opvoeding van kinderen tussen 0 en 6 jaar,* Rutgers WPF, 2012.

77 called the clitoris "very sensitive,": "Understanding Our Bodies—The Basics," lesson plan, *Rights, Respect, Responsibility: A K-12 Curriculum,* Advocates for Youth, 2017.

79 Germiest Body Part: "Study Finds Unexpected Bacterial Diversity on Human Skin," Press Release, National Institutes of Health, U.S. Department of Health and Human Services, May 28, 2009, https:// www.nih.gov/news-events/news-releases/study-finds-unexpected -bacterial-diversity-human-skin.

79 A sense of one's genitals as offensive: *Right from the Start: Guidelines for Sexuality Issues: Birth to Five Years,* Early Childhood Sexuality Education Task Force (New York: Sexuality Information and Education Council of the United States, 1998), 13, 47.

79 I saw real-life examples: Opening *Wipsite,* Melkweg, Amsterdam, March 17, 2016, https://www.melkweg.nl/nl/agenda/opening-de-wip site-17-03-2016. See also http://wipsite.nl.

82 Nurse and educator Julie Metzger describes: "Jonathan Zimmerman's *Too Hot to Handle: A Global History of Sex Education*," Radio Times, WHYY, April 9, 2015, minute 47:30, http://whyy.org/cms/radiotimes/2015/04/09/jonathan-zimmermans-too-hot-to-handle-a-global-history-of-sex-education.

82 personal-tour offerings: "Self-Exam: Vulva and Vagina," Our Bodies Ourselves, March 28, 2014, https://www.ourbodiesourselves.org/health-info/self-exam-vulva-vagina.

Chapter 6: The Doctor Is In

87 usually not more than four years: Nancy D. Kellogg, "Clinical Report—The Evaluation of Sexual Behaviors in Children," *Pediatrics* 124, no. 3 (September 2009): 992–998.

88 At a 1993 Colorado symposium: Francis Wardle and Kimberly Moore-Kneas, *Child-to-Child Sexual Behavior in Child Care Settings: Final Report of the Symposium Denver, Colorado, April 1993*, Children's World Learning Centers, Golden, Colorado, 1995.

89 In 1998, he published a landmark paper: William N. Friedrich et al., "Normative Sexual Behavior in Children: A Contemporary Sample," *Pediatrics* 101, no. 4 (April 1, 1998).

89 The story quickly hit: Susan Gilbert, "New Light Shed on Normal Sex Behavior in a Child," *New York Times*, April 7, 1998.

89 In a 1988 survey of more than 1,000 American students: Jeffrey J. Haugaard and Christina Tilly, "Characteristics Predicting Children's Responses to Sexual Encounters with Other Children," *Child Abuse & Neglect* 12, no. 2 (1998): 209–218.

89 A few years later, a similar survey: S. Lamb and M. Coakley, "'Normal' Childhood Sexual Play and Games: Differentiating Play from Abuse," *Child Abuse & Neglect* 17, no. 4 (July–August 1993): 515–526.

89 By 2002, a Swedish psychologist surveying: IngBeth Larsson and Carl-Göran Svedin, "Sexual Experiences in Childhood: Young Adults' Recollections," *Archives of Sexual Behavior* 31, no. 3 (June 2002): 263–273.

90 In a 1996 survey of American professionals: Jeffrey Haugaard, "Sexual Behaviors between Children: Professionals' Opinions and Undergraduates' Recollections," *Families in Society* 77, no. 2 (January 1996):

81–89. Prepublication research described in Wardle and Moore-Kneas, *Child-to-Child Sexual Behavior in Child Care Settings.*

90   "The tendency of our society": Wardle and Moore-Kneas, *Child-to-Child Sexual Behavior in Child Care Settings.*

91   "Mom taught us": Pattie Fitzgerald, *NO Trespassing—This Is MY Body* (Santa Monica, CA: Safely Ever After, 2011).

91   Cornelia Spelman instructs: Cornelia Spelman, *Your Body Belongs to You* (Chicago: Albert Whitman, 1997).

91   *My Body Is Private*: Linda Walvoord Girard, *My Body Is Private* (Chicago: Albert Whitman, 1984).

91   One children's book struck me: Kimberly King and Sue Ramà, *I Said No! A Kid-to-Kid Guide to Keeping Your Private Parts Private* (Weaverville, CA: Boulden, 2010).

92   and must not be permitted: See, for example, Steven P. Shelov and Tanya Remer Altmann, *Caring for Your Baby and Young Child: Birth to Age 5*, 5th ed., (New York: Bantam / American Academy of Pediatrics, 2009), 402–403.

93   excellent packet offered: *A Safer Family, A Safer World*, A Resource for Parents and Caregivers of Children 0–12 on Preventing Child Sexual Abuse, Harborview Center for Sexual Assault and Traumatic Stress, http://depts.washington.edu/hcsats/csabooklet.html.

94   They include the use of reasoning: "Sexual Violence: Risk and Protective Factors," Violence Prevention, Centers for Disease Control and Prevention, last updated March 22, 2017, https://www.cdc.gov/violenceprevention/sexualviolence/riskprotectivefactors.html.

94   a booklet professionals use: Toni Cavanagh Johnson, *Understanding Children's Sexual Behaviors: What's Natural and Healthy*, expanded 2015 (South Pasadena, CA: Toni Cavanagh Johnson, 2015).

94   "some sexologists even believe": Debra Haffner, *From Diapers to Dating: A Parent's Guide to Raising Sexually Healthy Children from Infancy to Middle School*, 2nd ed. (New York: William Morrow, 2008), 56–60.

95   Keeping something private means: Cory Silverberg, *Sex Is a Funny Word: A Book About Bodies, Feelings, and YOU* (New York: Seven Stories, 2015).

96   "It's natural to be interested": Laurie Krasny Brown and Marc Brown, *What's the Big Secret? Talking About Sex with Girls and Boys* (New York: Little, Brown, 2000), 14.

97 national education mandate: Beatrix, Koningin der Nederlanden, et al.; "Besluit van tot wijziging van het Besluit vernieuwde kerndoelen WPO, het Besluit kerndoelen onderbouw VO, het Besluit kerndoelen WEC, het Besluit kerndoelen WPO BES en het Besluit kerndoelen onderbouw VO BES in verband met aanpassing van de kerndoelen op het gebied van seksualiteit en seksuele diversiteit," October 18, 2012, https://zoek.officielebekendmakingen.nl/stb-2012 -470.html. See also Monique Vogelzang, "Omgaan Met Seksualiteit en Seksuele Diversiteit: Een Beschrijving van het Onderwijsaanbod van Scholen," Inspectie van het Onderwijs, Ministerie van Onderwijs, Cultuur, en Wetenschap, June 2016, https://www.rijksoverheid.nl/docu menten/rapporten/2016/06/01/omgaan-met-seksualiteit-en-seksuele -diversiteit-een-beschrijving-van-het-onderwijsaanbod-op-scholen.

98 a booklet for parents: *Seksuele Ontwikkeling van Kinderen 0-18 jaar* (Utrecht: Rutgers, 2016), 6, https://www.rutgers.nl/producten/ seksuele-ontwikkeling-van-kinderen-0-18-jaar.

99 the curriculum for four- and five-year-olds: "Les 10: Hoe zeg ik 'nee,'" Leskatern groep 1 en 2, *Relaties & Seksualiteit* (Utrecht: Rutgers WPF, 2013), 62.

99 In 2011, a Madison, Wisconsin, prosecutor: "Lawsuit Says Prosecutor Went Too Far in Charging Boy," Channel 3000, November 21, 2011, https://www.channel3000.com/news/lawsuit-says-prosecutor-went -too-far-in-charging-boy/162464344.

99 suspended a four-year-old boy: Jennifer Kent, "4-Year-Old Accused of Improperly Touching Teacher," KXXV-TV News Channel 25, November 2006, http://www.kxxv.com/story/5785699/4-year-old-accused -of-improperly-touching-teacher.

99 the legal ramifications for their children: *Raised on the Registry: The Irreparable Harm of Placing Children on Sex Offender Registries in the US* (New York: Human Rights Watch, May 1, 2013), https:// www.hrw.org/report/2013/05/01/raised-registry/irreparable-harm -placing-children-sex-offender-registries-us. See also Sarah Stillman, "The List: When Juveniles Are Found Guilty of Sexual Misconduct, the Sex-Offender Registry Can Be a Life Sentence," *New Yorker*, March 14, 2016, https://www.newyorker.com/magazine/2016/03/14/when-kids -are-accused-of-sex-crimes, and Eric Berkowitz, "Punishment That Doesn't Fit the Crime," *New York Times*, July 31, 2016, https://www

.nytimes.com/2016/07/31/opinion/sunday/punishment-that-doesnt
-fit-the-crime.html.

99 In a Q & A on the Dutch parenting website: Sanderijn van der
Doef, "Doktertje-spelen okee, maar hoe praat je daarover? (5
jr)," *Ouders Online*, November 12, 2010, https://www.ouders.nl/
vraagbaken/doktertje-spelen-okee-maar-hoe-praat-je-daarover-5-jr.

100 "fiddling in the doll corner": L. Douma, "Gefriemel in de Poppen-
hoek: Seksuele Opvoeding op de Basisschool," *Het Onderwijsblad*
17, October 30, 2010. https://www.schoolenveiligheid.nl/po-vo/ken
nisbank/gefriemel-in-de-poppenhoek.

100 "As adults, we almost can't help but": "Doktertje spelen: wel of niet?"
Interview with Marina van der Wal, *Vrouw*, May 3, 2014, https://
www.telegraaf.nl/nieuws/969779/doktertje-spelen-wel-of-niet.

100 following such a controversy: Even with a general acceptance of *doktertje spelen*, things can go awry. A Dutch kerfuffle on the topic of
child-to-child sexual abuse started in 2013 when the parents of a six-
year-old girl asked their day care center for advice on how often was
too often for *doktertje spelen* with the seven-year-old boy who was the
girl's best friend. The teacher advised the parents to keep the friends
apart, which the parents considered too drastic. As a result, the teacher
called the Bureau Jeugdzorg—the Dutch equivalent of Child Protective Services. The agency accused the parents of emotional neglect for
refusing to separate the friends. Eventually, the parents succeeded in
turning the blame around, and the Jeugdzorg was censured for making
a false accusation. See Anneke Stoffelen, "Jeugdzorg in de fout bij 'doktertje spelen' tussen meisje (6) en jongen (7)," *Volkskrant*, April 24,
2014, https://www.volkskrant.nl/binnenland/-jeugdzorg-in-de-fout-bij
-doktertje-spelen-tussen-meisje-6-en-jongen-7~a3640537.

101 In *NEE!*, a picture book: Sanderijn van der Doef, *NEE! Een boek over
Nee en Ja zeggen* (2009; reprint, Amsterdam: Ploegsma, 2015).

101 In *Ben jij ook op mij?* (*Do You Like Me Too?*): Sanderijn van der Doef,
Ben jij ook op mij? Een boek over seks, voor kinderen (1995; reprint,
Amsterdam: Ploegsma, 2015), 6–7.

Chapter 7: What (In)Equality Is Made Of

108 under the sway of pop psychology: John Gray, *Men Are from
Mars, Women Are from Venus: A Practical Guide for Improving*

Communication and Getting What You Want in Your Relationships (New York: HarperCollins, 1992); Louann Brizendine, *The Female Brain* (New York: Broadway Books, 2006); Louann Brizendine, *The Male Brain* (New York: Three Rivers, 2010).

109 several books I had waited much too long to discover: Caryl Rivers and Rosalind C. Barnett, *The Truth About Girls and Boys: Challenging Toxic Stereotypes About Our Children* (New York: Columbia University Press, 2011); Lise Eliot, *Pink Brain, Blue Brain: How Small Differences Grow into Troublesome Gaps—and What We Can Do About It* (Boston: Mariner Books, 2009); Cordelia Fine, *Delusions of Gender: How Our Minds, Society, and Neurosexism Create Difference* (New York: W. W. Norton, 2010); Cordelia Fine, *Testosterone Rex: Myths of Sex, Science, and Society* (New York: W. W. Norton, 2017); Rebecca M. Jordan-Young, *Brain Storm: The Flaws in the Science of Sex Differences* (Cambridge: Harvard University Press, 2010).

109 impact of media-darling gender theorists: *Boys' Brains vs. Girls' Brains: What Sex Segregation Teaches Students*, brochure, ACLU, May 2008, https://www.aclu.org/files/pdfs/womensrights/boysbrains_v_girls brains.pdf. See also Fine, *Delusions of Gender*; Eliot, *Pink Brain, Blue Brain*; Rivers and Barnett, *The Truth About Girls and Boys.*

109 asserting that boys and girls: Michael Gurian, *Boys and Girls Learn Differently! A Guide for Teachers and Parents* (San Francisco: Jossey-Bass, 2011); Leonard Sax, *Why Gender Matters: What Parents and Teachers Need to Know About the Emerging Science of Sex Differences* (New York: Doubleday, 2005; rev. ed.: New York: Harmony, 2017).

109 ballooned in the United States since 2000: "Single-Sex Schools/ Schools with Single-Sex Classrooms/What's the Difference?" National Association for Single Sex Public Education (now the National Association for Choice in Education), http://www.singlesexschools .org/schools-schools.htm.

110 "demonstrate[s] beyond reasonable doubt": Jennifer Connellan, Simon Baron-Cohen, Sally Wheelwright, Anna Batki, and Jag Ahluwalia, "Sex differences in Human Neonatal Social Perception," *Infant Behavior & Development* 23 (2000), 113–118.

110 "the null hypothesis is correct," Natalie Angier, "Insights From the Youngest Minds," profile of Elizabeth S. Spelke, *New York Times,*

April 30, 2012, http://www.nytimes.com/2012/05/01/science/insights -in-human-knowledge-from-the-minds-of-babes.html.

110 languish off the airwaves: Eliot, *Pink Brain, Blue Brain*, 10. When the decision about whether to publish scientific results is influenced by the outcome of the study—often, in the case of gender differences, when the null hypothesis is supported and no differences are shown—the research remains out of sight of the general public. This is called the "file-drawer problem."

110 "Would Brizendine have gotten this kind of pop": Emily Bazelon, "A Mind of His Own," *New York Times*, March 25, 2010, http://www .nytimes.com/2010/03/28/books/review/Bazelon-t.html.

110 "You don't have to be a genius": Naomi Wolf, *Misconceptions: Truth, Lies, and the Unexpected on the Journey to Motherhood* (New York: Anchor, 2003), 71.

111 young babies are already scanning: See, for example, Lisa A. Serbin et al., "Gender Stereotyping in Infancy: Visual Preferences for and Knowledge of Gender-Stereotyped Toys in the Second Year," *International Journal of Behavioral Development* 25, no. 1 (2001): 7–15.

111 The magnitude of those differences: Paul T. Costa Jr., Antonio Terracciano, and Robert R. McCrae, "Gender Differences in Personality Traits Across Cultures: Robust and Surprising Findings," *Journal of Personality and Social Psychology* 81, no. 2 (2001): 322–331.

111 "your brain is what you do with it,": Eliot, *Pink Brain, Blue Brain*, 6, 16.

112 asks for a 5 percent improvement: Priscilla Long, *The Writer's Portable Mentor* (Seattle: Wallingford, 2010), and Priscilla Long, *Minding the Muse: A Handbook for Painters, Composers, Writers, and Other Creators* (Seattle: Coffeetown, 2016).

113 "young children as 'gender detectives,'": Fine, *Testosterone Rex*, 182.

113 "The big mistake is to confuse": Fine, *Testosterone Rex*, 150.

113 "gender is a hierarchy,": Fine, *Testosterone Rex*, 193.

114 women recall being "tomboys": Peggy Orenstein, *Cinderella Ate My Daughter* (New York: Harper, 2011), 66–67.

114 a strategic childhood shift: May Ling Halim, Diane N. Ruble, and David M. Amodio, "From Pink Frilly Dresses to 'One of the Boys': A Social-Cognitive Analysis of Gender Identity Development and Gender Bias," *Social and Personality Psychology Compass* 5, no. 11 (November 2011): 933–949.

117 dissatisfied with their bodies: *Children, Teens, Media, and Body Image: A Common Sense Media Research Brief* (San Francisco: Common Sense Media, 2015), https://www.commonsensemedia.org/research/children-teens-media-and-body-image.

118 loved and safe: Lena Aburdene Derhally, "How (And Why) to Create Emotional Safety for Our Kids," *Washington Post*, March 23, 2016, https://www.washingtonpost.com/news/parenting/wp/2016/03/23/how-and-why-to-create-emotional-safety-for-our-kids; "Helping Your Child Develop a Healthy Sense of Self Esteem," American Academy of Pediatrics, https://www.healthychildren.org/English/ages-stages/gradeschool/Pages/Helping-Your-Child-Develop-A-Healthy-Sense-of-Self-Esteem.aspx and "Ways to Build Your Teenager's Self-Esteem," American Academy of Pediatrics, https://www.healthychildren.org/English/ages-stages/teen/Pages/Ways-To-Build-Your-Teenagers-Self-Esteem.aspx, both pages last updated November 21, 2015.

118 protecting them from early sexualization: *Report of the APA Task Force on the Sexualization of Girls*, Task Force on the Sexualization of Girls (Washington, DC: American Psychological Association, 2007), http://www.apa.org/pi/women/programs/girls/report-full.pdf.

118 "when parents...communicate": *Report of the APA Task Force*, 37.

118 When American girls as young as six: Christine Starr and Gail Ferguson, "Sexy Dolls, Sexy Grade-Schoolers? Media & Maternal Influences on Young Girls' Self-Sexualization," *Sex Roles* 67 (July 6, 2012).

119 "limit the culture box": Peggy Orenstein, "A New Generation of Girlie-Girls," public lecture, Town Hall, Seattle, February 15, 2012.

121 spatial lessons of sports and physical activity: Rivers and Barnett, "Math Wars," *The Truth About Girls and Boys*, 43–73.

122 I think of the ten-year study: Jacquelynne Eccles, Bonnie Barber, and Debbie Jozefowicz, "Linking Gender to Education, Occupation, and Recreational Choices: Applying the Eccles et al. Model of Achievement-Related Choices," in William B. Swann Jr., Judith H. Langlois, and Lucia C. Gilbert, editors, *Sexism and Stereotypes in Modern Society: The Gender Science of Janet Taylor Spence* (Washington, DC: American Psychological Association, 1998), 153–192.

122 "hardworking" in contrast to: Rivers and Barnett, *The Truth About Girls and Boys*, 62.

122 boys and girls internalize stereotypes: Lin Bian, Sarah-Jane Leslie, and Andrei Cimpian, "Gender Stereotypes About Intellectual Ability

Emerge Early and Influence Children's Interests," *Science* 355 (January 26, 2017): 389–391.

124 parents treat infant girls as more fragile: Rivers and Barnett, *The Truth About Girls and Boys*, 123–124.

124 mothers use more verbal and emotionally complex: Melissa Clearfield and Naree Nelson, "Sex Differences in Mothers' Speech and Play Behavior with 6-, 9-, and 14-Month-Old Infants," *Sex Roles* 54, nos. 1–2 (January 2006).

124 boys learn early not to be crybabies: Rivers and Barnett, *The Truth About Girls and Boys*, 136–138.

124 a "play-punch": "Questions Adolescent Boys Ask About Puberty," Ki Sung, *Stories Teachers Share* podcast, Mind/Shift, KQED, February 2, 2016, https://ww2.kqed.org/mindshift/2016/02/02/questions-adolescent-boys-ask-about-puberty.

128 noted the same phenomenon: Rina Mae Acosta and Michele Hutchison, *The Happiest Kids in the World: How Dutch Parents Help Their Kids (and Themselves) by Doing Less* (New York: Experiment, 2017), 190–191.

130 high association of their condition: C. Dhejne, R. Van Vlerken, G. Heylens, and J. Arcelus, "Mental Health and Gender Dysphoria: A Review of the Literature," *International Review of Psychiatry* 28, no. 1 (2016): 44–57, https://www.ncbi.nlm.nih.gov/pubmed/26835611.

130 Dutch transgender kids suffer fewer: "Poor Peer Relations Predict Parent- and Self-Reported Behavioral and Emotional Problems of Adolescents with Gender Dysphoria: A Cross-National, Cross-Clinic Comparative Analysis," https://link.springer.com/article/10.1007/s00787-015-0764-7.

130 Dutch kids raised in planned lesbian families: Henny M. W. Bos et al., "Children in Planned Lesbian Families: A Cross-Cultural Comparison Between the United States and the Netherlands," *American Journal of Orthopsychiatry* 78, no. 2 (April 2008): 211–219.

131 Still, Dutch feminists disagree: Claire Ward, "How Dutch Women Got to Be the Happiest in the World," *Maclean's*, August 19, 2011, http://www.macleans.ca/news/world/the-feminismhappiness-axis.

131 a sexual double standard still exists: Lisa Bouyeure, "De dubbele moraal bij seksuele opvoeding: Meisjes worden nog altijd met seksuele schaamte opgevoed" *De Volkskrant Magazine*, April 1, 2017.

131 In 2017, a nationwide campaign: Bouyeure, "De dubbele moraal bij seksuele opvoeding."

131 families in Canada and Sweden: Jessica Botelho-Urbanski, "Baby Storm Five Years Later: Preschooler on Top of the World," *Toronto Star*, July 11, 2016, https://www.thestar.com/news/gta/2016/07/11/baby-storm-five-years-later-preschooler-on-top-of-the-world.html; Tim Dowling, "The Swedish Parents Who Are Keeping Their Baby's Gender a Secret," *Guardian* (London), June 22, 2010, https://www.theguardian.com/lifeandstyle/2010/jun/22/swedish-parents-baby-gender.

131 Sweden, which currently ranks even higher: Selim Jahan, *Human Development Report 2016* (New York: United Nations Development Program [UNDP], 2016), 214, Table 5.

131 describes their work as a matter of democracy: Anna Leach, "'It's All About Democracy': Inside Gender Neutral Schools in Sweden," *Guardian* (London), February 2, 2016, https://www.theguardian.com/teacher-network/2016/feb/02/swedish-schools-gender-alien-concept.

132 In a 2016 TEDx talk, Rajalin said: Lotta Rajalin, *Gender-Neutral Pre-School: Something for My Kid?*, video, TEDx Tartu, February 4, 2016, 24:03, https://youtube.com/watch?v=/C1G1K7-kJxY.

132 I think that there might be a fear: Gabriella Martinson quoted in Frida Wikström, *Teachings for the Whole Life Spectra*, documentary, July 24, 2015, 9:10, https://www.youtube.com/watch?v=fJH0_P42C5c.

133 "No single factor": Fine, *Testosterone Rex*, 193.

133 The US gender gap is currently worse: *Human Development Report 2016*, 214, Table 5.

Chapter 8: Consent

136 "You can say no 100 times": Heather Burtman, "My Body Doesn't Belong to You," *New York Times*, June 16, 2017.

139 Planned Parenthood's 2015 video series: "Consent 101," YouTube playlist, Planned Parenthood, last updated November 1, 2016, https://www.youtube.com/playlist?list=PL3xP1jlf1jgJRkChwVOlwQcV0-UqcWiFV.

139 fielded a question about tickling: Kwame Anthony Appiah, "Should You Tell Uber Your Driver Was High?" The Ethicist, *New York Times*, March 1, 2017, https://www.nytimes.com/2017/03/01/magazine/should-you-tell-uber-your-driver-was-high.html.

140 The letters to the editor: "The 3.5.17 Issue," The Thread, *New York Times Magazine*, March 17, 2017, https://www.nytimes.com/2017/03/17/magazine/the-3-517-issue.html.

141 American adults are confused: Bianca DiJulio et al., "Survey of Current and Recent College Students on Sexual Assault," Henry J. Kaiser Family Foundation, June 12, 2015, https://www.kff.org/other/poll-finding/survey-of-current-and-recent-college-students-on-sexual-assault; PPFA Consent Survey Results Summary, Planned Parenthood, October 2015, https://www.plannedparenthood.org/files/1414/6117/4323/Consent_Survey.pdf.

141 Most important is an enthusiastic *yes*: Zhana Vrangalova, "Everything You Need to Know About Consent That You Never Learned in Sex Ed," *Teen Vogue*, April 18, 2016, https://www.teenvogue.com/story/consent-how-to. For more on affirmative consent, see Jaclyn Friedman and Jessica Valenti, *Yes Means Yes!: Visions of Female Sexual Power and A World Without Rape* (Berkeley: Seal Press, 2008), and Jaclyn Friedman, *Unscrewed: Women, Sex, Power, and How to Stop Letting the System Screw Us All* (Boston: Seal Press, 2017).

141 "When kids play such games as Red Rover": Rivers and Barnett, *The Truth About Girls and Boys*, 115.

Chapter 9: No Cooties Allowed

144 highly gender-segregated: Eleanor E. Maccoby and Carol Nagy Jacklin, "Gender Segregation in Childhood," in *Advances in Child Development and Behavior*, edited by E. H. Reese, 20 (New York: Wiley, 1987), 239–287.

145 a modern phenomenon: See Jared Diamond, *The World Until Yesterday: What Can We Learn from Traditional Societies?* (New York: Penguin, 2012), 200–201.

145 hostility from their peers: D. Bruce Carter and Laura A. McCloskey, "Peers and the Maintenance of Sex-Typed Behavior: The Development of Children's Conceptions of Cross-Gender Behavior in Their Peers," *Social Cognition* 2, no. 4 (1984): 294–314.

146 "It truly does not serve them": Deborah Roffman, *Talk to Me First: Everything You Need to Know to Become Your Kids' "Go-To" Person about Sex* (Boston: Da Capo Lifelong, 2012), 87.

146 "It may only be temporary": Tischa Neve, "Vriendschap tussen
meisje en jongen; klasgenootjes noemen het verkering," *J/M Ouders*, accessed February 16, 2017, https://www.jmouders.nl/opvoeden/
gedrag/vriendschappen/vraag/vriendschap-tussen-meisje-en-jongen
-klasgenootjes-noemen-het-verkering.

146 Psychologists studying four-year-olds: Lisa A. Serbin, Illene J.
Tonick, and Sarah H. Sternglanz, "Shaping Cooperative Cross-Sex
Play," *Child Development* 48, no. 3 (September 1977): 924–929.

146 A mix of styles, researchers say: Amanda J. Rose and Karen D. Rudolph, "A Review of Sex Differences in Peer Relationship Processes:
Potential Trade-offs for the Emotional and Behavioral Development
of Girls and Boys," *Psychological Bulletin* 132, no. 1 (2006): 98–131.

146 "might make it more difficult for boys and girls": Serbin, Tonick, and
Sternglanz, "Shaping Cooperative Cross-Sex Play," 924.

147 receive a simple classroom talk: "Wij zijn vriendjes," lesson plan, *Kriebels in je buik*, Groep 2, Sociale en emotionele ontwikkeling, Rutgers
Kenniscentrum Seksualiteit, 2017, https://www.kriebelsinjebuik.nl.

149 boys and girls learn by experience how to relate: Rose and Rudolph,
"A Review of Sex Differences in Peer Relationship Processes: Poten-
tial Trade-offs for the Emotional and Behavioral Development of
Girls and Boys," 125; Serbin, Tonick, and Sternglanz, "Shaping Co-
operative Cross-Sex Play," 924; Marion K. Underwood and Lisa H.
Rosen, "Gender, Peer Relations, and Challenges for Girlfriends and
Boyfriends Coming Together in Adolescence," *Psychology of Women
Quarterly* 33, no. 1 (January 28, 2009): 16–20.

151 It's a paradigm under challenge: *Boys' Brains vs. Girls' Brains: What
Sex Segregation Teaches Students*, brochure, ACLU, May 2008,
https://www.aclu.org/files/pdfs/womensrights/boysbrains_v_girls
brains.pdf.

151 no educational advantage: "Single-Sex Versus Coeducational Schooling: A Systematic Review," US Department of Education, Office of
Planning, Evaluation and Policy Development, Policy and Program
Studies Service, Washington, DC, 2005, http://www.ed.gov/about/
offices/list/opepd/reports.html.

151 "Today, much of the so-called 'science'": Juliet A. Williams,
"What's Wrong with Single-Sex Schools? A Lot," *Los Angeles*

Times, January 25, 2016, http://www.latimes.com/opinion/op-ed/la
-oe-0125-williams-single-sex-schools-20160125-story.html.

151 boys who attend all-male high schools: Christie P. Karpiak et al., "University Students from Single-Sex and Coeducational High Schools: Differences in Majors and Attitudes at a Catholic University," *Psychology of Women Quarterly* 31, no. 3 (September 2007): 282–289.

152 "Too often the classroom is a place": Caryl Rivers and Rosalind C. Barnett, *The Truth About Girls and Boys: Challenging Toxic Stereotypes About Our Children* (New York: Columbia University Press, 2011), 161.

153 not only romantic relationships but also professional ones: Clare M. Mehta and JoNell Strough, "Sex Segregation in Friendships and Normative Contexts Across the Life Span," *Developmental Review* 29 (2009): 201–220.

153 routinely guess wrong: Ashton M. Lofgreen et al., "Situational and Dispositional Determinants of College Men's Perception of Women's Sexual Desire and Consent to Sex: A Factorial Vignette Analysis," *Journal of Interpersonal Violence* (November 2017).

156 girls adopt more boy-typed behaviors: Amanda J. Rose, "Structure, Content, and Socioemotional Correlates of Girls' and Boys' Friendships," *Merrill-Palmer Quarterly* 53, no. 3 (July 2007): 489–506.

157 "Teach them that there are certain discussion topics": Wendy Buckler, "Boy-Girl Friendships," Focus on the Family, 2015, https://www.focusonthefamily.com/parenting/schoolage-children/boy-girl-friendships.

157 In a 2015 episode on menstruation: "Ongesteld," *De Dokter Corrie Show*, School TV (NTR) April 12, 2015, 19:38, https://www.schooltv.nl/video/de-dokter-corrie-show-ongesteld.

158 discussed whether boy-girl friendships matter: Allison Benedikt and Gabriel Roth, "The 'Child Care War Machine' Edition," *Mom and Dad Are Fighting* (podcast), *Slate*, February 2, 2017, http://www.slate.com/articles/podcasts/mom_and_dad_are_fighting/2017/02/boy_girl_friendships_and_the_cost_of_child_care_on_mom_and_dad_are_fighting.html.

161 the loss of deep same-gender friendships: See Jennifer Finney Boylan, "From Best Man to Puzzled Woman," *New York Times*, April 7, 2017, https://www.nytimes.com/2017/04/07/style/modern-love-jennifer

-finney-boylan.html; Ira Glass, "Infinite Gent," Act Two, "Testosterone," *This American Life*, August 30, 2002, https://www.thisameri canlife.org/220/testosterone/act-two-0.

161 men's and women's opinions on the appropriateness: Claire Cain Miller, "It's Not Just Mike Pence; Americans Are Wary of Being Alone with the Opposite Sex," *New York Times*, July 1, 2017, https:// www.nytimes.com/2017/07/01/upshot/members-of-the-opposite -sex-at-work-gender-study.html.

Chapter 10: Spring Fever

165 widely used curriculum: *Kriebels in je buik*, Rutgers Kenniscentrum Seksualiteit, 2017, https://www.kriebelsinjebuik.nl.

165 internationally agreed sexuality-education standards: *Kriebels in je buik*, Algemene introductie, 3.

166 Schools in the Netherlands: *Kriebels in je buik*, Algemene introductie, 4.

166 a fit in the Netherlands: *Dutch Lessons in Love, Part 1: Sixty Years of Sexual Evolution in the Netherlands*, video, Rutgers, July 11, 2015, 17:32, https://youtu.be/50izsaMwcrs.

167 "As a teacher, you don't have to be afraid": *Kriebels in je buik*, Algemene introductie, 9.

168 hundreds of elementary schools: Elsbeth Reitzema, phone call with author, March 21, 2017.

171 Eventually the curriculum also teaches: "Verliefdheid en seksuele oriëntatie," lesson plan, *Kriebels in je buik*, Groep 8, Sociale en emotionele ontwikkeling.

172 The manual reminds teachers: "Jongens en meisjes," lesson plan, *Kriebels in je buik*, Groep 2, Sociale en emotionele ontwikkeling, 6.

172 a story about pregnancy, birth, and how babies: "Hoe worden kindjes geboren?" lesson plan, *Kriebels in je buik*, Groep 2, Voortplanting en gezinsvorming, 6.

173 sometimes doctors help: "Hoe worden kindjes geboren?" lesson plan, *Kriebels in je buik*, Groep 2, Voortplanting en gezinsvorming, 6.

173 fully wanted and enjoyed: G. Martinez, C. E. Copen, and J. C. Abma, "Teenagers in the United States: Sexual activity, Contraceptive Use, and Childbearing, 2006–2010 National Survey of Family Growth," *Vital and Health Statistics* 23, no. 31 (October 2011), https://www.cdc.gov/

nchs/data/series/sr_23/sr23_031.pdf; Amy T. Schalet, *Not Under My Roof: Parents, Teens, and the Culture of Sex* (Chicago: University of Chicago Press, 2011), 5–8.

174 Other key lessons for seven- and eight-year-olds: lesson plans, *Kriebels in je buik*, Groep 4.

175 Eight- and nine-year olds go on: lesson plans, *Kriebels in je buik*, Groep 5.

175 In the fifteen-minute episode: "Verliefd!" *Huisje Boompje Beestje*, School TV (Teleac), April 27, 2007, 15:00, https://www.schooltv.nl/video/huisje-boompje-beestje-verliefd.

176 "The Dutch concept of *verliefd zijn*": Schalet, *Not Under My Roof*, 36.

176 She quotes one Dutch mother: Schalet, *Not Under My Roof*, 36.

176 In another public-television clip: "Verliefd: Hoe voelt dat?" School TV (NTR), July 2, 2007, 3:05, https://www.schooltv.nl/video/verliefd-hoe-voelt-dat.

176 it's just as normal to fall in love: "Ik ben verliefd," lesson plan, *Kriebels in je buik*, Groep 4, Sociale en emotionele ontwikkeling.

Chapter 11: The Joy of Sex Ed

186 Fewer than half of all US schools: *Results from the School Health Policies and Practices Study 2014*, US Department of Health and Human Services, Centers for Disease Control and Prevention (CDC), 2015, Table 1.2, 11, https://www.cdc.gov/healthyyouth/data/shpps/pdf/shpps-508-final_101315.pdf.

186 As of 2018: "Sex and HIV Education," State Laws and Policies, Guttmacher Institute, as of April 1, 2018, https://www.guttmacher.org/state-policy/explore/sex-and-hiv-education.

186 As of 2014, programs in half of US middle schools: *Results from the School Health Policies and Practices Study 2014*, Table 1.19, 21.

186 "engage in a shoe-related activity.": Sanford Johnson, "How to Put on a Sock," video, 1:51, https://www.youtube.com/watch?v=06kT9yfj7QE.

186 proliferate in the states with the highest: Compare "Teen Birth Rate by State," CDC, last updated February 1, 2018, https://www.cdc.gov/nchs/pressroom/sosmap/teen-births/teenbirths.htm, to "Sex and HIV Education," Guttmacher Institute, https://www.guttmacher.org/state-policy/explore/sex-and-hiv-education.

186 only in a negative light: "Sex and HIV Education."

187 Most schools fail to meet: Zewditu Demissie et al., *School Health Profiles 2014: Characteristics of Health Programs Among Secondary Schools*, US Department of Health and Human Services, Centers for Disease Control and Prevention, 2015, https://www.cdc.gov/healthyyouth/data/profiles/pdf/2014/2014_Profiles_Report.pdf.

187 students receive 13.5 hours *total*: *Results from the School Health Policies and Practices Study 2014*, Table 1.13, 17.

187 a marked drop from a decade ago: *Results from the School Health Policies and Practices Study 2014*, Table 11.1, 134.

187 Even at six years old: Sandra L. Caron and Carie Jo Ahlgrim, "Children's Understanding and Knowledge of Conception and Birth: Comparing Children from England, the Netherlands, Sweden, and the United States," *American Journal of Sexuality Education* 7, no. 1 (2012): 16–36.

187 report that students practice communication: *Results from the School Health Policies and Practices Study 2014*, Table 1.15, 18.

187 American adolescents get pregnant: "About Teen Pregnancy," Centers for Disease Control and Prevention, last updated May 9, 2017, https://www.cdc.gov/teenpregnancy/about/index.htm.

187 Eight in ten American teens compared to nine in ten Dutch: "Sexual Activity, Contraceptive Use, and Childbearing of Teenagers Aged 15–19 in the United States," data brief, National Center for Health Statistics, July 2015, https://www.guttmacher.org/fact-sheet/american-teens-sexual-and-reproductive-health; "Main Conclusions: *Sex Under the Age of 25*," Rutgers and Soa Aids Nederland, 2017, http://seksonderje25e.nl/page/summary_sex_under_25.

188 only about half of sexually experienced US teenagers: Laura Duberstein Lindberg, Isaac Maddow-Zimet, and Heather Boonstra, "Changes in Adolescents' Receipt of Sex Education, 2006–2013," *Journal of Adolescent Health* 58 (2016): 621–627.

188 Most of that education goes to white students: Pamela K. Kohler, Lisa E. Manhart, and William E. Lafferty, "Abstinence-Only and Comprehensive Sex Education and the Initiation of Sexual Activity and Teen Pregnancy," *Journal of Adolescent Health* 42 (2008): 344–351.

188 as effective as no sex ed: John S. Santelli et al., "Abstinence-Only-Until-Marriage: An Updated Review of U.S. Policies and Programs and Their Impact," *Journal of Adolescent Health* 61 (2017): 273–280. http://www.jahonline.org/article/S1054-139X(17)30260-4/fulltext.

188 $20 billion annually: "Counting It Up: The Public Costs of Teen Childbearing 2013," data brief, The National Campaign to Prevent Teen and Unplanned Pregnancy (renamed Power to Decide in 2017), December 2013, https://powertodecide.org/sites/default/files/resources/primary-download/counting-it-up-key-data-2013.pdf.

188 half of all new STI cases: Adolescent Sexual and Reproductive Health in the United States, fact sheet, Guttmacher Institute, September 2017, https://www.guttmacher.org/fact-sheet/american-teens-sexual-and-reproductive-health.

188 three times lower than in the United States: "Rape at the National Level, Number of Police-Recorded Offences," data table (rate per 100,000 population 2003–2008), United Nations Office on Drugs and Crime, http://www.unodc.org/documents/data-and-analysis/Crime-statistics/Sexual_violence_sv_against_children_and_rape.xls.

188 a century ago offered: See Jonathan Zimmerman, Too Hot to Handle: A Global History of Sex Education (Princeton, NJ: Princeton University Press, 2015).

190 The core objectives: Beatrix, Koningin der Nederlanden et al., "Besluit van tot wijziging van het Besluit vernieuwde kerndoelen WPO, het Besluit kerndoelen onderbouw VO, het Besluit kerndoelen WEC, het Besluit kerndoelen WPO BES en het Besluit kerndoelen onderbouw VO BES in verband met aanpassing van de kerndoelen op het gebied van seksualiteit en seksuele diversiteit," October 18, 2012, https://zoek.officielebekendmakingen.nl/stb-2012-470.html.

190 One option is to advocate for it: "Why Sex Ed? A Parent's Guide to Understanding Sex Education in Your School, 2017 Toolkit," Advocates for Youth, http://www.whysexed.org/wp-content/uploads/2017/10/FoSE-Toolkit-102017.pdf.

191 profile of Metzger: Bonnie Rochman, "Let's Talk (Frankly) About Sex," New York Times Sunday Magazine, March 25, 2015, https://www.nytimes.com/2015/03/29/magazine/lets-talk-frankly-about-sex.html.

191 a mom in Nebraska: Julie Metzger, interview with the author, Seattle, March 9, 2017.

192 In 2018 it cost $80: Great Conversations, 2018, https://www.greatconversations.com/programs-and-registration.

194 courses designed for senior citizens: Amy Johnson, interview with the author, May 5, 2017.

196 argue that independent, private approaches: "Jonathan Zimmerman's *Too Hot To Handle: A Global History of Sex Education*," Radio Times, WHYY, April 9, 2015, minute 35:40 http://whyy.org/cms/radiotimes/2015/04/09/jonathan-zimmermans-too-hot-to-handle-a-global-history-of-sex-education.

196 capable of doing a fine job: See, for example, Al Vernacchio, *For Goodness Sex: Changing the Way We Talk to Teens About Sexuality, Values, and Health* (New York: Harper Wave, 2014).

196 international laws and standards: For a synthesis, see Santelli et al., "The Human Right to Sexual Health Information" (subsection), "Abstinence-Only-Until-Marriage: An Updated Review of U.S. Policies and Programs and Their Impact," *Journal of Adolescent Health* 61 (2017): 273–280.

197 Various polls and surveys have shown: "Survey Says: Investing in Results," fact sheet, The National Campaign to Prevent Teen and Unplanned Pregnancy, January 2015, https://powertodecide.org/what-we-do/information/resource-library/survey-says-investing-results-january-2015; see also discussion in Norman A. Constantine, "Converging Evidence Leaves Policy Behind: Sex Education in the United States," *Journal of Adolescent Health* 42 (2008): 324–326; and *Sex Education in America General Public/ Parents Survey* (NPR/Kaiser/Kennedy School 2004).

197 "full of pornographic content": "What Is Comprehensive Sex Education?" Save Nebraska Children, last accessed February 2, 2018, http://www.savenebraskachildren.com/about.html.

197 along with the Catholic Archdiocese of Omaha: Timothy F. McNeil, "Children Can Opt-Out of OPS Sex Ed Classes," Archdiocese of Omaha, last accessed February 2, 2018, https://archomaha.org/news/faith-at-work/children-can-opt-ops-sex-ed-classes.

197 fliers and petitions: "Parents' Group in Omaha Fights Radical Sex-Ed Curriculum, Distributes "Opt-Out" Forms Outside Every Middle School in the City," Mass Resistance, December 4, 2016, http://www.massresistance.org/docs/gen3/16d/omaha-schools-sex-ed/index.html and http://www.massresistance.org/docs/gen3/16d/omaha-schools-sex-ed/docs/NFV-Flyer.pdf, both last accessed February 2, 2018.

198 One speaker, who described herself: Omaha Public Schools, "Board of Education Meeting [Part 1] - January 4, 2016," video, posted January 5, 2016, 2:59:59, https://www.youtube.com/watch?v=ByVTsj5Wr4Q.

198   at least one student reported: Brenda Council (Adolescent Health Project Manager, Women's Fund of Omaha), phone interview with the author, April 26, 2017.

198   used toothbrushes: Tara Culp-Ressler, "5 Offensive Analogies Abstinence-Only Lessons Use to Tell Teens Sex Makes Them Dirty," *ThinkProgress*, April 7, 2014, https://thinkprogress.org/abstinence-only-course-in-texas-tells-kids-that-having-sex-makes-them-like-a-chewed-up-piece-of-gum-79bba598feab; Honeydew Wilkins, "Like a Pair of Old, Worn-Out Shoes," video, January 19, 2016, 2:06, https://www.youtube.com/watch?v=OoxTygEG85c.

198   the nation's top spot for STI rates: Blythe Bernhard, "St. Louis Drops to Second Place for Nation's Highest STD Rates," *St. Louis Post-Dispatch*, September 26, 2017, www.stltoday.com.

198   quickly persuade school officials: Michele Munz, "More Schools Cancel Christian Sex Ed Program; Emotions Run High at Public Meetings," *St. Louis Post-Dispatch*, March 10, 2017, www.stltoday.com.

198   "What I would really like": Michele Munz, "Christian Anti-Abortion Group Is Providing Sex Ed at Area Public Schools; Parents and Students Wonder If That's a Good Idea," *St. Louis Post-Dispatch*, March 6, 2017, www.stltoday.com.

199   "God's standard of abstinence": Bridget Van Means, *God's Masterpiece… You*, video, Grace Church St. Louis, 37:26 (minute 8:00), published January 20, 2014, last accessed February 4, 2018, https://www.youtube.com/watch?v=y1XjWl-WTdk.

199   Personal Responsibility Education Program (PREP): "Competitive PREP Fact Sheet—March 2017," fact sheet, Adolescent Pregnancy Prevention Program, Family & Youth Services Bureau, Administration for Children & Families, US Department of Health and Human Services (HHS), https://www.acf.hhs.gov/fysb/programs/adolescent-pregnancy-prevention/programs/prep-competitive.

199   the Teen Pregnancy Prevention Program (TPP): "About the Teen Pregnancy Prevention (TPP) Program," Office of Adolescent Health, Office of the Assistant Secretary for Health, HHS, last updated February 13, 2017, https://www.hhs.gov/ash/oah/grant-programs/teen-pregnancy-prevention-program-tpp/about/index.html.

200   People who receive CSE: Pamela K. Kohler, Lisa E. Manhart, and William E. Lafferty, "Abstinence-Only and Comprehensive Sex Ed-

ucation and the Initiation of Sexual Activity and Teen Pregnancy," *Journal of Adolescent Health* 42 (April 2008): 344–351, http://www .jahonline.org/article/S1054-139X(07)00426-0/fulltext; "Effective HIV and STD Prevention Programs for Youth: A Summary of Scientific Evidence," fact sheet, National Center for HIV/AIDS, Viral Hepatitis, STD, and TB Prevention and Division of Adolescent and School Health, CDC, October 1, 2010, https://www.cdc.gov/healthyyouth/ sexualbehaviors/pdf/effective_hiv.pdf.

200 abstinence organizations such as ThriVe: "Sexual Risk Avoidance Education (SRAE) Grantees FY2017," Family & Youth Services Bureau, Administration for Children & Families, HHS, October 19, 2017, https://www.acf.hhs.gov/fysb/sexual-risk-avoidance-grantees-fy2017.

200 In 2017, the Trump administration: Elizabeth Chuck, "Trump Administration Abruptly Cuts Funding to Teen Pregnancy Prevention Programs," *NBC News*, August 25, 2017, www.nbcnews.com.

200 its own stream of grant money: "Funded Agencies," DASH Home, CDC, August 1, 2016, https://www.cdc.gov/healthyyouth/partners/ index.htm.

201 define core standards: *National Sexuality Education Standards: Core Content and Skills, K–12*, Future of Sex Education Initiative (2012), http://www.futureofsexed.org/documents/josh-fose-standards-web.pdf.

201 American-produced, K-12 comprehensive sex ed curriculum: *Rights, Respect, Responsibility: A K-12 Sexuality Education Curriculum*, Advocates for Youth, 2015, http://www.advocatesforyouth.org/3rs-curric -lessonplans.

206 "a Christ-centered ministry": "Our Center," Care Net Pregnancy Centers of Okanogan County, 2018, last accessed February 4, 2018, http://pregnantandscared.net/about-us/about-our-center.

206 free AOUHM lessons: "Care Net's Youth Prevention Program," Free Services, Care Net Pregnancy Centers of Okanogan County, 2018, last accessed February 4, 2018, http://pregnantandscared.net/ be-informed/youth-prevention-program; "Curricula," Choosing the Best: The Leader in Abstinence-Centered SRA Education, last accessed February 4, 2018, http://www.choosingthebest.com/curricula.

206 comprehensive middle school curriculum: "WHY Get Real?," Get Real: Comprehensive Sex Education That Works, last accessed February 4, 2018, http://www.getrealeducation.org/.

Chapter 12: Safe Haven

212 nine out of ten Dutch parents: Amy T. Schalet, *Not Under My Roof: Parents, Teens, and the Culture of Sex* (Chicago: University of Chicago Press, 2011), 77.

212 "really wanted": G. Martinez, C. E. Copen, and J. C. Abma, "Teenagers in the United States: Sexual Activity, Contraceptive Use, and Childbearing, 2006–2010 National Survey of Family Growth," https://www.cdc.gov/nchs/data/series/sr_23/sr23_031.pdf.

212 Dutch boys *and* girls: Schalet, *Not Under My Roof,* 8.

212 "what it means to be a virgin": Heather Corinna, *S.E.X.: The All-You-Need-to-Know Sexuality Guide to Get You Through Your Teens and Twenties,* 2nd ed. (Boston: Da Capo Lifelong, 2016), 208.

213 "As out there as it may seem,": Corinna, *S.E.X.,* 208.

213 more than half still say they wish: Bill Albert, *With One Voice 2012: America's Adults and Teens Sound Off About Teen Pregnancy,* The National Campaign to Prevent Teen and Unplanned Pregnancy (August 2012), http://success1st.org/uploads/3/4/5/1/34510348/wov_2012.pdf.

213 In a 2017 Gallup poll...morally acceptable: Jeffrey M. Jones, "Americans Hold Record Liberal Views on Most Moral Issues," Gallup, May 11, 2017, http://news.gallup.com/poll/210542/americans-hold-record-liberal-views-moral-issues.aspx.

215 "a mutually faithful": Sec. 510. [42 U.S.C. 710], "Separate Program for Abstinence Education," Compilation of the Social Security Laws, Social Security Administration, last accessed February 6, 2018, https://www.ssa.gov/OP_Home/ssact/title05/0510.htm.

215 But recent research debunks: K. Paige Harden and Jane Mendle, "Adolescent Sexual Activity and the Development of Delinquent Behavior: The Role of Relationship Context," *Journal of Youth and Adolescence* 40, no. 7 (November 2010): 825–838; K. Paige Harden, "A Sex-Positive Framework for Research on Adolescent Sexuality," *Perspectives on Psychological Science* 9, no. 5 (2014): 455–469; R. M. Anderson, "Positive Sexuality and Its Impact on Overall Well-Being," *Bundesgesundheitsblatt—Gesundheitsforschung—Gesundheitsschutz* 56, no. 2 (February 2013): 208–214: "The results indicate that sexual health, physical health, mental health, and overall well-being are all

positively associated with sexual satisfaction, sexual self-esteem, and sexual pleasure."

215 "challenging of gender inequality.": Schalet, *Not Under My Roof*, 11–12.

216 "Sixteen is a beautiful age.": Schalet, *Not Under My Roof*, 133.

216 too deep in the details: Marina van der Wal and Bram Bakker, *Vrij(be)wijs: Help je kind en puber op weg bij liefde en seks* (Utrecht: Kosmos, 2017), 266.

216 By trading in strict prohibitions for "soft" power: Schalet, *Not Under My Roof*, 152–153, 188.

216 "hookup culture": See Lisa Wade, *American Hookup: The New Culture of Sex on Campus* (New York: Norton, 2017); Peggy Orenstein, *Girls & Sex: Navigating the Complicated New Landscape* (New York: HarperCollins, 2016).

219 preserve a close-knit family: Schalet, *Not Under My Roof*, 135, 183.

219 equally assertive at telling partners: Hanneke de Graaf and Ciel Wijsen, *Seksuele gezondheid in Nederland 2017*, Rutgers (2017), 50; *102 vragen uit het onderzoek 'Seks onder je 25e*, Soa Aids Nederland and Rutgers WPF (2012), 25–26.

219 "simply telling kids sex is fine": Ariel Levy, *Female Chauvinist Pigs: Women and the Rise of Raunch Culture* (New York: Simon & Schuster, 2005), 167.

222 list of such discussion topics: Corinna, "The Sexual Readiness Checklist," in *S.E.X.*, 186–187.

225 "groaning" downstairs: Van der Wal and Bakker, *Vrij(be)wijs*, 153.

225 "Or you'll hear noises. So be it." Van der Wal and Bakker, *Vrij(be)wijs*, 189.

226 "teenager's cottage": Christopher Alexander et al., *A Pattern Language: Towns—Buildings—Construction* (New York: Oxford University Press, 1977), 723.

Conclusion: Bringing It Home

229 "Cultures can change": Lisa Wade, "Hookup Culture on College Campuses," public lecture, Town Hall, Seattle, January 30, 2017.

234 gender-stereotypical beliefs: For example, see Eva S. Lefkowitz et al., "How Gendered Attitudes Relate to Women's and Men's Sexual

Behaviors and Beliefs," *Sexuality & Culture* 18, no. 4 (December 2014): 833–846.

237 "Something happens for girls": Elizabeth Debold, Marie C. Wilson, and Idelisse Malavé, *Mother-Daughter Revolution: From Betrayal to Power* (Reading, MA: Addison-Wesley, 1993), 10.

243 twenty-five *days*: Hillary Clinton, *What Happened* (New York: Simon & Schuster, 2017), 87.

Index

abortions, comprehensive sexuality education and reduced demand for, 166

abstinence-only-until-heterosexual-marriage (AOUHM), 186, 188, 206, 215

Best Choice curriculum, 198, 199

federal funding for, 200

ACLU (American Civil Liberties Union), challenging single-sex public schooling, 151

Acosta, Rina Mae, 128

adolescents

Dutch and American attitudes toward sexuality among, 176

first sexual experience, 213, 223, 245–246

having sex in parental home, 224–225

preparing for sexual intimacy, 211–212, 213

sexuality education for, 240–247

See also sex between adolescents; teenage pregnancy

advice for parents. *see* sexuality education advice for parents

Advocates for Youth, 190, 202

"age-appropriate," sex education and, 52, 59

Alexander, Christopher, 226

Algemene Onderwijsbond (teachers' union), 100

Amaze.org, 194, 239

American Academy of Pediatrics, 41

American culture

body shame and, 20

confusion of sexuality with eroticism and shame in, 23

physical contact and intimacy in, 52

American Library Association (ALA)

European illustrations and American market, 24

challenges to *My Mom's Having a Baby!*, 57–58

American parents

discomfort in talking about sex with children, 40–41, 42

view of sex between adolescents, 212, 213–215

See also parents

American Psychological Association, 118

Amsterdam Mamas Facebook group, 28, 34

Answer, 190

antisocial behavior, Dutch rejection of, 130

Appiah, Kwame Anthony, 139–140

Aunt Flow, 244

baby and toddlerhood, sexuality
    education for, 231–235
babysitting, stereotypes affecting
    use of male, 124–127
Bakker, Bram, 225
Barbé, Belle, 79
Barnett, Rosalind C., 109,
    141, 152
Baron-Cohen, Simon, 110
bathing, communal, 25–26
Bazelon, Emily, 110
Beatrix (queen), 24
Benedikt, Allison, 158–159
*Ben jij ook op mij? (Do You Like
    Me Too?)* (van der Doef),
    101–102
Best Choice (sex education
    curriculum), 198, 199
Biel, Jessica, 194
birds and bees talk, confusion about
    morality and, 60–63
Birds & Bees & Kids, 53
birth control. *See* contraception
Blozen Mag (Blushing Allowed)
    (Brons-van der Wekken), 42
bodily functions, Dutch comfort
    with acknowledging, 24–25
body parts
    inability of many adults to name
        reproductive, 70
    naming reproductive, 3–4, 5, 9,
        45–49, 233–234
    normalizing, 232, 233
body positivity
    learning correct terminology for
        body parts and, 47
    in Netherlands, 23–24

body shame
    in Netherlands, 26
    in United States, 20
    women and, 70
body sovereignty, 138–139
Bonjour Jolie, 244
boundaries, practice keeping, 93
boys
    as babysitters, 124–127
    harmful stereotypes about, 126
    higher status of, 114–115
    lesson discussing differentiating
        girls from, 169–172
    nurturing and, 123–127
    stereotype that are more brilliant
        than girls, 122
    valuation of, 120–121
Brain Storm (Jordan-Young), 109
bras, first, 243
Brizendine, Louann, 108, 110
Brons-van der Wekken,
    Sarina, 42
Brown, Laurie Krasny, 95–96
Brown, Marc, 95–96
Burtman, Heather, 136
Butler, Dori Hillestad,
        54–55, 57
    responses to criticism of *My
        Mom's Having a Baby!*,
        58–59

Care Net Pregnancy Center of
    Okanogan County, 206
Central Michigan University,
    students at *3Rs* training,
    203–205
cervix, 70

childhood gender segregation, 144,
    145–146, 148–149
childhood love, 162–163
childhood sexual exploration
    boundary between child sexual
        abuse and, 89, 90
    child-to-child, 85–90
    Dutch attitudes toward, 97–102
    how to address, 88–90
    lack of messages supporting,
        92–93
    messages supporting as positive,
        94–97
    rules for, 97–99, 102–104, 236
    safety issues, 89, 90–94,
        101–102
    skills learning in, 94
childlikeness, Dutch focus on
    preserving, 60
children
    balancing freedom with
        protection, 32–35
    desire to preserve innocence of,
        58–60
    gender segregation of young
        children in public locker
        rooms, 26, 27, 29–31
    public nudity and, 21–23,
        28–30
    raising in gender neutral
        environment, 128–133
    report on welfare of, around the
        world, 60
    right to sexuality education,
        196–197
    self-pleasuring and, 69, 71–73,
        77, 78

sexuality education for baby and
    toddlerhood, 231–235
sexuality education for
    elementary ages, 238–240
sexuality education for
    preschoolers, 235–238
sexually informed, 63–67
sneaking photos of, 34–35
using mirror to see genitals,
    80–82
See also adolescents
children's books
    body positivity in Dutch,
        23–24
    childhood sexual exploration as
        theme in, 91–93
    sex education, 54–55
    on sexuality, 101–102
child sexual abuse
    boundary between healthy
        childhood sexual exploration
        and, 89, 90
    fears of, 31–32, 39, 90, 92
Cinderella Ate My Daughter
    (Orenstein), 119
Clinton, Hillary, 243
clitoridectomy, 75–76
clitoris, 45
    defined, 74
    failure to acknowledge role in
        female pleasure, 73–75
    female circumcision, 75–76
    female pleasure and, 73–76,
        77–78, 82–83
color, gender and, 115, 128, 132
communal bathing, in Netherlands,
    25–26

comprehensive sexuality education
(CSE)
*Family Life and Sexual Health
(FLASH)* curriculum, 183
gender equality and, 239
*Kriebels in je buik (Butterflies in
Your Stomach)* curriculum 76,
165–166
*Lang leve de liefde (Long Live
Love)* curriculum, 178
in Netherlands, 166–167
Our Whole Lives (OWL)
curriculum, 193
Rights, Respect, Responsibility
curriculum, 201–205, 238
in United States, 201–205,
238–239
condom, 56, 188, 207
condom dispenser, 229–230
consent, 135–142
body sovereignty and, 139
early lessons about, 135–138,
233, 235–236
pestering of girls and, 135–136
teaching about, 140–142, 172,
239
tickling and, 139–141,
235–236
contraception
teaching elementary students
about, 173
teaching young children about,
55–56
for teens having sex, 187–188,
225–226, 245
Corinna, Heather, 212–213, 239
courtship, 219

cross-gender friendships, 143–163
default concept of as romantic, 159
during elementary age years, 240
encouraging, 145–163
gender equality and, 144,
146–147, 152
platonic, 159–161
skills learned from, 153, 159
"cunt shaming," 79

Delusions of Gender (Fine), 109
Denmark, gender equality in,
133–134
De Telegraaf (newspaper), 100
Dils, Laurie, 190, 200
Dobson, James, 157
De Dokter Corrie Show (television
program), 157–158, 196
dress
adolescents and fashion, 241–243
focus on what people are doing
not wearing, 237–238
gender neutral, for kids, 9, 12,
128–129
Dunn, Erin, 29, 30
Dutch parents
comfort level of fathers in talking
about children's sexuality,
43–44
focus on preserving
childlikeness, 60
hands-off approach to children's
explorations about pleasure
and their bodies, 77
view of sex between adolescents,
212, 215–216, 218–219
See also parents

"Dutch Protocol," 130
Dutch sex education curricula. *See*
    Kriebels in je buik (Butterflies
    in Your Stomach) (sex
    education curriculum)
Dutch teenagers, fewer pregnancies,
    STIs, and risky behaviors
    among, 16, 166

Elders, Joycelyn, 76
elementary ages, sexuality
    education for, 238–240
Eliot, Lise, 109, 111
The Embarrassment of Riches
    (Schama), 60
eroticism
    confusion of nudity with, 27
    confusion of with sexuality and
        shame, 23
    sex education and separating sex
        from, 53–54
The Eve Appeal, 70

The Family Book (Parr), 235
Family Life and Sexual Health
    (FLASH) curriculum,
    183–184
family nudity, 19–21, 37
fathers, talking to children about
    their body and sexuality,
    43–44. *See also* parents
The Female Brain (Brizendine), 108
Female Chauvinist Pigs (Levy), 219
female genital mutilation (FGM)/
    female circumcision, 75–76
female pleasure, clitoris and, 73–76,
    77–78, 82–83

Fine, Cordelia, 109, 113–114, 133
"first moon" celebrations, 194,
    244–245
first-period kits, 244
Fitzgerald, Pattie, 91
Focus on the Family, 58, 157
foreskin, 70
Fox & Friends (television
    program), 58
freedom, balancing with protection,
    32–35
Fremont Solstice Parade, 36–37
Friedrich, William N., 89
friendships, same-gender, 144,
    160–161. *See also* relationships
Friz, Caleb, 198
From Diapers to Dating (Haffner),
    94
funds, for sex education programs,
    199–200
The Future of Sex Ed
    Initiative, 190

games, gender lessons hidden in,
    112
gender, as a hierarchy, 113–114
gender dysphoria, 130
gender equality
    comprehensive sexuality
        education and, 239
    consent and, 142
    cross-gender friendships and,
        144, 146–147, 152
    fostering in children, 11, 234–235
gender gap
    in STEM, 108
    in United States, 133–134

gender inequality
  2016 United Nations Human
    Development Report, 134
  disparate status and, 112–116
  explanations/justifications for,
    107–112
  girls as nurturing and, 123–127
  lack of knowledge and ownership
    of genitals and, 81
  leveling the field and, 127–134
  looks and self-esteem and,
    116–121
  ritual coverings and, 27
  STEM-success stories,
    121–123
gender neutral
  dress, 9, 12
  raising children, 128–133
gender-neutral language, using with
  children, 237
gender-nonconforming children,
  129–130
gender-segregated schools, 109,
  144, 151
gender stereotypes, 108–112
  about brilliance, 122
  avoiding with babies and
    toddlers, 234
  avoiding with preschoolers,
    236–237
  learning, 110–112, 113
genitals
  children playing with own, 69,
    71–73
  gender inequality and lack of
    ownership of own, 81
  proper names of, 45–49

question of hand washing after
    touching, 78–79
  using mirror to see, 80–82
Gerber, Andrea, 139, 141
Get Real sex education curriculum,
    206–207
gezelligheid, 7–8
Gilkerson, Luke, 73–74
girls
  coercion of, 135–136
  expectations about nurturing
    and, 123–127
  higher status of boys and,
    114–115
  lesson discussing differentiating
    boys from, 169–172
  looks and self-esteem and,
    116–121
  sexualization of, 118–119,
    241–242
  social stereotypes about,
    127–128
  STEM and, 107–108
  stereotype that are less brilliant
    than boys, 122
  valuation of, 120–121
Girls & Sex (Orenstein), 44–45
golden rule, 10
Gray, John, 108
Gray's Anatomy, 73
Great Conversations (puberty
    class), 43, 44, 81, 191–193
Green, Hank, 14
Gurian, Michael, 109, 151

Haffner, Debra, 59, 94–95
Hancock, Justin, 73

The Happiest Kids in the World
(Hutchison & Acosta), 128
Harper, Douglas, 74
Harris, Robie, 92–93
hen (gender-neutral pronoun), 132
HIV, comprehensive sexuality
education as defense against,
166
HIV education, 183
home, allowing teens to have sex in
the parental, 224–225
"hookup culture," 216
Hotel Sophie (television show), 196
HPV, prevention of, 207
Huffington Post (website), 160
Huisje Boompje Beestje (television
program), love-themed
episode of, 175–176
Human Rights Watch, 99
Hutchison, Michele, 128

Ik vind jou lief (I Like You) (van der
Doef), 56
indecent exposure, 36, 37
innocence
definitions of for children, 58, 60
desire to preserve children's,
58–60
Innocenti Report Card series, 60
intelligence, internalizing gender
stereotypes about, 122
intercourse
age at first, 212
teaching children about, 49, 51–53
intimacy
sex and, 245
sex education about, 51–52, 54

intoxicated sex, 245
I Said No! (King), 91
It's So Amazing (Harris), 92–93

J/M voor Ouders website, 146
Johnson, Amy, 191, 193
Johnson, Sanford, 186
Johnson, Toni Cavanagh, 94
Jordan-Young, Rebecca, 109
Juicebox (app), 194

Kama Sutra, 14
Keller, Sharon, 35
Kesler, Kari, 139, 140–141
King, Kimberly, 91
*Kriebels in je buik (Butterflies in
Your Stomach)* (sex education
curriculum), 76, 165–166
lesson discussing differentiating
of girls and boys, 169–172
lessons fostering self-esteem, 175
lessons on love, 173–177

labia, 45
Lang, Amy, 53, 54, 72, 73
Lang leve de liefde (Long Live Love)
sex education curriculum, 178
Lehman, Rob, 124
Levin, Diane, 159
Levy, Ariel, 219
locker rooms at public swimming
pools, gender segregation of
young children in, 26–27,
29–31
LOLA, 244
Long, Priscilla, 112
looks, self-esteem and, 116–121

Los Angeles Times (newspaper), 151
love
childhood, 162–163, 240
teaching about, 173–177
lovemaking, talking about, 51–52

The Male Brain (Brizendine),
108, 110
male gaze phenomenon, 136, 237
Mann, Sally, 27
Margolis, Krista, 199
Martinsson, Gabriella, 132–133
masturbation, 76, 239
McBride, Brittany, 203
medical visits, teaching consent
and, 141–142
*Men Are from Mars, Women Are
from Venus* (Gray), 108
menstruation
education about, 157–158
"first moon" parties, 194, 244–245
first period, 244–245
subscription period-supply
delivery services/first-period
kits, 244
Merriam-Webster's, 74
#MeToo movement, 138
Metzger, Julie, 81, 191, 192, 193
Misconceptions (Wolf), 110–111
Mississippi First, 186
mixed-gender sleepovers, 154,
161–162, 212, 219–220, 224,
246
Mol, Kiki, 217
Mom and Dad Are Fighting
(podcast), 158–159
Moore, Tracy, 63–64

morality, birds and bees talk and
confusion about, 60–63
Mother-Daughter Revolution
(Debold), 237
Mulvey, Laura, 237
Muslims in Netherlands, sex
education and, 168–169,
178, 181
My Body Is Private (Girard), 91
My Mom's Having a Baby! (Butler),
54–55, 57
criticism of, 57–59

National Sexuality Education
Standards (NSES), 201–202, 238
National Survey of Family Growth,
187
Nebraskans for Founders' Values, 197
NEE! (van der Doef), 101, 102
NEMO (Amsterdam), sex and
puberty exhibit, 13–16, 39
Netherlands
acceptance of public nudity in,
21–23
attitudes toward childhood
sexual exploration in, 97–102
attitudes towards sex between
teenagers, 212, 215–216,
218–219
body positivity in, 23–24
comfort with acknowledging
bodily functions in, 24–25
communal bathing in, 25–26
comprehensive sexuality
education in, 166–167
Dutch attitude towards sex, 9–10
gender equality in, 134

gender roles in, xvii, 130–131
normalization of sex in, 16
parenting style in, 6–7
raising children in gender neutral
  environment in, 128–131
sex education in schools in,
  96–97, 165–178, 180–181,
  189–190, 196
sexual double standard in, 130–131
sexual openness in, 9
See also under Dutch
Neve, Tischa, 146
New York Times Magazine,
  139–140, 191
New York Times (newspaper), 45,
  89, 136, 161
No Child Left Behind Act (2001), 151
normalization of sex, in
  Netherlands, 16
No Trespassing—This is MY Body
  (Fitzgerald), 91
Nottingham, Su, 204
Not Under My Roof (Schalet), 176,
  212
nudity
  acceptance of public nudity in
    Netherlands, 21–23
  confusion with eroticism, 27
  discomfort with public nudity in
    United States, 28–30, 36
  family, 19–21, 37, 236
  nurturing, expectations about girls
    and, 123–127

O. School (website), 194
Obama, Barack, 59
Office of Adolescent Health, 199

Online Etymology Dictionary, 74
Open Road Alliance, 202
O'Reilly, Bill, 59–60, 138
The O'Reilly Factor (television
  program), 59
Orenstein, Peggy, 44–45, 119
Ouders Online, 99
ourbodiesourselves.org, 82
Our Whole Lives (OWL) (sex
  education curriculum),
  193–194
Oxford English Dictionary, 74

Pacific Science Center (Seattle), 15
Palo Alto Weekly (newspaper), 31
parental consent, for Dutch
  sexuality education, 169
parenting styles, in Netherlands, 6–7
parents
  desire of American parents
    for sex education for their
    children, 197
  fear of sexually informed children
    offending others, 63–67
  fears about teens and sex,
    214–216
  preparing daughters and sons
    for sexual intimacy, 211–212,
    219–220
  as role models, 242–243
  as source of sexuality education,
    178–179
  supporting teens who are having
    sex, 226–227
  See also American parents; Dutch
    parents; sexuality education
    advice for parents

parent-teen relationships, sex
    and puberty and, 216,
    217–219
Parr, Todd, 235
Pateros K-12 school, sex education
    at, 205–208
A Pattern Language (Alexander),
    226
Pediatrics (journal), 89
The PeepShow, 14–16
penis
    defined, 74
    identifying, 45, 46, 48–49, 70
periods. See menstruation
Personal Responsibility Education
    Program (PREP), 199
pestering, of girls, 135–136
Philippart, Heidi, 232–233
photographing children at play,
    34–35
Pink Brain, Blue Brain (Eliot), 109,
    111
"pink tax," 243
Planned Parenthood, 139, 141
    Teen Council, 194
Planned Parenthood League of
    Massachusetts, 206
platonic relationships between men
    and women, 159–161
"playing doctor," 85–88. See also
    childhood sexual
    exploration
"play-punch," 124
pleasure, clitoris and, 73–76, 77–78,
    82–83
pornography, 53, 74, 178, 190, 214,
    241, 245

pregnancy
    lessons on, 172–173
    unintended/unwanted, 166,
        187–188
    See also teenage pregnancy
preschool years, sexuality education
    for, 235–238
privacy, children's self-pleasuring
    and, 72–73
private parts, advising children to
    keep private, 91–93
Psychology Today (magazine), 160
Pubermania (van Essen & Mol),
    217
puberty
    advice for parents about
        discussing, 240–241
    Dutch film about, 15–16
    Great Conversations class about,
        43, 44, 81, 191–193
    relationships between parents
        and children during, 217–219
pubic hair, 241
public nudity
    in Netherlands, 21–23
    US laws against, 36
    in United States, 28–30
    in Washington State, 36

Rajalin, Lotta, 131–132, 133, 134
rape culture, 34
Real Talk (app), 194
reciprocity in intimate partnerships,
    245
Reitzema, Elsbeth
    on childhood sexual exploration,
        96–98, 99–100, 101

on depicting intimate side of
sexuality, 54
on description of clitoris in sex
education curricula, 76
on embarrassing puberty
moments, 244
on teaching young children
about intercourse, 52–53
relationships
comprehensive sexuality
education and, 166
parent-teen, 216, 217–219
teaching children about healthy,
142, 239
reproduction, teaching about,
172–173, 175
to preschoolers, 235
Rights, Respect, Responsibility (3Rs)
(sex education curriculum),
201–205, 238
training for teachers, 202–205
ritual coverings, objectification and
gender inequality and, 27
Rivers, Caryl, 109, 141, 152
Rodriguez, Sarah B., 75
Roffman, Deborah, 72–73,
145–146
Room One, 206
Roth, Gabriel, 158–159
Rutgers (sexual and reproductive
health foundation), 52
sex education curriculum (*see
Kriebels in je buik (Butterflies
in Your Stomach)* (sex
education curriculum))
use of Rutgers curriculum for
Spring Fever Week, 96–97

safety issues, childhood sexual
exploration and, 89, 90–94,
101–102
same-gender friendships
steering children toward, 144
transgender adults and, 160–161
Save Nebraska Children, 197
Sax, Leonard, 109, 151
Scarleteen (website), 194, 212, 222,
239
Schalet, Amy, 176, 212, 215, 216,
218, 219
Schama, Simon, 60, 76
schools
as best place for comprehensive
sexuality education, 178–180
childhood sexual exploration in
Dutch, 99–100
gender neutral, in Sweden,
131–133
gender-segregated, 109, 144, 151
reasons why sex education
should be in, 189–190
See also sex education in schools
Schroeder, Elizabeth, 142, 200, 202,
203
Science (journal), 122
self-esteem
lessons fostering, 175
looks and, 116–121
self-objectification, focus on girls'
looks and, 120
self-pleasuring, children and, 69,
71–73, 77, 78
self-sexualization of girls, media
and, 118–119
self-socialization, 113

Sesamstraat (television series), 24
sex
 in American culture, 17
 definitions of, 212–213
 describing on clinical level, 51
 discomfort of American parents
  in discussing, 40–41, 42
 Dutch attitude towards, 9–10
 relationship gaps and, 245
 sex education and separating
  from eroticism, 53–54
S.E.X. (Corinna), 212–213, 222,
  239
Sex, Etc. (website), 194
sex and puberty exhibit, at NEMO,
  13–16, 39
sex between adolescents
 age at first intercourse, 212
 American parents' view of, 212,
  213–215
 contraception and, 225–226
 Dutch parents' view of, 212,
  215–216, 218–219
 Melissa's and Kendra's stories,
  220–224
 objections to, 214–215
 parental support for teen having
  sex, 226–227
 parent-teen relationships and,
  216, 217–219
 preparing teens for,
  211–212, 213
 locations where permitted,
  224–225
sex differences, assumptions about
  inherent, 108–110
sex-ed apps, 194

sex education
 "age appropriate," 52, 59
 in American schools, 183–189,
  190, 196, 197–208, 238–239
 children's books and, 23–24,
  54–55, 91–93, 101–102
 children's right to, 196–197
 cross-gender, 157–158
 discomfort of American parents
  in discussing sex with
  children, 40–41, 42
 on Dutch public television,
  157–158
 in Dutch schools, 96–97,
  165–178, 180–181
 how children interpret sexual
  information, 53–54
 intimacy aspect of, 51–52,
  54
 necessity of, 44–45
 private initiatives in United
  States, 191–196
 public funding for, 199–200
 resources for, 239
 teaching about intercourse,
  51–53
 teaching correct reproductive
  terminology, 3–4, 5, 9, 45–49,
  233–234
 teaching young children about
  birth control, 55–56
 trauma of birds and bees talk
  and, 60–63
 unlearning imagined stories
  about sex, 62–63
 who should deliver,
  178–180

See also abstinence-only-until-
heterosexual-marriage
(AOUHM); comprehensive
sexuality education (CSE);
sexuality education advice for
parents
sex education curricula
abstinence-only-until-
heterosexual-marriage, 186,
188, 198, 199
Best Choice, 198, 199
*Family Life and Sexual Health
(FLASH)*, 183–184
Get Real, 206–207
Our Whole Lives, 193–194
Rights, Respect, Responsibility,
201–205, 238
sexual risk avoidance education,
186
*See also Kriebels in je buik
(Butterflies in Your Stomach)*
(sex education curriculum)
sex education in schools,
178–180
bipartisan support for, 42
in Netherlands, 168–178,
180–181, 189–190, 196
pushback against, 197–198
in United States, 183–189, 190,
196, 197–208
sex-ed websites, 194
Sex Is a Funny Word (Silverberg),
66–67, 95
sexual abuse of children, fear of,
31–32, 39, 90, 92
sexual double standard, in
Netherlands, 130–131

sexuality
childhood sexual exploration and
adult, 90
confusion with eroticism and
shame, 23
lack of conversation about in
United States, 17
sexuality education advice for
parents, 41–42
adolescence, 240–247
baby and toddlerhood, 231–235
elementary ages, 238–240
preschool, 235–238
sexuality-education standards, 165
Sexuality Information and
Education Council of the
United States, 190
sexualization of girls
in adolescence, 241–242
protecting girls from early,
118–119
sexual pleasure
clitoris and, 73–76, 77–78, 82–83
girls and, 71–72
right to, 76
sexual risk avoidance (SRA)
education, 186
sexual violence
risk factors for perpetration of,
93–94
sex education and, 188
shame
body, 20, 26, 70
confusion with eroticism, 23
locker-room gender segregation
for young children and, 31
sense of genitals as dirty and, 79

Shape (magazine), 160
Silverberg, Cory, 66–67, 95
Simkin, Penny, 194–195
single-sex schools, 109, 144, 151
sleepovers, mixed-gender, 154,
　161–162, 212, 219–220,
　224, 246
slut shaming, 34
Smitten Kitten (sex toy store),
　194
snippa (vulva), 46
snopp (penis), 46
Sonneveld, Marilyn, 79
So Sexy So Soon (Levin), 159
Spelke, Elizabeth S., 110
Spelman, Cornelia, 91
sports, STEM and spatial lessons of,
　121–122
Spring Fever Week, sexuality
　education during. *See Kriebels
　in je buik (Butterflies in Your
　Stomach)* (sex education
　curriculum)
states, sex education requirements
　and, 186–187
status, gender inequality and,
　112–116
STEM (science, technology,
　engineering, and math)
　girls and, 107–108
　success in encouraging girls in,
　121–123
STIs (sexually transmitted
　infections)
　abstinence-only-until-
　　heterosexual-marriage and,
　186, 187, 188

comprehensive sexuality
　education as defense against,
　166
sex education about, 206–207
subscription period-supply delivery
　services, 244
Summers, Lawrence H., 110
Sweden, gender equality in,
　131–133
Switzerland, gender equality in,
　133–134

Tabú (website), 194
*The Talk: 7 Lessons to Introduce
　Your Child to Biblical Sexuality*
　(Gilkerson), 73–74
Talk to Me First (Roffman), 72–73,
　146
teenage pregnancy
　abstinence-only-until-
　　heterosexual-marriage
　　education and, 186, 187
　programs to reduce, 199–200
　sex between teenagers and
　　worries about, 214
Teen Facts (sex and puberty
　exhibit), 13–16, 39
Teen Pregnancy Prevention
　Program (TPP), 199–200
television, body functions on
　Dutch, 24
ten Hoeve, Henk, 168, 180
testes, 70
Testosterone Rex (Fine), 109, 113
Thompson, Carol, 54–55
ThriVe St. Louis, 199, 200
Tia (app), 194

tickling, consent and, 139–141, 235–236

toddlerhood, sexuality education for, 231–235

toilet learning, contributing to child's self-esteem, 231

tomboys, awareness of boys' higher social status and being, 114–115

Too Hot to Handle: A Global History of Sex Education (Zimmerman), 196

topless freedom for women, 30

topless sunbathing, 26, 27

transgender adults, same-gender friendships and, 160–161

transgender children, 129–130

Trump, Donald, 138, 151

The Truth About Girls and Boys (Rivers & Barnett), 108, 152

Tryst Network (website), 194

Turner Foundation, 202

2Voices, 232

Understanding Children's Sexual Behaviors (Johnson), 94

UNESCO sexuality-education standards, 165

UNICEF, 60

unintended/unwanted pregnancy comprehensive sexuality education as defense against, 166

rates of, in United States, 187–188

Unitarian Universalist Church, 193

United Church of Christ, 193

United Nations Human Development Report, 134

United States
attitudes toward sex between teenagers in, 212, 213–215

comprehensive sexuality education in, 238–239

female genital mutilation in, 75

gender equality in, 133–134

private sex education programs in, 191–196

sex education in schools, 183–189, 190, 196, 197–208, 238–239

US Centers for Disease Control and Prevention (CDC)
HIV, STI, and pregnancy prevention benchmarks, 187

risk factors for perpetration of sexual violence, 93–94

talking to children about sexuality and, 41

US Department of Health and Human Services, 199

vagina, 45, 70, 170–171

Vagina (Wolf), 69

valuation of girls and boys, 120

van der Doef, Sanderijn, 56, 101–102

van Essen, Ingrid, 217

Van Means, Bridget, 199

van der Wal, Marina, 100, 225

victim blaming, women and, 136

virginity
Dutch teen perspectives on, 14

meanings of, 212–213

Volkskrant (newspaper), 131
Vrij(be)wijs (Bakker & van der
    Wal), 225
vulva, 45, 46, 48–49, 70

Week van de Lentekriebels (Spring
    Fever Week), sexuality
    education during, 96–97,
    168–178, 180–181
Weinstein, Harvey, 138
WestWind Foundation, 202
*What's the Big Secret? Talking
    About Sex with Girls and Boys*
    (Brown & Brown), 95–96
What to Expect: The Toddler Years
    (Eisenberg, et al.), 92
Whitcomb, Sean, 37
"Why Sex Ed?" (online toolkit), 190
Willem-Alexander (king), 24–25

Williams, Juliet A., 151
Wipsite (website), 79, 196
Wolf, Naomi, 69, 76, 110–111
women
    body shame and, 70
    portrayal in American media,
        10–11
World Health Organization
    on right to sexual health
        information and pleasure, 76
    sexuality-education standards,
        165
Wurtele, Sandy K., 40

Yellowberry brand, 243
Your Body Belongs to You
    (Spelman), 91

Zimmerman, Jonathan, 196

About the Author

© Jessica Peterson

Bonnie J. Rough is the author of the Minnesota Book Award-winning memoir *Carrier: Untangling the Danger in My DNA,* as well as *The Girls, Alone: Six Days in Estonia,* named one of the Best Kindle Singles of 2015. Her work has appeared in numerous anthologies and periodicals including the Best American series, the *New York Times, Huffington Post, The Sun,* and *Brain, Child.* An essayist, memoirist, and journalist, Rough has been the recipient of a Bush Foundation Artist Fellowship and a McKnight Artist Fellowship for Writers, among other honors. Born and raised in the Pacific Northwest, she has lived in the Midwest and in the Netherlands and now resides in Seattle with her family. www.bonniejrough.com.